The Cults From *A* to *Zen*

In this quick-reference guide, you'll find what you need to know about . . .

The Western Cults

- Mormonism
- Jehovah's Witnesses
- Christian Science

The Eastern Cults

- Transcendental Meditation
- The Church of Scientology
- Hare Krishna

The New Age Cults

- Theosophy
- The Forum/est
- The Church Universal and Triumphant

   . . . and more!

Josh McDowell & Don Stewart bring you the latest information on the cults, and then show you how to share the truth of Jesus Christ with cult followers.

Also available from Here's Life Publishers—

THE
DECEIVERS

Josh McDowell
& Don Stewart

Assisted by Kurt Van Gorden

Here's Life Publishers

First Printing, April 1992

Published by
HERE'S LIFE PUBLISHERS, INC.
P. O. Box 1576
San Bernardino, CA 92402

Cover design by David Marty Design

Library of Congress Cataloging-in-Publication Data
McDowell, Josh.
    The deceivers : what cults believe, how they lure followers / Josh
McDowell and Don Stewart.
        p.   cm.
    Includes bibliographical references.
    ISBN 0-89840-342-1
    1. Cults—Controversial literature. 2. Christian sects—
Controversial literature. I. Stewart, Don Douglas. II. Title.
BP603.M36   1992
291.9—dc20   92-9770
                                                          CIP

Unless designated otherwise, Scripture quotations are from *The New American Standard Bible*, © The Lockman Foundation 1960, 1962, 1963, 1968, 1971, 1972, 1975, 1977.
    Scripture quotations designated KJV are from the *King James Version*.
    Scripture quotations designated NIV are from *The Holy Bible: New International Version*, © 1973, 1978, 1984 by the International Bible Society. Published by Zondervan Bible Publishers, Grand Rapids, Michigan.
    Scripture quotations designated RSV are from *The Revised Standard Version*, © 1952 by the National Council of the Churches of Christ. Published by Thomas Nelson, Inc., Nashville, Tennessee.
    Scripture quotations designated TLB are from *The Living Bible*, © 1971 by Tyndale House Publishers, Wheaton, Illinois.

For More Information, Write:

L.I.F.E.—P.O. Box A399, Sydney South 2000, Australia
Campus Crusade for Christ of Canada—Box 300, Vancouver, B.C., V6C 2X3, Canada
Campus Crusade for Christ—Pearl Assurance House, 4 Temple Row, Birmingham, B2 5HG, England
Lay Institute for Evangelism—P.O. Box 8786, Auckland 3, New Zealand
Campus Crusade for Christ—P.O. Box 240, Raffles City Post Office, Singapore 9117
Great Commission Movement of Nigeria—P.O. Box 500, Jos, Plateau State Nigeria, West Africa
Campus Crusade for Christ International—100 Sunport Lane, Orlando, FL 32809, U.S.A.

Contents

Why This Book?

O ver the years we have had many requests to write a book on the various alternatives to Christianity—the cults, non-Christian religions, secular religions, and the occult. This volume is an enlarged revision of our former work *Understanding the Cults*.

Frequently we are challenged by people of other religious beliefs when we affirm the uniqueness and finality of the Christian faith. They argue that Christianity is compatible with other religions and cults, and that we should not stress the uniqueness of Jesus Christ as being the only way a person can know the true and living God.

This book demonstrates that Christianity is *not* compatible with cults. Our work, *Handbook of Today's Religions*, demonstrates the incompatibility of Christianity and non-Christian religions, secular religions, and the occult. It is in this sense that we have titled this book *The Deceivers*. We are not suggesting that the founders of these groups deceive their followers with intent. In fact, some of them may have begun a sincere search for truth, but ended up playing in Satan's sideshow.

It should also be pointed out that it is not Christianity that has attacked the cults, but rather, the cults have attacked Christianity. The result is that orthodox Christianity has had to go on the defensive, presenting its truth to combat the deviations the cults wish to perpetrate as historic Christian doctrine.

The
Scope
of
Our Study

This book is intended to be a general reference work for those who are interested in knowing what various groups believe and why those beliefs are not compatible with biblical Christianity. It is not intended to be an exhaustive treatise on any one group or a comprehensive guide to all alternatives to Christianity. Rather, we have confined ourselves to deal with specific groups with which we have had the most contact. However, because we haven't dealt with a particular group doesn't mean we advocate its beliefs.

In addition, it has been necessary for us to limit ourselves to evaluating the central beliefs of each chosen group, spending little time dealing with its history, organization, methods, or secondary beliefs, unless specifically related to their doctrines in a fashion that this warrants consideration. Not all chapters will be the same length. We have examined the conversion methods of the cults and have devoted the most space to the largest and most aggressive. The lesser aggressive cults will have a brief treatment, containing the basic facts that separate the group from Christian fellowship.

Our desire is for this work to serve as a useful reference and springboard for further study. We have also prepared an extensive bibliography to give the reader further help if he wishes to know more about any one group.

The
Proper
Attitude

We live in a society where a person has the freedom to follow the religious belief of his or her choice. We have no quarrel with this. However, when individuals or groups publicly claim they are now God's true work here upon the earth, and orthodox Christianity, which has existed throughout the centuries, is now wrong, we feel we must answer such challenges. They have the freedom to say it, but as Christians we have the responsibility to answer them.

The Bible commands us to "be ready always to give an answer to every man that asketh you a reason of the hope that is in you with meekness and fear" (1 Peter 3:15, KJV). This work is that answer to those who have attacked historic Christianity and place their own beliefs above it. We are not attacking these groups; we are merely answering their accusations. An example of the type of accusations we are answering can be found in the writings of The Church of Jesus Christ of Latter-day Saints, better known as the Mormons:

> Every intelligent person under the heavens that does not, when informed, acknowledge that Joseph Smith, Jr., is a prophet of God, is in darkness and opposed to us and to Jesus and His kingdom on the earth (Brigham Young, *Journal of Discourses,* 8:223).

> What does the Christian world know about God? Nothing . . . Why, so far as the things of God are concerned, they are the veriest fools; they know neither God nor the things of God (John Taylor [third president of the Mormon Church], *Journal of Discourses,* 13:225).

We cannot allow these types of accusations to pass. They must be answered. However, in answering the charges made by the cults and other non-Christian groups, we desire to do so without resorting to name-calling or sarcasm. It is possible to disagree with a person's beliefs and yet love the person holding those beliefs.

What we oppose is the teaching of these groups, not the people in the groups nor their right to believe whatever they want. We speak out because the Bible commands us to "contend earnestly for the faith which was once for all delivered to the saints" (Jude 3).

Finally, the apostle Paul has exhorted us to "prove all things; hold fast that which is good" (1 Thessalonians 5:21, KJV).

1

What Is
a
Cult?

T he term *cult* has gained a diverse definition over the last century. This is true especially since the 1950s when the secular media began to examine groups and label them as cults due to adverse behavior. *Time* magazine (September 3, 1951, p. 51) called the faddish following of L. Ron Hubbard's book *Dianetics* a cult two years before he incorporated it as the religion of Scientology. *Time's* basis for calling it a cult seemed to be Hubbard's high-volume sales in the self-help book market.

We must never abandon the legitimate use of a term simply because of its misuse by others. Psychologists have tried to define a cult as a group that alters one's behavior and psychological outlook on life. Sociologists have defined a cult as a group that does not fit the norms of a given society. Both of these recent endeavors fail to address what is essential to all cults, that is theology. Thus, we will use the theological definition as the only one that addresses all aspects of life, thought, and behavior.

The word *cult* is from the Latin word *cultus*, which literally means to worship or show reverence to something. According to the *Oxford English Dictionary*, it gained acceptance in the seventeenth century and again in the mid-nineteenth century as a representation of a particular religious group. The first book to deal with several cults in one volume is William Irvine's *Timely Warnings* (1917), later retitled as *Heresies Exposed* (1919). In this volume Irvine correctly identifies the need to understand cults theologically with the Bible as our standard to separate truth from error. "Almost every heresy," he said, "in its last analysis, does just this, it interposes a veil between needy man and a waiting God" (tenth edition, p. 8). Irvine's book says the "great foundational truths of the gospel will be denied" by the cults (p. 6).

There have been other writers who have evaluated several cults in a single text. No author is perhaps better known for this than Dr. Walter R. Martin, who spent forty years of his life exposing the errors of the cults. He wrote:

A cult, then, is a group of people polarized around someone's interpretation of the Bible and is characterized by major deviations from orthodox Christianity relative to the cardinal doctrines of the Christian faith, particularly the fact that God became a man in Jesus Christ (*Martin Speaks Out on the Cults*, p. 17).

What Irvine, Martin, and others have said of the cults is true. We must approach our study from God's Word, for the apostle Paul warned there would be false Christs and a false gospel that would attempt to deceive the true church and the world:

For if one comes and preaches another Jesus whom

we have not preached, or you receive a different spirit which you have not received, or a different gospel which you have not accepted, you bear this beautifully . . . for such men are false apostles, deceitful workers, disguising themselves as apostles of Christ. And no wonder, for even Satan disguises himself as an angel of light. Therefore it is not surprising if his servants also disguise themselves as servants of righteousness; whose end shall be according to their deeds (2 Corinthians 11:4,13-15).

While it is not impossible to give a clear definition of a modern religious cult, the elusiveness of the meaning is due to the constantly changing parameters of the groups with which we are dealing. In light of the new groups we must refine our definition. The Bible is altogether rejected by some cults. Others cults make no claim to the Christian church, since they stem from a different world view. We will provide what we think is a definition that fits all cults whether they are an offshoot of Christianity, Hinduism, Buddhism, Taoism, or Islam.

DEFINITION: A cult is a group of people basing their beliefs upon the world view of an isolated leadership, which always denies the central doctrines of Christianity as taught from the Bible.

We will classify the cults in this study into three categories: Western Cults, Eastern Cults, and New Age Cults. Some of the teachings of these cults will overlap, but we will use their foundational world view for classification.

Western Cults. The western cults are those that usually break off from Christianity and deny the essential doctrines of our faith. They will use the Bible as one of their sources and Jesus Christ as a central figure. Usually they claim that they are the only true representation of Christianity existing.

Eastern Cults. These cults do not claim the Bible or

Jesus Christ as necessary in their structure, but instead they are a break off of some eastern philosophy. Their foundation is usually rooted in Hinduism, Buddhism, or Taoism. Sometimes they will claim compatibility with Christianity, but in essence their world view is in oriental philosophy.

New Age Cults. The New Age cults usually try to unify eastern and western thinking, therefore they will have a melting pot of beliefs. The Bible is valued only when it advances their cause, Jesus is quoted only when beneficial, and the world view is usually monistic or pantheistic.

Why Do Cults Prosper?

Cults grow in membership due to adopting methods of proselytizing similar to Christian evangelism. The Jehovah's Witnesses spent 835,426,538 hours distributing literature in 1990. They publish more than fifty-five million issues of *Watchtower* and *Awake* magazines each month in 128 languages.

The Mormon Church has 40,000 full-time missionaries propagating the doctrines of Joseph Smith. They are growing so rapidly that the *Mormon Church Almanac* proudly touts a third of a million baptisms annually, of which three quarters of those baptized were formerly Protestant.

The *Christian Science Monitor* newspaper has gained respectability in all levels of government, the business world, and households far and near. It publishes an international edition and has expanded to a well-produced television program.

These facts tell us that the cults are using every available means to gain new members, but why do people join cults? There are four basic reasons people join the cults: intellectual, emotional, social and spiritual (cf., Kurt Van Gorden, with Ronald Enroth, ed., *Evangelizing the Cults*, Ann Arbor, MI: Servant Publications, 1990, p. 140).

Intellectual Reasons People Join Cults

God gave us the ability to be intellectual. He expects us to use our reasoning processes (Isaiah 1:18), but sin has distorted our ability to think correctly about God and His message. Paul says that many people are forever learning but are not able to come to a knowledge of the truth (2 Timothy 3:7). The cults step in with intellectual answers to satisfy man's fallen nature.

In an unsure world cults provide authoritative answers to man's basic questions: *Who am I? Why am I here? Where am I going?* This does not mean they give correct answers; it only means they provide a false security in the philosophies of the world.

Many cults prey on ignorance and try to impress the uninformed with pseudo-scholarship. An example is The Way International's founder, Victor Paul Wierwille, who quoted profusely from Hebrew and Greek sources in an attempt to give the impression of scholarship. We also find the door-to-door representatives of Jehovah's Witnesses giving a similar impression of knowledge. To combat this, the believer must know what he believes and why he believes it and thus be able to expose the cult's teachings.

Emotional Reasons People Join Cults

Genesis 1:26,27 tells us we are made in God's image and likeness, both male and female. Our emotions are a gift from God that He did not give to animals. From this we derive love, joy, peace, kindness, and other qualities. Sin has distorted our emotional makeup and produced hatred, depression, restlessness, selfishness, and other bad qualities. Cults appeal to man's basic emotional need. All of us need to be loved and to sense meaningful direction in our lives. Individuals who experience an identity crisis or have emotional problems are particularly susceptible to cults. Often when a person is grieving over the death of a loved one, the cults target him or her as easy prey for the hunt.

The cults take advantage of this and offer ready-made, but ultimately unsatisfying, solutions. Most cults tell their followers what to believe, how to behave and what to think, and emphasize dependence upon the group or leader for their emotional stability. A former teacher for Unity School of Christianity, who is now a born again Christian, wrote of her experience to one of the writers on this project.

"It was the love," Mrs. D. said, "which first enticed me into Unity. I was in a place of just having been divorced and I was feeling down about myself. Unity says that you are special and needed. They teach you how to love yourself and others." Eventually this woman was able to separate her emotions from the written truth of God's Word, so she left Unity to follow the true Jesus. Her testimony gives us hope that God's Holy Spirit can filter through the emotional entrapment of cults and free the soul to bow to King Jesus.

Social Reasons People Join Cults

We do not often think about our social life in relationship to God's creative purpose, but God made us to be social beings. The cults exploit the social needs that God instilled in us. The family unit was conceived by God through the creation of Adam and Eve as husband and wife. When people began to multiply and spread out, clans and villages developed, and consequently these became cities and nations. It is from our social influence that we spawn our relationship to humanity and we fulfill our desire to be part of a group or become active in society.

When their group-life is disrupted, be it due to a dysfunctional family, a bad church atmosphere, burn-out in the work place, or plain disgust with political issues, people want to drop out of society, and the cults are there to catch them.

One of the writers, Kurt Van Gorden, was a former member of the Children of God cult. At the time he joined the movement he had already been a Christian for a year, but the church he attended did not have an active plan for evangelizing others. Kurt's desire to spread the gospel was challenged one day when he met the Children of God. They were doing what he thought Christians ought to do, so he joined them on that basis. About six months later Kurt was able to distinguish between their activism and their false doctrines, so he repented and came back into Christian fellowship and attended a Campus Crusade for Christ Bible study.

The cults take advantage of other social factors, such as when the hypocrisy or sin of some Christian leader becomes public. The Jehovah's Witnesses spotlight these subjects in nearly every issue of *Awake* magazine, as if to reassure members that they have made the right move by rejecting "Christendom." They commit the logical fallacy of composition (assuming the parts are the same as the whole) and reject Christianity because of the members of the church. See our section on hypocrites in *Answers to Tough Questions* (San Bernardino, CA: Here's Life Publishers, 1980), pp. 127-128.

Spiritual Reasons People Join Cults

The cults are devoid of spiritual truth, but they make every effort to satisfy man's spiritual needs. Many Christians are not disciples of God's Word and have joined cults as a result of not knowing the scrip-

tural foundations of Christianity. Perhaps they belong
to a denomination spoiled through liberal theology. If
the church fails to carefully and seriously provide
spiritual truth and biblical exposition, those with
spiritual needs will find other avenues of fulfillment.

Many people involved in the cults were raised in
Christian churches but were untaught in basic Christian
doctrine. Chris Elkins, a former Unification Church
"Moonie" member, points this out:

> In most cults, a majority of the members left a main-
> line, denominational church. Perhaps in the church's
> attempt to explain why its members are leaving and join-
> ing cults, brainwashing is seen as an easy out.
>
> My contention is that brainwashing is really not the
> issue. In most cases we would be hard-pressed to isolate
> any element in the methodology of a cult that is not
> present in some form in mainstream churches. For Chris-
> tians, the main issue with cults should be theology.
>
> Many of us accepted Christ at an early age. We had a
> child's understanding of Jesus, the Bible and salvation.
>
> That is okay for children and new Christians. But
> many of us older Christians are still babies spiritually.
> We have not learned to feed ourselves, much less anyone
> else (*Christian Life*, August 1980).

2

The
Characteristics
of a
Cult

E xtensive travel throughout the United States and abroad has made us aware of certain features that characterize the cults. These include:

Authoritative Differences

One of the distinctive marks that flags cultism today is the role of cultic leaders as new prophets, apostles, messiahs, or the sole channel of truth. This authoritative leadership is supported by new revelation that is either equal or superior to that of the Bible. If the Bible stands in the way of the leadership it is often altered to weaken its otherwise clear message. Cults accomplish this by retranslating the Bible into an unscholarly translation, or by redefining biblical words which keeps the cult members in darkness.

Isolated Leadership

Cults are usually characterized by central leader

figures who consider themselves messengers of God with unique access to the Almighty. Since the leader has such a special relationship with God, he can dictate the theology and behavior of the cult. Consequently, he exercises enormous influence over the group.

This strong leadership leads the cult follower into total dependence upon the cult for belief, behavior, and lifestyle. When this falls into the hands of a particularly corrupt leader, the results can be tragic, as with the mass suicide of 912 people under Jim Jones and the People's Temple in Jonestown, Guyana. The more dramatic the claims of a cult leader, the more possibility of a tragic conclusion.

The cult leaders isolate their authority from historic Christianity. They set their stage with an open frontal attack of historic Christianity. Their argument is that the church has departed from the true faith, and that they alone provide God's true direction. Joseph Smith, founder of Mormonism, said all the churches are wrong and he alone was to restore true faith. The founders of Jehovah's Witnesses, Christian Science, and other cults claim the same thing: Christianity is wrong and they are right. Each one isolates himself from biblical teachings and his group from Christianity.

Additional Scripture

Many cults promote the false idea that God has revealed something special to them. Sometimes it is in the form of a vision, at other times they have a special written message. The cults thrive on new revelation that supersedes the Bible because they have an innate desire for modern man to have modern revelation. What they fail to realize, however, is that the Bible does speak to modern man: "The counsel of the Lord stands forever, the plans of His heart from generation to generation" (Psalm 33:11). Rather than obeying God's

Word, cults always contradict it with their new message.

Joseph Smith added three works, *The Book of Mormon, The Pearl of Great Price* and *Doctrines and Covenants*. Thus, the Bible is *not* truly their final source of authority.

Mary Baker Eddy, founder of Christian Science, claimed that her writings were inspired from God and she was only the scribe. The Bible is demeaned as having no more value "than the history of Europe and America."

The Unification Church believes the Bible to be incomplete, while Rev. Moon's *Divine Principle* is the true authoritative source. On page 233 of the *Divine Principle* it is labeled the "complete Testament" in opposition to the Old and New Testaments. Regardless of whether the Bible is superseded by other works or reinterpreted by a cult leader, a sure mark of a cult is that the final authority on spiritual matters rests on something other than the plain teachings of Holy Scripture.

Altering the Bible

Another mark of the cults is how they change what is actually written within the Bible. This is a different category from their new revelation. It is one thing to claim additional Scripture, but it is another to change the words God spoke.

The cults do this in one of two ways: They retranslate the Bible by inferior and unreliable scholarship (making it say what they want it to say), or they redefine the terms of the Bible, clouding its message.

Only a few of the cults publish their own Bible. The Mormons, Jehovah's Witnesses, Christadelphians, and The Way International are among the few. The other cults are satisfied with redefining the terms of the Bible which, in effect, destroys the valid translation.

Examples of how cults redefine terms are plentiful. When a Christian Scientist reads the Bible, it is only through the filter of Mary Baker Eddy's definitions (i.e., God is Mind, Jesus is not the Christ, Baptism is submergence in truth, etc.).

These and other cults justify their existence by claiming they have something more than just the Bible and its "inadequate message." The cults have no objective, independent way to test their teachings and practices. Contrary to this, the Bible warns us about those who would attempt to alter or add to the Word of God (Proverbs 30:5,6; Galatians 1:6-9). As members of the universal Christian church, we can and should test all of our teachings and practices objectively and independently by God's infallible Word, the Bible (Acts 17:11).

Prophecy, Signs, and Wonders

As Christians we believe in a supernatural God who works within a natural world. The Bible attests to God's demonstration of His anointing upon an individual by giving special knowledge of future events (prophecy) or by accompanying his message with signs and wonders (miracles). Since the leaders of cults wish to place themselves in a similar position as the prophets of the Bible, it is not surprising that they will attempt to prove their anointing with prophecies of future events or special signs, such as healings, or wonders, such as miraculous events.

The prophets and apostles of the Mormon Church have made several dated predictions of future occurrences. The Watchtower Bible and Tract Society, beginning with their founder Charles Taze Russell, has predicted the date of Christ's return and the battle of Armageddon with specific dates. Herbert W. Armstrong, founder of the Worldwide Church of God, has made several predictions of world events. The Church of Christ, Scientist boldly published *A Century of Christian Science Healings*, announcing the healings of hundreds of people through Mary Baker Eddy's methodology. The Way International boasted of signs and wonders, including people raised from the dead. The followers of Sun Myung Moon are immersed in visions of the "True Parents" (Moon and his wife) during prayer, and often spirits are manifested in their presence. The New Age cults and Unity School of Christianity speak of astounding healings that defy common explanation. An advanced class of Transcendental Meditation devotees, *Siddhis*, claim the miraculous events of walking through walls and levitation.

Are these people really giving accurate predictions and prophecies? Are these events miraculous? What is a Christian to make of this and how do we explain what seems to be paranormal phenomena? These events hold a tight grip on the lives of many cult members who believe that these signs are proof of God's blessing.

The Christian is commissioned to test all things by God's Word. Our first caution comes out of Deuteronomy 13:1-3:

> If a prophet or a dreamer of dreams arises among you and gives you a sign or a wonder, and the sign or the wonder comes true, concerning which he spoke to you, saying, "Let us go after other gods (whom you have not known) and let us serve them," you shall not listen to the words of that prophet or that dreamer of dreams; for the Lord your God is testing you to find out if you love the Lord your God with all your heart and with all your soul.

In the above passage we must take note that some of the "signs or wonders" of the deceiver will actually happen. Some of the so-called miraculous events will be nothing more than slight-of-hand tricks by polished showmen. Former followers of Jim Jones reported that his healings were staged dramas and that the "cancers" extracted from his followers were actually animal parts (Phil Kerns, *People's Temple, People's Tomb*, Plainfield, NJ: Logos, 1979, p. 86).

On the other hand, some of the signs may only be accountable to the forces of darkness set in opposition to God's Kingdom. Whether it is man's deceptive trick or the demonic powers at work, some of the events will have the appearance of a *bona fide* miracle. Our passage in Deuteronomy tells us that God allows this to happen in order for our devotion and love to be tested. Some people, who are experientially oriented, will not follow after the true God, but will go after other gods on the basis of the so-called signs and wonders.

Our second caution comes from Deuteronomy 18:20-22:

> "But the prophet who shall speak a word presumptuously in My name which I have not commanded him to speak, or which he shall speak in the name of other gods, that prophet shall die." And you may say in your heart, "How shall we know the word which the Lord has not spoken?" When a prophet speaks in the name of the Lord, if the thing does not come about or come true, that is the thing which the Lord has not spoken. The prophet has spoken it presumptuously; you shall not be afraid of him.

God's message is clear—stay away from false prophets. No prophet of the Bible ever predicted an event that failed in one degree. This is not true of the prophets and leaders of the cults. None have ever had 100 percent accuracy. Joseph Smith gave at least ten well documented false prophecies. The Watchtower Bible and Tract Society has fourteen false predictions. Mr. Armstrong has given at least ten false predictions.

How does the Bible tell us to detect a false prophet? If even one of their predictions fail, then we know they were not sent by God.

The authoritative difference between the cults and Christianity forms a wide chasm. They supplant the biblical structure of the church with isolated unaccountable leadership. They reduce the effectiveness of the written Word of God through new translations and redefining terms. They minimize the authority of the Bible by adding new scriptures that have a superior position.

Doctrinal Differences

The apostle Paul told his companion Titus "to exhort in sound doctrine and to refute those who contradict" (Titus 1:9).

In the opening of the second chapter, he reiterates his comment: "Speak the things which are fitting for sound doctrine" (2:1). The doctrinal differences between cults and Christianity are many. We believe that Christians should focus only on the major tenets of our faith in determining where a group stands in relationship to the gospel message. On that note, we tend not to discuss blood transfusions with Jehovah's Witnesses or polygamy with Mormons. Even though these subjects may be intellectually stimulating and may lead to an ultimate discussion about man's sinfulness and our Savior's love, we suggest you stick with the essentials, such as the Trinity, deity of Jesus Christ, His atonement and bodily resurrection, the person and deity of the Holy Spirit, salvation by grace, and the doctrines of heaven and hell.

The Cults on the Nature of God (Trinity)

All non-Christian cults have either an inadequate view or outright denial of the Holy Trinity. The biblical doctrine of the Trinity, one God in three Persons, is usually attacked as being pagan or of satanic origin.

The Christian Scientists, Jehovah's Witnesses, and The Way all deny the Trinity, saying it is of pagan origin. The Mormons use the word "trinity" to mean three gods among many gods. The Moonies use the word "trinity" to mean Father, Mother, and Son.

Cults, therefore, are marked by their denial of the Trinity, their confusion of the Persons, and their deviation on the nature of God. In echo of Dr. Walter Martin's many lectures on the cults, "You may be wrong on many points of doctrine, but if you are wrong on the nature of God, you are wrong enough to lose your soul for all eternity."

The Cults on Jesus' Deity, Atonement, and Resurrection

One characteristic that is common to all cults is their false teaching about the person, nature, and work of Jesus Christ. The apostle Paul warned about following after "another Jesus" (2 Corinthians 11:4). The "other Jesus" will never pass in heaven. The only way we can be certain that we are following the true Jesus is to maintain the biblical description given to Him. When anyone detracts from the genuine identity of Jesus, he has "another Jesus" with no saving power. Merely attaching the name Jesus to a nonbiblical person only places the cults in the same position as a false teacher in Paul's day.

The Bible makes it clear that Jesus was God in human flesh, second person of the Holy Trinity, who lived a sinless life on earth and died as a sacrifice for the sins of the world. Three days after his crucifixion, Jesus rose bodily from the dead. Fifty days afterward He ascended into heaven, where He now sits at the right hand of the Father, interceding on behalf of believers. He will, one day, return bodily to planet earth and judge the living and the dead while setting up His eternal kingdom.

Some cults say that Jesus was "created" as a god, or that He is only god-like. None of them will say He is eternal as God. The Mormons, as an example, teach that Jesus was one god among many gods, thus denying His eternal nature as the one God. The Jehovah's Witnesses believe Jesus was created as a god known as Michael the Archangel. The Christian Scientists, The Way, and the Moonies all deny the deity of Jesus, saying He was godly, but not God.

On the atonement of Christ, the cults deny the power of the cross. The Mormons believe that the blood of Christ covers only certain sins, but not all sins. The Jehovah's Witnesses and Moonies see it as an important event that began the redemption process, but each individual must finish the work himself.

Several of the cults deny the bodily resurrection of Jesus. Jehovah's Witnesses, Christian Scientists, and Moonies deny it.

No matter what the particular beliefs of any cult may be, the one common denominator they all possess is a denial of the biblical teaching on the true deity, atonement, and resurrection of Jesus Christ.

The Cults on the Person of the Holy Spirit

God's nature has three Persons, or centers of personal identity, the Father, the Son, and the Holy Spirit. By "person" we do not mean body, we mean all the characteristics of personhood—reasoning, will, and emotions. The Holy Spirit is identified with these attributes in the same way that the Father and Son are.

The cults wrestle with the Holy Spirit in several ways. The early Mormons divided the Holy Ghost from the Holy Spirit saying that the Holy Ghost was a spirit-man and offspring of their heavenly parents, while the Holy Spirit was the mind of the Father and Son.

The Jehovah's Witnesses, Christian Scientists, The Way and Moonies deny the Holy Spirit as a person or as God. The Mormons believe the Holy Ghost is a person in human form, who was born in heaven as one of several gods.

Sadly, the cults have missed out on the communion, love, and fellowship the Christian has with the Holy Spirit. He who guides us into all truth (John 16:13) and convicts us of sin, righteousness, and judgment (John 16:8) has been disdained by the cults. To be born of the Spirit is the gift of God, but to shun and blaspheme the Holy Spirit is damnation.

The Cults on Salvation by Works

One teaching that is totally absent from all the cults is the gospel of the grace of God. No one is taught in the cults that he can be saved from eternal damnation by simply placing his faith in Jesus Christ. It is always belief in Jesus Christ and "do this" or "follow that." All cults attach something to the doctrine of salvation by grace through faith.

It might be mandatory baptism and obedience to the laws and ordinances of the gospel, as in Mormonism. It might be the auditing process of Scientology. It might be the mantras, meditations and chants of Transcendental Meditation and the New Age. It might be the good works of the Jehovah's Witnesses and Moonies. But it is never taught that faith in Christ alone will save anyone. Christianity teaches that good works will follow those who are saved (Ephesians 2:10), but we are not saved on the basis of baptism (1 Corinthians 1:17), works (Titus 3:5), or keeping the law (Romans 8:3).

The Cults on Heaven and Hell

All of the cults have altered the biblical teachings of heaven and hell. Heaven has become a state of mind in the New Age and Mind Science cults, while it has become an interplanetary confederacy of gods in Mormonism and to Hare Krishna devotees. Hell is non-literal for the Mind Sciences, New Age, Jehovah's Witnesses, and The Way International. It is limited to Satan and those who commit the unpardonable sin in Mormonism.

None of the cults teach the glory of heaven as the reward for those who place their faith in Jesus Christ. None of them teach eternal damnation and punishment in hell for the unbeliever.

Interpretation Differences

Very few Christians have witnessed to any large number of people without the objection being presented, "Well, that's just your interpretation." For years we have observed the impasse of two parties accusing one another of private interpretation. It is almost as if Christians are afraid to admit they interpret the Bible. There is nothing wrong with interpreting it, so long as the interpretation is correct. The next time someone charges you with interpreting the Bible, you may wish to tell him, "Yes, I have a good reason for mine. What reason do you have for yours?"

Interpretation is nothing to shy away from unless you have no basis for why you interpret a passage as you do. The cults lack any truly biblical concept for interpreting the Bible. This is not so in Christianity, but pastors and Bible teachers have not given enough guidelines on why Christians should interpret the Bible in certain ways.

The noted Christian apologist Dr. John Warrick Montgomery expresses that when we have sound, literal interpretive methods, then we are following in the footsteps of Jesus and the apostles, for they too believed in a literal Word of God:

> The total trust Jesus and the apostles displayed toward Scripture entails a precise and controlled hermeneutic. They subordinated the opinions and traditions of their day to Scripture; so must we. They did not regard Scripture as erroneous or self-contradictory; neither can we. They took its miracles and prophecies as literal fact; so must we. They regarded Scripture not as the product of editors and redactors but as stemming from Moses, David, and other immediately inspired writers; we must follow their lead. They believed that the events recorded in the Bible happened as real history; we can do no less (*Faith Founded on Fact*, Nashville, TN: Thomas Nelson Publishers, 1978, p. 223).

The following guidelines are not exhaustive, nor do they replace a seminary class in hermeneutics, but they will fit most applications. Upon interpreting any passage of Scripture there are three main items to keep in mind: 1. Text; 2. Context; 3. Background. The text tells us what the words say. The context tells us how the words are used. The background tells us about the people, places and environment.

Scripture Text

There are three ways in which we study the text. We will give an example of each way from the New Testament. The first way we study a text is the *literary genre*, meaning the stance, mood, or style that the text is written in. We must recognize that the mood or style is inspired as well as the words written. If God wrote through English writers instead of Hebrew, then we would expect Him to use all styles of speech available, be it idioms, prose, poetry, allegory, figures of speech, quotations or narrative. Jesus acknowledged figures of speech in John 6:48; 10:7; 15:5. We take figures of speech in a normal and literal sense for the point it conveys. In our book *Reasons Skeptics Should Consider Christianity* (San Bernardino, CA: Here's Life Publishers, 1981), we give four examples of common figures of speech (pp. 36-37).

The second way we look at the text is *word study*, for ultimate meaning. We must recognize that the words in the text are not accidental. Jesus said even the jot and tittle will not pass away (Matthew 5:18, KJV). Many good study aids are available for word studies of the Old and New Testaments. Whether it is the beginner with *Strong's Concordance* and *Vine's Expository Dictionary*, or the student of languages with his lexicons, through this we see the comparative, synonymous, etymological and historical uses of a given word.

The third way we look at the text is to study the *grammar*. The grammar tells us how the word is used in its literal and normal sense. How it relates to other words in the sentence is important, as Paul brings out in his argument about the plural usage of a noun (Galatians 3:16).

Scripture Context

There are three kinds of context we may look at. The first is the *immediate context*, which usually includes the paragraph immediately preceding and following the text. How does it relate to the subject? Without the context of the Sermon on the Mount, we might mistake Jesus to teach absolute human perfection instead of love like our heavenly Father (Matthew 5:48).

The second kind of context is the *wider context* of the whole book. The chapters and verses were placed in our Bible for easy reference, but not always according to correct division of thoughts and structure (see 1

Corinthians 11:1 in NIV for an example of corrected verse structure). Without the wider context we may think that 1 John 3:6 tells us Christians are sinless, but the wider context of the book (1 John 1:8-10) tells us otherwise.

The third kind of context is the *complete context* of the whole Bible. No verse is an island standing by itself in the sea of Scripture. Sometimes we need to look at the context of the whole Bible to understand a verse. In Genesis 3:9, one may think that God is limited in knowledge, since he asked Adam, "Where are you," but in the complete context of the Bible we see that God is omniscient (Isaiah 46:10; Psalm 139:1-6). Therefore, we see that God's question to Adam was not His lack of knowledge, but was purposed to get Adam to confess his sin. We take the passage literally, but the complete context shows us the application.

Scripture Background

There are three kinds of background we might look for in studying a text of Scripture. The first is the *cultural background*, which includes social, legal, religious, and political manners and customs. It is through knowing the culture that we can explain how Joseph sought a divorce from Mary, even though they were only engaged (Matthew 1:18-20). (cf., Josh Mc-Dowell, *A Ready Defense* [San Bernardino, CA: Here's Life Publishers, 1990], p. 86.)

The second kind of background is the *historical elements*. These are the things we find in extra-biblical history and archaeology. Testimony mounts annually as to the locations and content of cities mentioned in the Bible. Even the evidence of Solomon's porch, that was available at the time of Christ, is archaeological in nature and testifies to the temple Solomon built (John 10:23).

The third kind of background is the *environmental elements.* This is the fauna, flora, geography and topography. Some of this may only be discovered archaeologically and some remains the same today. In topography we read the literal account that Jesus went up to Jerusalem (Luke 19:28), which remains the same today. Many plants and animals are the same (Psalm 23; Matthew 13:26).

As we have gone through this list most of us can recall sermons we have heard where these rules of hermeneutics were applied. In repeating the sermon content to a friend we were unaware, perhaps, that we were using these proper rules of interpretation. When a cultist challenges your interpretation in the literal Word of God, at least you have a sound reason for why you do so.

Cults, Interpretation, and Semantics

None of the cults have a standard hermeneutic from which they develop a consistent interpretation of the Bible. Usually their proof-texts are out of context, to justify the peculiar doctrines of the cult. Without an objective and reasonable way to understand what the Bible teaches, the cult member is at the mercy of the theological whims of the cult leader.

In their endeavor to look like the Christian church, cults have had to take on our terminology but abandon our meanings. This game of semantics may be resolved when you engage in a dialogue by asking the other party what he means by his terms. Keep on questioning until you feel safe that a definition has been determined. Then you should refer to the contrasting definitions as you continue your dialogue. This will help you to keep the two world views in perspective while you talk. As an example, when speaking to a Mormon who has mentioned his heavenly father, you should ask him if the father is an exalted man. You may have to do this more than once to get the affirmation. As you share your faith and refer to this distinction, the Mormon will realize that when you speak of salvation through the God of the Bible, you are not speaking of the same thing he is.

Conclusion

Most of these features will be present in every cult. The sure mark of a cult is what it does with the person, nature and work of Jesus Christ. All cults ultimately deny the fact that Jesus Christ is God the Son, second Person of the Holy Trinity, who paid our penalty for sin at Calvary's cross, and arose on the third day triumphant over death.

3

The
Beliefs
of
Orthodox
Christianity

For the last two thousand years, the Christian church has held certain beliefs to be vital to one's faith. While there is some doctrinal disagreement within the three branches of Christendom—Roman Catholic, Eastern Orthodox and Protestant—there is a general agreement among them as to the essentials of the faith. Whatever disagreement the church may have among its branches, it is insignificant compared to the heretical non-Christian beliefs of the cults. We offer this section as a yardstick to compare the errant beliefs of the cults.

The Doctrine of Authority

When it comes to the matter of final authority there is agreement among the major branches of Christianity with regard to the divine inspiration of the Old and New Testaments. However, the Roman Catholic and Eastern Orthodox branches of the church go somewhat beyond the Bible as to their source of authority.

Roman Catholic. The historic Roman Catholic Church accepts the sixty-six books of the Old and New Testaments as the inspired Word of God. They also accept the Apocrypha as being inspired of God. Further, they consider church tradition just as authoritative as the Scriptures. (In a previous work, we have dealt with reasons why we do not accept the Apocrypha as sacred Scripture [see *Answers to Tough Questions,* pp. 36-38]).

Eastern Orthodox. The historic Eastern Orthodox Church also accepts the sixty-six books of the Old and New Testaments as God's inspired revelation. They add that their church is the custodian of God's Word and the rightful interpreters.

Protestant. The historic Protestant Church holds that Scripture alone is the final authority on all matters of faith and practice. The Lutheran formula of Concord put it this way: "We believe, confess, and teach that the only rule and norm, according to which all dogmas and doctrines ought to be esteemed and judged, is no other whatever than the prophetic and apostolic writings both of the Old and of the New Testaments."

Scripture itself testifies that it is complete in what it reveals and the standard and final authority on all matters of doctrine and practice:

All Scripture is inspired by God and profitable for teaching, for reproof, for correction, for training in righteousness (2 Timothy 3:16).

But know this first of all, that no prophecy of Scripture is a matter of one's own interpretation, for no prophecy was ever made by an act of human will, but men moved by the Holy Spirit spoke from God (2 Peter 1:20,21).

You shall not add to the word which I am commanding you, nor take away from it, that you may keep the commandments of the Lord your God which I command you (Deuteronomy 4:2).

I testify to everyone who hears the words of the prophecy of this book: if anyone adds to them, God shall add to him the plagues which are written in this book; and if anyone takes away from the words of the book of this prophecy, God shall take away his part from the tree of life and from the holy city, which are written in this book (Revelation 22:18,19).

The Doctrine of God

The doctrine of God is the same in all three branches of Christianity. The Westminster Shorter Catechism (question 6) reads, "There are three persons in the Godhead: the Father, the Son, and the Holy Ghost; and these three are one God, the same in substance, equal in power and glory."

The Athanasian Creed elaborates on the doctrine of the Trinity:

> We worship one God in Trinity, and Trinity in Unity; Neither confounding the Persons, nor dividing the Substance [Essence]. For there is one Person of the Father, and another of the Son, and another of the Holy Ghost. But the Godhead of the Father, of the Son, and of the Holy Ghost is all one, the Glory equal, the Majesty co-eternal. Such as the Father is, such is the Son, and such is the Holy Ghost. The Father uncreate, the Son uncreate, and the Holy Ghost uncreate . . . The Father eternal, the Son eternal, and the Holy Ghost eternal. And yet they are not three Gods, but one God . . . the Unity in Trinity and the Trinity in Unity is to be worshipped.

In a previous work, *Answers to Tough Questions*, we explained in a simple way the biblical doctrine of the Trinity. We are reprinting it here as an attempt to clarify what orthodox Christianity believes regarding the nature of God:

> One of the most misunderstood ideas in the Bible concerns the teaching about the Trinity. Although Chris-

tians say that they believe in one God, they are constantly accused of polytheism (worshipping at least three
gods).

The Scriptures do *not* teach that God wears three different masks while acting out the drama of history. What
the Bible does teach is stated in the doctrine of the Trinity
as: there is *one* God who has revealed Himself in three
persons, the Father, the Son and the Holy Spirit, and
these three persons are the one God.

Although this is difficult to comprehend, it is nevertheless what the Bible tells us, and is the closest the finite
mind can come to explaining the infinite mystery of the
infinite God, when considering the biblical statements
about God's being.

The Bible teaches that there is one God and only one
God: "Hear, O Israel! The Lord is our God, the Lord is
one!" (Deuteronomy 6:4); "There is one God" (1 Timothy
2:5, KJV); "Thus says the Lord, the King of Israel and his
Redeemer, the Lord of hosts: 'I am the first and I am the
last, and there is no God besides Me' " (Isaiah 44:6).

However, even though God is one in His essential
being or nature, He is also three persons: "Let us make
man in our image" (Genesis 1:26, KJV); "Then the Lord
God said, Behold, the man has become like one of us"
(Genesis 3:22, RSV).

God's plural personality is alluded to here, for He
could not be talking to angels in these instances, because
angels could not and did not help God create. The Bible
teaches that Jesus Christ, not the angels, created all
things (John 1:3; Colossians 1:16; Hebrews 1:2).

In addition to speaking of God as one, and alluding
to a plurality of God's personality, the Scriptures are
quite specific as to naming God in terms of three persons.
There is a person whom the Bible calls the Father, and
the Father is designated as God the Father (Galatians
1:1).

The Bible talks about a person named Jesus, or the
Son, or the Word, also called God: "The Word was God"

(John 1:1, KJV). Jesus "also was calling God His own Father, making Himself equal with God" (John 5:18).

There is a third person mentioned in the Scriptures called the Holy Spirit, and this person—different from the Father and the Son—is also called God ("Ananias, why has Satan filled your heart to lie to the Holy Spirit? . . . You have not lied to men but to God" [Acts 5:3,4, RSV]).

The facts of the biblical teaching are these: There is one God. This one God has a plural personality. This one God is called the Father, the Son, the Holy Spirit, all distinct personalities, all designated God. We are therefore led to the conclusion that the Father, Son and Holy Spirit are one God, the doctrine of the Trinity.

Dr. John Warwick Montgomery offers this analogy to help us understand this doctrine better:

> The doctrine of the Trinity is not "irrational"; what *is* irrational is to suppress the biblical evidence for Trinity in favor of unity, or the evidence for unity in favor of Trinity.
>
> Our data must take precedence over our models—or, stating it better, our models must sensitively reflect the full range of data.
>
> A close analogy to the theologian's procedure here lies in the work of the theoretical physicist: Subatomic light entities are found, on examination, to possess wave properties (W), particle properties (P), and quantum properties (h).
>
> Though these characteristics are in many respects incompatible (particles don't diffract, while waves do, etc.), physicists "explain" or "model" an electron as PWh. They have to do this in order to give proper weight to all the relevant data.
>
> Likewise the theologian who speaks of God as "three in one." Neither the scientist nor the theologian expects you to get a "picture" by way of his model; the purpose of the model is to help you take into account *all* of the facts, instead of perverting reality through super-imposing an apparent "consistency" on it.
>
> The choice is clear: either the Trinity or a "God" who is only a pale imitation of the Lord of biblical and confessional Christianity (*How Do We Know There Is a God?*, pp. 14,15).

The Person of Jesus Christ

Two thousand years ago, Jesus asked His disciples the ultimate question: "Who do you say that I am?" (Matthew 16:15) Central to the Christian faith is the identity of its founder, Jesus Christ, and it is of monumental importance to have a proper view of who He is.

Jesus Was Human

The Christian church has always affirmed that, although He was supernaturally conceived by the Holy Spirit, God in human flesh, Jesus Christ was also fully man. The teaching of the Scriptures is clear with regard to His humanity:

• He grew intellectually and physically.

Jesus kept increasing in wisdom and stature, and in favor with God and men (Luke 2:52).

• He desired food.

And after He had fasted forty days and forty nights, He then became hungry (Matthew 4:2).

• He became tired.

Jesus therefore, being wearied from his journey . . . (John 4:6).

• He needed sleep.

And behold, there arose a great storm in the sea, so that the boat was covered with the waves; but He Himself was asleep (Matthew 8:24).

• He cried.

Jesus wept (John 11:35).

• He died.

But coming to Jesus, when they saw that He was already dead, they did not break his legs (John 19:33).

Therefore, it is made plain by Scripture that Jesus

was genuinely human. He possesses all the attributes of humanity.

Jesus Was God

Jesus of Nazareth was a man but He was more than just a man. He was God in human flesh. While the Scriptures clearly teach He was a man, they likewise make it clear that He was God.

Jesus Made Divine Claims

There are many references by Jesus and His disciples concerning who He was:

In the beginning was the Word, and the Word was with God, and the Word was God (John 1:1).

Jesus said to him, " . . . He who has seen Me has seen the Father" (John 14:9).

Jesus said to them, "Truly, truly, I say to you, before Abraham was born, I am" (John 8:58).

. . . looking for the blessed hope and the appearing of the glory of our great God and Savior, Christ Jesus (Titus 2:13).

From now on I am telling you before it comes to pass, so that when it does occur, you may believe that I am He (John 13:19).

Jesus Exercised Divine Works

Jesus' friends and enemies were constantly amazed at the works He performed. In John 10, Jesus claims, "I and the Father are one." Then when the Jews again attempted to stone Him, "Jesus answered them, 'I showed you many good works from the Father; for which of them are you stoning Me?' The Jews answered Him, 'For a good work we do not stone You, but for blasphemy; and because You, being a man, make Yourself out to be God' " (John 10:30-33).

Some of the works attributed to Christ as well as to God are:

1. Christ created all things (John 1:3; Colossians 1:16; Hebrews 1:10).

2. Christ upholds all things (Colossians 1:17; Hebrews 1:3).

3. Christ directs and guides the course of history (1 Corinthians 10:1-11).

4. Christ forgives sin (Mark 2:5-12; Colossians 3:13).

5. Christ bestows eternal life (John 10:28; 1 John 5:11).

6. Christ will raise the dead at the resurrection (John 11:25; John 5:21,28,29).

7. Christ will be the judge of all men in final judgment (John 5:22,27; Matthew 25:31-46; 2 Corinthians 5:10).

Jesus Possessed Divine Attributes

By Demonstration

Jesus not only claimed to be God, but He also demonstrated that He had the ability to do things that only God could do.

• Jesus exercised authority over nature.

And being aroused, He rebuked the wind and said to the sea, "Hush, be still." And the wind died down and it became perfectly calm. And He said to them, "Why are you so timid? How is it that you have no faith?" And they became very much afraid and said to one another, "Who then is this, that even the wind and the sea obey Him?" (Mark 4:39-41)

- Jesus reported events which occurred when He was far away from the scene.

Nathanael said to Him, "How do You know me?" Jesus answered and said to him, "Before Philip called you, when you were under the fig tree, I saw you." Nathanael answered Him, "Rabbi, You are the Son of God; You are the King of Israel." Jesus answered and said to him, "Because I said to you that I saw you under the fig tree, do you believe? You shall see greater things than these" (John 1:48-50).

- Jesus knew the very thoughts of people.

But He knew what they were thinking (Luke 6:8).

- Jesus had authority over life and death.

And He came up and touched the coffin; and the bearers came to a halt. And He said, "Young man, I say to you, arise!" And the dead man sat up, and began to speak. And Jesus gave him back to his mother. And fear gripped them all, and they began glorifying God, saying, "A great prophet has arisen among us!" and "God has visited His people!" (Luke 7:14-16)

By Association

Not only did Christ demonstrate the ability to do the things only God could do, but the attributes which were attributed to God were also attributed to Jesus Christ. These attributes are found both in the Old Testament prophecies attributed to the Messiah, the Christ, and in the New Testament as direct references to Jesus. Old Testament prophecies which refer to Jesus Christ and His attributes can be examined in Chapter 9 in *Evidence That Demands a Verdict* (San Bernardino, CA: Here's Life Publishers, 1979). Here the direct New Testament references will be considered.

The customary division of the attributes of God into metaphysical and moral is assumed here.

As regards metaphysical attributes we may affirm

firstly that God is self-existent; secondly that He is immense (or infinite). In regard to immensity to infinity He is eternal, unchangeable, omnipresent, omnipotent, perfect, incomprehensible, omniscient.

As regards moral attributes God is holy, true, loving, righteous, faithful and merciful. In these respects man differs from the ideal of manhood in the sense that He is the Author of these qualities. They are un-derived in Him. It will not be deemed necessary here to go beyond mere proof that all these attributes of God existed in Him. If the metaphysical attributes of God exist in Christ, then the moral attributes are un-derived and infinite in degree. Emphasis therefore will be laid on the metaphysical attributes.

Jesus' several statements of His oneness with the Father bear upon this subject, especially John 16:15: "All things that the Father has are Mine." This is a marvelous claim. This explains why in the previous verse (John 16:14) He could say that the work of the Holy Spirit is to glorify Christ: "He shall glorify Me for He shall take of Mine, and shall disclose it to you." Beyond Christ there is nothing to know about the character of God (John 14:9).

Christ possesses the metaphysical attributes of God.

These attributes involve what might be called the essence of God. (The following is not an exhaustive list.)

1. *Self-existence*

Christ has the quality that He is not dependent on anyone or anything for His existence, and all other life is dependent on Him: "I am the life" (John 14:6). He does not say, "I have" but "I am." There is no life from amoeba to archangel apart from Christ. These verses must be explained against the background of the name

Jehovah (Yahweh) as explained in Exodus 3:13-15 and 6:2-9. (Also see Colossians 1:15-23.)

2. *Eternal*

When used of created things this adjective means without end. As used of God, of course, it means without beginning or end. Some clear evidence is found in 1 John 5:11-20:

> And the witness is this, that God has given us eternal life, and this life is in His Son. . . . And we know that the Son of God has come, and has given us understanding, in order that we might know Him who is true, and we are in Him who is true, in His Son Jesus Christ. This is the true God and eternal life.

Also see John 8:35; Hebrews 13:8; 1 John 1:2; Micah 5:2; and Isaiah 9:6.

3. *All-knowing*

This attribute, also known as omniscience, is the quality of having all knowledge. Biblical evidence for omniscience attributed to Christ is found in three areas.

First is the opinion of the disciples: "Now we know that You know all things, and have no need for anyone to question You; by this we believe that You came from God" (John 16:30). Also compare John 21:17.

Second, the testimony of Scripture: " 'But there are some of you who do not believe.' For Jesus knew from the beginning who they were who did not believe, and who it was that would betray Him" (John 6:64); "In whom are hidden all the treasures of wisdom and knowledge" (Colossians 2:3). Also see John 2:23-25 and 1 Corinthians 1:25.

Third, from examples in Scripture: "But Jesus, aware of their reasonings, answered and said to them,

'Why are you reasoning in your hearts?' " (Luke 5:22).
Also see John 4:16-19; John 21:6; and Matthew 17:24-27.

Often people refer to Matthew 24:36 as an exception, to illustrate that Christ was not all-knowing.
However, many scholars, including Augustine, understand the word *know* here to mean "to make known or
declare." This is a proper meaning of the text. Thus
Jesus is stating that it is not among his instructions from
the Father to make this known at this time (Shedd, *Dogmatic Theology II*, 276).

4. *All-powerful*

This means God can do anything not forbidden by
His divine nature. For example, God cannot sin, for He
is holy and righteous. Allowing for this exception, God
can do anything (Mark 10:27). Another name for this attribute is omnipotence.

Christ claimed equality with God in this area:

Jesus therefore answered and was saying to them,
"Truly, truly, I say to you, the Son can do nothing of
Himself, unless it is something He sees the Father doing;
for whatever the Father does, these things the Son also
does in like manner" (John 5:19).

Jesus is called the Almighty: "I am the Alpha and
the Omega," says the Lord God, "who is and who was
and who is to come, the Almighty" (Revelation 1:8).
Compare this with Revelation 1:17,18; 22:12,13; and
Isaiah 41:4.

5. *Present everywhere*

This is commonly called omnipresence. This
means God is everywhere, there is no place where He is
not present. What is important here is to note this does
not mean God is everything. Rather, He is everywhere.
God is separate from His creation.

For where two or three have gathered together in My name, there I am in their midst (Matthew 18:20).

And lo, I am with you always, even to the end of the age (Matthew 28:20).

Christ possesses the moral attributes of God.

These are attributes which deal with the character of God. Again, this list is not complete.

1. *Holy*

This means that God is pure, He cannot sin, and He is unspoiled by evil or sin either by act or nature. Christ also possesses this attribute: "And the angel answered and said to her, 'The Holy Spirit will come upon you, and the power of the Most High will overshadow you; and for that reason the holy offspring shall be called the Son of God' " (Luke 1:35).

2. *Truth*

Truth is the quality of being consistent with your words and actions and having those words and actions correspond to the real world. Thus it means you never lie. Christ's claims were strong here. He not only claimed to know the truth, He claimed He was the truth. The truth can never lie.

Jesus said to him, "I am the way, and the truth, and the life; no one comes to the Father, but through Me" (John 14:6).

And to the angel of the church in Philadelphia write: "He who is holy, who is true, who has the key of David, who opens and no one will shut, and who shuts and no one opens, says this" (Revelation 3:7).

3. *Love*

This means that love, unconditional in its nature, is an attribute of God. Here again bold statements are made with regard to Christ's love:

For God so loved the world, that He gave His only begotten Son, that whoever believes in Him should not perish, but have eternal life (John 3:16).

A new commandment I give to you, that you love one another, even as I have loved you, that you also love one another. By this all men will know that you are My disciples, if you have love for one another (John 13:34,35).

4. *Righteous*

God is a righteous or just God. Righteousness means a standard. God's standard of love, justice, holiness is what He expects of us. Only God's righteous standard is acceptable to Him. God is righteous and God can only accept righteous people before Him, yet He alone can be perfectly righteous, so Christ was accepted as our righteousness, as a perfect substitute:

Much more then, having now been justified by His blood, we shall be saved from the wrath of God through Him (Romans 5:9).

For if by the transgression of the one, death reigned through the one, much more those who receive the abundance of grace and of the gift of righteousness will reign in life through the One, Jesus Christ. So then as through one transgression there resulted condemnation to all men, even so through one act of righteousness there resulted justification of life to all men. For as through the one man's disobedience the many were made sinners, even so through the obedience of the One the many will be made righteous. And the Law came in that the transgression might increase; but where sin increased, grace abounded all the more, that, as sin reigned in death, even so grace might reign through righteousness to eternal life through Jesus Christ our Lord (Romans 5:17-21).

My little children, I am writing these things to you that you may not sin. And if anyone sins, we have an Advocate with the Father, Jesus Christ the righteous (1 John 2:1).

In the future there is laid up for me the crown of righteousness, which the Lord, the righteous Judge, will award to me on that day; and not only to me, but also to all who have loved his appearing (2 Timothy 4:8).

Then Christ's righteous sacrifice demonstrates His deity by His acceptance by God.

Now, concerning the moral attributes, some say, "I love unconditionally" or "I tell the truth, but that doesn't make me God." So why does it make Christ God? This question is answered by understanding two concepts, one having to do with God's nature, the other with our nature.

God's attributes are qualities that are all true of God and do not exist in isolation. In other words, God's justice exists with God's love. One does not exclude the other. Thus, the attributes which represent the character of God are affected by those qualities which are true of His essence.

So if God is love and God is infinite (another attribute not touched on here) then God's love is infinite. This is in contrast to man. Man may love, but his love is not infinite.

Second, man's basic nature is sinful and has the tendency to continue to sin. Thus although man may act righteously at times, on his own, or may love unconditionally, ultimately he is bounded by and infected with his sin nature which results in disobedience to God's standard.

Jesus Received Worship as God

Jesus allowed Himself to be worshipped, something that is reserved for God alone:

You shall fear only the Lord your God; and you shall worship Him, and swear by His name (Deuteronomy 6:13).

Then Jesus said to him, "Begone, Satan! For it is written, you shall worship the Lord your God, and serve Him only" (Matthew 4:10).

"Where is He who has been born King of the Jews? For we saw His star in the east, and have come to worship Him" . . . And they came into the house and saw the Child with Mary His mother; and they fell down and worshipped Him (Matthew 2:2,11).

And behold, Jesus met them and greeted them. And they came up and took hold of His feet and worshipped Him (Matthew 28:9).

And when they saw Him, they worshipped Him (Matthew 28:17).

And he said, "Lord, I believe. And he worshipped Him (John 9:38).

Jesus Is God Yahweh

Attributes ascribed to Yahweh in the Old Testament are also used in reference to Jesus in the New Testament, demonstrating that Jesus is Yahweh.

"THERE IS ONE GOD" (1 Corinthians 8:6)

GOD IS . . .		JESUS IS . . .
Genesis 1:1		John 1:1-3
Job 33:4	**CREATOR**	Colossians 1:12-17
Isaiah 40:28		Hebrews 1:8-12
Isaiah 41:4	**FIRST**	Revelation 1:17
Isaiah 44:6	**&**	Revelation 2:8
Isaiah 48:12	**LAST**	Revelation 22:13
Exodus 3:13,14		John 8:24, 58
Deuteronomy 32:39	**I AM**	John 13:19
Isaiah 43:10	**(EGO EIMI)**	John 18:5
Genesis 18:25		2 Timothy 4:1
Psalm 96:13	**JUDGE**	2 Corinthians 5:10
Joel 3:12		Romans 14:10-12

Psalm 47		Matthew 2:1-6
Isaiah 44:6-8	**KING**	John 19:21
Jeremiah 10:10		1 Timothy 6:13-16
Psalm 27:1		John 1:9
Isaiah 60:20	**LIGHT**	John 8:12
Psalm 106:21		John 4:42
Isaiah 43:3,11	**SAVIOR**	Acts 4:10-12
Isaiah 45:21-23		1 John 4:14
Psalm 23		John 10:11
Psalm 100:3	**SHEPHERD**	Hebrews 13:20
Isaiah 40:11		1 Peter 5:4
(ibid., p. 89)		

The teaching on the person of Jesus Christ from the Scripture is very clear. He was fully God and at the same time fully man. Any deviation from this position is not only unscriptural, it is also heretical. Those who attempt to make Jesus something less than God cannot go to the Bible for their justification. Therefore, if one takes the Bible seriously, one must conclude that Jesus of Nazareth was God in human flesh.

For further material and sources see *More Than a Carpenter* (Wheaton, IL: Tyndale House Publishers, 1980), Chapter 1, and *Evidence That Demands a Verdict*, Chapter 6.

The Atonement

Within all branches of Christianity there is agreement that the deity of Christ was a perfect satisfaction to God as just and substitutionary punishment for the sins of the world:

Therefore as in Adam we had fallen under sin, the curse, and death, so we are delivered from sin, the curse, and death in Jesus Christ. His voluntary suffering and death on the cross for us, being of infinite value and merit, as the death of one sinless, God and man in one person, is both a perfect satisfaction to the justice of God, which had condemned us for sin to death, and a fund of infinite merit, which has obtained him the right, without prejudice to justice, to give us sinners pardon of our sins, and grace to have victory over sin and death (the longer catechism of the Eastern Orthodox Church, answer to question 208).

His Bodily Resurrection

The doctrine of the bodily resurrection is so central to Christianity that Paul said if it did not happen then all of our preaching and faith is in vain (1 Corinthians 15:14). In our former work, *Answers to Tough Questions*, we state the importance of the resurrection:

> The sign of the resurrection was meant to set Jesus apart from anyone else who ever lived, and it would designate Him the Son of God (Romans 1:4).

> The accounts of His appearances are recorded for us by eyewitnesses to whom Jesus appeared alive over a forty-day period after His pubic crucifixion. As the scriptural account sets forth to these "he shewed Himself alive after His passion by many infallible proofs, being seen of them forty days, and speaking of the things pertaining to the kingdom of God" (Acts 1:3, KJV).

> Writing about A.D. 56, the apostle Paul mentions the fact that more than 500 people had witnessed the resurrected Christ at one time and most of them were still living when he wrote (1 Corinthians 15:6). This statement is somewhat of a challenge to those who might not have believed, since Paul is saying that there are many people yet living who could be interviewed to find out if Christ had indeed risen (pp. 47-48).

The Deity of the Holy Spirit

Central to the Christian faith is the teaching that the Holy Spirit is personal and is God, the third person of the Holy Trinity. The doctrine that the Holy Spirit is a person is clearly taught in Scripture. Notice the following examples of personal attributes displayed by the Holy Spirit. He can be grieved (Ephesians 4:30), resisted (Acts 7:51) and lied to (Acts 5:3). Moreover, the Holy Spirit can speak (Acts 21:11), think (Acts 5:3) and teach (Luke 12:12). Thus, the Holy Spirit is personal.

Furthermore, the Holy Spirit is spoken of in the Bible as a divine person. The Holy Spirit has the attributes of God, for He is all-powerful (Luke 1:35-37), eternal (Hebrews 9:14), and all-knowing (1 Corinthians 2:10,11). The Scriptures teach that lying to the Holy Spirit is lying to God (Acts 5:3,4).

The Holy Spirit also was involved in divine works, including creation (Genesis 1:2, Job 33:4), the new birth (John 3:5), the resurrection of Christ (Romans 8:11) and the inspiration of the Bible (2 Peter 1:20,21). Finally, to blaspheme against the Holy Spirit is an unforgivable sin (Matthew 12:31,32). The conclusion is that the Holy Spirit is God, the third person of the Holy Trinity.

The Doctrine of Man

The doctrine of man is succinctly expressed in the Westminster Shorter Catechism that "God created man, male and female, after his own image, in knowledge, righteousness, and holiness, with dominion over the creatures."

We relate how man fell from his created status in our book, *Answers to Tough Questions*:

> An infinite-personal God created the heavens and the earth (Genesis 1:1) and man in his own image (Genesis 1:26). When He had finished creating, everything was good (Genesis 1:31).
>
> Man and woman were placed in a perfect environment, with all their needs taken care of. They were given only one prohibition; they were not to eat of the fruit of

the tree of the knowledge of good and evil, lest they die (Genesis 2:17).

Unfortunately, they did eat of the tree (Genesis 3), and the result was a fall in four different areas. The relationship between God and man was now broken, as can be seen from Adam and Eve's attempt to hide from God (Genesis 3:8).

The relationship between man and his fellow man was severed, with both Adam and Eve arguing and trying to pass the blame to someone else (Genesis 3:12,13).

The bond between man and nature also was broken, with the ground producing thorns and thistles and the animal world no longer being benevolent (Genesis 3:17, 18). Man also became separated from himself, with a feeling of emptiness and incompleteness, something he had not experienced before the fall (pp. 62-63).

The Doctrine of Salvation

The doctrine of salvation is linked with the atoning death of Christ on the cross. While all major branches of Christianity agree that Christ's death was satisfactory to God as a sacrifice for the world's sins, there is a disagreement on how that sacrifice is appropriated. We believe the Bible teaches that salvation is by grace, a free gift of God to all those who believe in Christ. Those who receive Christ by faith have their sins forgiven and become children of God, a new creation in Christ Jesus:

> For by grace you have been saved through faith; and that not of yourselves, it is the gift of God; not as a result of works, that no one should boast (Ephesians 2:8,9).

> He saved us, not on the basis of deeds which we have done in righteousness, but according to His mercy, by the washing of regeneration and renewing by the Holy Spirit (Titus 3:5).

> But as many as received Him, to them He gave the

right to become children of God, even to those who believe in His name (John 1:12).

In Him we have redemption through His blood, the forgiveness of our trespasses, according to the riches of His grace (Ephesians 1:7).

Therefore if any man is in Christ, he is a new creature; the old things passed away; behold, new things have come (2 Corinthians 5:17).

Since salvation is a free gift from God, no one can add anything to the completed work of Christ to receive it. It is received by faith and faith alone.

The Doctrine of the Church

The Westminster Confession of Faith contains a statement about the church that is accepted by all branches of Christendom:

The catholic or universal Church, which is invisible, consists of the whole number of the elect, that have been, are, or shall be gathered into one, under Christ the head thereof, and is the spouse, the body, the fullness of Him that filleth all in all. The visible Church, which is also catholic or universal under the gospel (not confined to one nation, as before under the law), consists of all those, throughout the world, that profess the true religion, and of their children, and is the kingdom of the Lord Jesus Christ, the house and family of God, out of which there is no ordinary possibility of salvation.

The true church is made up of all those individuals who have put their trust in Christ as their Savior. It is not merely the attending of church or having a name on the membership list that make one a member of Christ's true church. Only the transforming work of the Holy Spirit in the heart of the repentant sinner qualifies one for membership in the true body of Christ.

Conclusion

As Bible-believing Christians, we know that God is personal, eternal, and triune. However, the cults each deny one or more of the essential Bible doctrines we have discussed. Beware of any group or individual that changes essential doctrines. The Bible's teachings cannot be exploited at the whim of any group or individual. It contains "the faith once for all delivered to the saints" (Jude 3), and one who changes its divine pronouncements acts like those condemned in 2 Peter 3:16: "The untaught and unstable distort, as they do also the rest of the Scriptures, to their own destruction."

Introduction

to

Western Cults

I n this section we will deal with the cults that claim to be the true representation of the Christian church. Usually a western cult will begin in Europe, America, or Australia. Our study will entail those that have memberships of more than 100,000 people. Those groups with the largest following will naturally deserve the most attention, therefore, the order will be: Mormonism, Jehovah's Witnesses, Christian Science, Unity School of Christianity, Unification Church ("Moonies"), Unitarian Universalist, and The Way International.

The western cults reveal a consistent trend:

1. Isolated leadership

2. Extrabiblical revelation

3. Alteration of the Bible

4. Denial of essential Christian doctrine

59

5. The claim that the Chrisitian church is wrong

Some people may question why Unity School of Christianity and the Unification Church are classified as western cults, since both groups are influenced by oriental philosophy. Our reason is clear: Unity, although it teaches reincarnation, claims to be the true Christian church; and Sun Myung Moon claims to fulfill biblical messiahship, even though he interprets the Bible through Taoism.

4

Mormonism

The Church of Jesus Christ of Latter-day Saints is one of the largest, wealthiest, and most respected of any western cult. Popularly known as the Mormon Church, they derive their nickname from the first of their extrabiblical revelations, *The Book of Mormon*. The religious environment of America in the early nineteenth century opened the floodgate for a variety of divergent movements, among which Mormonism has been the most successful. The Mormon Church claims to be the only true Christian church, in fact, the "restored" church, while declaring that all Christian denominations are false.

History

Joseph Smith, Jr., the founder of Mormonism, was born in Sharon, Vermont, December 23, 1805. Smith was the fourth of ten children of Joseph and Lucy Mack Smith. In 1814 the family moved to Palmyra, New York (about twenty-five miles east of Rochester). Four years later they moved to nearby Manchester, where later Smith would claim to have several angelic revelations leading to the establishment of the Mormon Church.

Palmyra, New York, had three denominations (Baptist, Methodist, and Presbyterian) nestled among the homes of their community. Most of the Smith family joined the Presbyterians, but Joseph focused mostly on the differences and attended a Methodist church for a short time. It is Joseph's view of the denominational differences that set the stage for his alleged first vision.

Mormonism and New Revelation

Mormonism is built on extrabiblical revelation. If Joseph Smith had not convinced his companions that God spoke directly to him, then Mormonism would not be with us today. There are three ways in which Joseph Smith claimed that God spoke to him as with no other living man: visions, prophecy, and the gift and power to translate. This resulted in his extrabiblical revelations of *The Book of Mormon*, *Doctrine and Covenants*, *Pearl of Great Price*, and the *Inspired Version* of the Bible. These, along with the King James Version of the Bible, are referred to as the "standard works" of the Mormon Church.

Visions

Joseph Smith purported to have several visions throughout his lifetime. Some of these visions became a part of their scriptures called the *Pearl of Great Price* and the *Doctrine and Covenants*. A few of his visions and revelations are not recorded in either standard work and are found only in journals, diaries, and their *History of the Church*. Several of these visions and revelations were received while Smith was gazing into a "peep stone." Peep stone gazing was not uncommon in the early 1800s. Usually a special stone would be placed in a hat and the person would look at the stone to receive a revelation or vision.

Prophecy

Most of the prophecies of Joseph Smith can be found in the *Doctrine and Covenants*. Smith was fond of giving forth a new prophecy for any situation, some of these are not found in the standard works, but only in their *History of the Church* and other historical documents.

Gift and Power to Translate

Some of Smith's new revelations came through what the Mormons call the "gift and power to translate." Most of the time this was done while Smith was looking into his peep stone. This "gift and power" was used for *The Book of Mormon*, parts of the *Pearl of Great Price* and the *Inspired Version* of the Bible.

The First Vision of 1820

In 1820 Joseph allegedly received a vision that became the basis for the founding of the Mormon Church. According to Mormon history, the background of Joseph's first vision was a revival that broke out in the spring of 1820, in Palmyra, New York. Smith portrays this revival as a "division amongst the people, some crying, 'Lo, here!' and others, 'Lo, there!' Some were contending for the Methodist faith, some for the Presbyterian, and some for the Baptist" (*Pearl of Great Price, Joseph Smith—History*, 1:5).

Joseph, being fourteen years old at the time, often said to himself, "What is to be done? Who of all these parties are right; or, are they all wrong together? If any one of them be right, which is it, and how shall I know it?" (ibid., 1:10)

As Joseph's story proceeds, he was reading the Bible and happened upon James 1:5: "If any of you lack wisdom, let him ask of God, that giveth to all men liberally, and upbraideth not; and it shall be given him" (KJV). He took this passage to mean that he should go to the woods and pray for an answer about which church he should join. The actual context of James 1:5 is set against Smith's interpretation, because the wisdom James speaks of is concerning why we go through trials.

Nevertheless, Smith went to the woods to pray and was overcome by a demonic attack: "Thick darkness gathered around me, and it seemed to me for a time as if I were doomed to sudden destruction" (ibid., 1:15).

Immediately afterward he said a light appeared over his head with two personages descending in the light. The Father pointed to the Son and introduced him. Smith continued:

> My object in going to inquire of the Lord was to know which of all the sects was right, that I might know which to join . . . I asked the Personages who stood above me in the light, which of all the sects was right (for at this time it had never entered into my heart that all were wrong)—and which I should join. I was answered that I must join none of them, for they were all wrong; and the Personage who addressed me said that all their creeds were an abomination in his sight; that those professors were corrupt (ibid., 1:18,19).

Biblical Analysis of Smith's First Vision

We find in Joseph Smith's first vision that all the Christian churches are said to be wrong. Smith's question reveals his lack of knowledge about denominations and the church.

The denominations of Christianity teach the same doctrines of the Trinity, deity of Jesus Christ, Person of the Holy Spirit, atonement, resurrection, and salvation by grace. The Bible allows latitude on peripheral issues (Romans 14:1-5; Colossians 2:16,17; and 1 Corinthians 12:12-27) which is usually what denominations differ over. Christian organizations like Campus Crusade for Christ are proof of Christian unity, because the members are from several denominations, yet we focus upon a unified work in Christ.

We have already mentioned in Chapter 1 that the test for a true prophet includes complete accuracy and following the true God (Deuteronomy 13:1-5; 18:20-22). We would like to add Isaiah 8:20 to this: "To the law and to the testimony! If they do not speak according to this word, it is because they have no dawn." This test is important because it tells us that all of their current words must agree with what God has already said.

Joseph Smith's first vision fails to pass the test of Scripture. Smith claims that he saw God the Father, which is contrary to John 1:18; 6:46 ("No man has seen God"); and 1 Timothy 6:16 ("whom no man has seen or can see"). Smith claims that the Father had a body, which is contrary to Colossians 1:15 ("the image of the invisible God"). Smith claimed that Jesus said all the churches were wrong, which is contrary to Matthew 16:18: "I will build my church; and the gates of hell shall not prevail against it" (KJV). One could hardly believe that the same Jesus who illustrated the continuation of the church in the parables of Matthew 13 would contradict himself in a vision to Joseph Smith and say that all the churches were wrong. The apostle Paul also shows that the church will be here throughout all ages (Ephesians 3:21).

The Birth of Mormonism

In what looks like a well orchestrated sequence of events, Joseph, with the help of a few assistants, was able to start his own church. The story from the account in the *Pearl of Great Price* says that Joseph Smith had an angel awaken him from his sleep on September 21, 1823. This angel, later identified as Moroni, a supposed character in *The Book of Mormon*, told Smith that a record of the people on this continent was written on golden plates and buried near his home.

Moroni showed Joseph the plates that were buried in the hill Cummorah, but forbade him to receive them for four years. The golden plates were said to be buried in a stone box along with two stones set in silver bows that were attached to a breastplate. Moroni told Smith that these stones were the Urim and Thummim, and these are used by "seers" for the purpose of translation (*Pearl of Great Price*, 1:27-54).

He finally received the golden plates, the stones, and the breastplate on September 22, 1827, and began translating the characters. The language on the plates was said to be "reformed Egyptian hieroglyphics," which no one had heard of before or after the time of Smith. The resulting *Book of Mormon*, published March 26, 1830, is the foundational scripture in the Mormon Church and her 125 splinter groups.

On April 6, 1830, at Fayette, New York, "The Church of Christ" was officially organized with six members. Their first name, The Church of Christ, was changed in 1832 to The Church of the Latter-day Saints and again in 1834 to its current name, The Church of Jesus Christ of Latter-day Saints.

Acting on the preconceived notion that the Christian church was false, Smith set out to restore all of its missing parts: prophet, seer, revelator, apostles, seventy, baptism, priesthood, temples, and additional scripture. Mormonism gained its greatest stronghold when nearly an entire congregation of the early Disciples of Christ, including their noted preacher Sidney

Rigdon, converted to Joseph Smith's newly found religion. This took place in Kirtland, Ohio, in October of 1830. From that time forward Smith never lacked good, well polished preachers.

What began as an organization of six men in a log cabin at Fayette, New York, has grown to an empire of eight million people with an income in excess of $3,000,000 daily. Their missionary program takes more than 40,000 missionaries around the world, and they baptize about a third of a million people annually.

The Mormon Church Structure

Priesthood Authority

Moroni had told Smith that possession and use of the stones constitutes a "seer." Smith evidently did not feel that this gave him enough authority, so it was decided that the proper priesthood and authority to baptize needed to be restored to the church. On May 15, 1829, Joseph Smith and Oliver Cowdery, one of the scribes for *The Book of Mormon*, claimed that John the Baptist appeared to them near Harmony, Pennsylvania, and instructed them to baptize each other in the Sesquihanna River. With this baptism came the authority of the Aaronic Priesthood.

A short time afterward, Peter, James and John also visited Smith and Cowdery while in Pennsylvania. The purpose of this visitation was to restore the Melchizedek Priesthood, which gives them the "power to lay on of hands for the gift of the Holy Ghost."

These two priesthoods, central to Mormon theology, are for male members of their church and originally were for white males only. Men of other races were forbidden to have the Mormon priesthoods until a new revelation was given to their prophet in 1978. The only class currently forbidden to have the priesthood in Mormonism is women.

Prophet, Seer, Revelator

The top ranking official of the Mormon Church is their prophet. He is sometimes referred to as a seer or revelator and he has two companions, a first and second counselor. The three of them make up the First Presidency of the Mormon Church. The new prophet is chosen from the president of their twelve apostles upon the death of the current prophet.

Joseph Smith, the first prophet of the Mormon Church, added several new doctrines to his young church. Some of their questionable practices and doctrines drew criticism from neighboring communities.

From the earliest of times Smith had a cloud of controversy following him from state to state. In New York and Pennsylvania he was a known "glass looker," which is an occultic practice of looking into a stone for lost or buried treasure. In 1826 he was tried and convicted of this in a court of law.

If we listen to the Mormon viewpoint of history at Temple Square, Salt Lake City, Utah, about the persecution of the early Mormon Church, one could easily become misled and think that the Mormon Church was persecuted for no apparent reason. This argument is contrary to fact. Their position on the persecution of Joseph Smith and the early Mormons reads like an incomplete novel. Missing from most Latter-day Saint books is the court conviction of Smith's glass-looking, his failed banking scheme in Kirtland, Ohio, his polygamy before the revelation, his organized armies in Missouri and Illinois, and the ordered destruction of the printing presses that opposed him in Nauvoo, Illinois. Documented proof of these and other events is available in *The Changing World of Mormonism* (Jerald and Sandra Tanner, Chicago: Moody Press, 1980).

On June 27, 1844, a mob of about 200 people, their faces blackened to avoid recognition, stormed the jail and shot Joseph and his brother Hyrum, killing both men. Joseph did not die without a fight. According to the church's own account he shot three men in the mob, of which two later died (*History of the Church*, 6:617,618).

After the death of Joseph Smith, the baton of leadership was passed to Brigham Young, the president of the twelve apostles.

Young led the group westward in a journey which saw many hardships including Indian attacks, exposure, and internal strife. On July 24, 1847, they arrived at Salt Lake Valley in Utah which became the headquarters of the Mormon Church. By the time of Young's death in 1877, the membership had grown from 20,000 in Illinois to 150,000 in Utah.

Living Prophets

There have been twelve other prophets of the Mormon Church since the time of Joseph Smith. Currently leading the Latter-day Saints is their thirteenth prophet, Ezra Taft Benson. The next person in line will be Howard W. Hunter, who is the current president of the twelve apostles.

The living prophet is by all means the most important figure in present-day Mormonism. Ezra Taft Benson, their living prophet, said in a speech on February 26, 1980, at Brigham Young University, that the living prophet is "more vital to us than the standard works." This is not unusual for Mormons. In 1945 the official magazine of the Mormon Church said this: "When our leaders speak, the thinking has been done. When they propose a plan—it is God's plan. When they point the way, there is no other which is safe. When

they give directions, it should mark the end of the controversy" (*Improvement Era*, June 1945, p. 354).

Twelve Living Apostles

The Mormon Church takes the position that a
church must have apostolic succession by direct laying
on of hands or it is not the church of Jesus Christ. The
way they get around the gap between the first century
and 1830 is by having the apostles of the first century
return to earth (Harmony, Pennsylvania) and pass on
the authority of the church by laying hands upon
Joseph Smith and Oliver Cowdery. It is their contention
that if a church does not have twelve living apostles
then it cannot be the true church. These twelve men follow the First Presidency in authority.

The First Quorum of Seventy

Directly under the rank of the council of twelve
apostles is the first quorum of seventy. These selected
seventy men of the Mormon Church are supposed to be
the modern-day counterpart for the seventy that Jesus
sent out in Luke 10. These men, along with the apostles
and presidency of the Mormon Church, constitute what
is considered the General Authorities. When there is a
need for a final answer on an issue, any General
Authority may be consulted.

Under their direction is a second quorum of seventy, the stake presidency at local church buildings, and
the bishops, who are over the wards within the stake.

Biblical Analysis of the Mormon Church Structure

In looking over the structure of the Mormon
Church we must remember what Paul said in 1 Thessalonians 5:21: "But examine everything carefully; hold
fast to that which is good." We realize within Christian
denominations there has been debate over ecclesiastical

hierarchy and the order of the church service, but in Mormonism we are not speaking of the same thing. Since Smith claims to restore what was not restorable, he would first have to show that God intended the succession of prophets, apostles and seventies in the original before he can restore it.

In examining the founder of the Mormon Church any Christian should immediately be alarmed that Joseph Smith was convicted of an occultic practice, glass looking, between the time of his first vision and the founding of his church. Peep stone gazing and glass looking was not an isolated incident in Smith's life. Much has been written on it, and one author has photographs of two of Joseph Smith's actual seer stones. (See D. Michael Quinn, *Early Mormonism and the Magic World View*, Salt Lake City: Signature Press, 1985.)

The question of the priesthood and authority in Mormonism is also answered in the Bible. The Mormons cannot hold the Aaronic priesthood because it was limited to the descendants of Aaron. The purpose of the Aaronic priesthood was to do priestly services and especially to offer the sacrifices for the people of Israel (Hebrews 5:1-3). The need for the Aaronic priesthood was done away with through the sacrifice of Jesus on the cross (Hebrews 7:27). There was a change of the law and the priesthood concerning it (Hebrews 7:12).

Since the purpose of the Aaronic priesthood was fulfilled through the cross, Jesus was established as the High Priest of the Christian faith, after the order of Melchizedek (Hebrews 7:11-18). He continues forever after the order of Melchizedek (Hebrews 7:17) and has an unchangeable priesthood (7:24). No Mormon can hold the Melchizedek priesthood since Jesus will never vacate his position as our high priest.

The only priesthood mentioned in the Bible for the Christian is found in 1 Peter 2:5-10. Therein we find the royal and holy priesthood for the believer. It is not limited to white males, but is for all believers. Our authority comes from being children of the true and living God. John 1:12 tells us: "But as many as received Him, to them He gave the right [authority] to become the children of God, even to those who believe in His name." Our authority is not a result of our priesthood, but from what our Savior did for us.

Do we need a prophet to lead the Christian church? In a real sense we do have a prophet leading Christianity—His name is Jesus. Jesus is our prophet (Acts 2:22), our priest (Hebrews 7:12), and our king (Revelation 17:14). The Mormons have a false concept that we need an Old Testament type prophet, such as Moses, to lead Christianity. They often appeal to Amos 3:7 as proof of this, but their proof text is out of context. What Amos is telling us is that God will never allow a calamity to happen to Israel without first telling the prophet.

Probably the strongest argument against the idea of a prophet is Luke 16:16: "The Law and the Prophets were proclaimed until John." Jesus said that the last of the Old Testament prophets was John the Baptist. Hebrews 1:1 echoes this: "God, after He spoke long ago to the fathers in the prophets . . . in these last days has spoken to us in His Son." The prophets were for those before the time of Christ.

The apostles Jesus chose were the foundation of the church. When Judas killed himself he was replaced by Matthias (Acts 1:26). When we look at Ephesians 2:20, it tells us about the foundation of the church, "having been built upon the foundation of the apostles and prophets, Christ Jesus Himself being the corner stone." The church has been continuing in its building since the days of the apostles. We do not tear out the foundation each time an apostle dies and fill it with a new foundation.

Another problem develops over the seventy in the Mormon Church. The passage they take this from is found in one place, Luke 10:1. The best of the Greek manuscripts have seventy-two instead of seventy. The *New American Standard Bible* and *New International Version* bear this out. The Mormon Church has built part of its restoration on an inferior text, which becomes especially problematic since Smith claimed to retranslate the Bible through the gift and power of God, and he never corrected the verse.

The Scriptures of Mormonism

The Mormon Church has four accepted scriptures they call their Standard Works: The Bible, *The Book of Mormon, Doctrine and Covenants,* and *Pearl of Great Price.*

The Bible

The eighth Article of Faith for the Mormon Church states, "We believe the Bible to be the Word of God in so far as it is translated correctly" (*Pearl of Great Price,* p. 60). *The Book of Mormon* claims that the Catholic Church has taken away parts of the Word of God: "Many parts which are plain and most precious; and also many covenants of the Lord have they taken away. And all this have they done that they might pervert the right ways of the Lord" (1 Nephi 13:26*b*,27).

Orson Pratt, an early apostle of the Mormon Church, put it this way: "Who knows that even one verse of the whole Bible has escaped pollution, so as to convey the same sense now that it did in the original?" (*Orson Pratt's Works,* 1891, p. 218)

This general distrust for the Bible has led Mormons to place more confidence in the other standard works of their church. Joseph Smith made an attempt to correct the errors he thought were in the Bible by translating it through "the gift and power of God." The Mormon claim that the Bible has been changed beyond recovery of the original text is totally false (see *Answers to Tough Questions*, pp. 4-6).

Smith began his work on the Bible in the spring of 1831. On July 2, 1833, the *History of the Church* records: "We this day finished the translation of the scriptures." Plans were made to publish the translation (*Doctrine and Covenants*, 94:10), but it failed to see the presses until 1867, when a splinter group of the Mormon Church published it. The Utah Mormon Church refused to adopt Smith's finished work until 1984 when parts of it were added to the footnotes of their King James Version.

The apostle John gives a warning about adding to or taking from the book of Revelation:

> If anyone adds to them, God shall add to him the plagues which are written in this book; And if anyone takes away from the words of the book of this prophecy, God shall take away his part from the tree of life and from the holy city, which are written in this book (22:18*b*,19).

This verse becomes a self-condemning charge against the prophet Smith. In the Bible published by the Mormon Church, the book of Revelation has the following verses with "JST" in the footnote, indicating a change in text from the Joseph Smith Translation: Revelation 1:1,20; 2:1,22,26,27; 3:1,2; 4:4,5,6; 5:6; 6:1,14; 9:14; 12:1; 13:1; 19:15,18,21; 20:6.

Rev. John D. Nutting wrote a comparison of the Hebrew and Greek manuscripts of the Bible with Smith's version. He discovered that the changes Smith made in the Bible are not supported by any Old or New

Testament manuscript. Smith was uneducated in the languages of the Bible and was not qualified to translate it (available from Utah Gospel Mission, P. O. Box 1901, Orange, CA 92668).

The Book of Mormon

The Book of Mormon is also considered inspired: "We also believe *The Book of Mormon* to be the Word of God" (*Articles of Faith*, number 8). Joseph Smith called it the "most correct of any book on the earth" (*Teachings of the Prophet Joseph Smith*, Salt Lake City: Deseret Press, 1949, p. 194).

The Book of Mormon is supposedly about the early inhabitants of the Americas and contains the fullness of the gospel and the "plain and precious things missing" from the Bible. The American Indians, called Lamanites in *The Book of Mormon*, were originally of Jewish descent. Most of the book is centered around Lehi and his family, who supposedly left Jerusalem in 600 B.C. Rebellion caused them to separate company, the unrighteous became dark-skinned because of their sins, the righteous Nephites remained "white and delightsome."

The two factions began to war and battle with one another, eventually the dark-skinned Lamanites won. Before Moroni, the last Nephite, died he took the records of his people, which were engraved in reformed Egyptian hieroglyphics, and buried them in the hill Cummorah. He enters the story again in 1823 and appears as an angel to Smith, who is told to translate it.

It is a compilation of fifteen books written in the same style as the King James Version of the Bible. What gives it a sound of authority are the many verses and entire chapters of the Bible scattered throughout its text. Smith attempted to make it more acceptable by having three men sign testimonies that God's voice told them the translation is true and they "saw the golden plates."

The testimony of the three witnesses (Oliver Cowdery, David Whitmer and Martin Harris) is published at the beginning of *The Book of Mormon*. What is not commonly discussed among the Mormons is how these three witnesses later *changed their testimony*. The witness Oliver Cowdery became an attorney and died in 1850, never opposing these poetic lines found in a Mormon publication, *Times and Seasons*: "Does it prove there is no time,/Because some watches will not go? ... /Or *The Book of Mormon* not His word,/Because denied by Oliver" (2:482). David Whitmer, who wrote two booklets on Mormonism and Brigham Young, said, "In June, 1829, the Lord called Oliver Cowdery, Martin Harris and myself as three witnesses, to behold *the vision of the angel*" (*An Address to All Believers in Christ*, 1887, p. 32).

It is not insignificant that Whitmer said the three men had a vision. Martin Harris, the third witness, sheds more light on this: "While praying I passed into a state of entrancement, and in that state I saw the angel and the plates" (Anthony Metcalf, *A New Witness for Christ in America*, Salt Lake City: Bookcraft Publishers, 1959, vol. 2, p. 348). The *Book of Mormon* witnesses have proven their story unreliable by changing their testimony "from seeing the angel with golden plates" to a vision and entrancement.

The translation of *The Book of Mormon* appears to be through a process of divination rather than knowing languages. The Mormon history collection *Compressive History of the Church* portrays the translation process as mechanical: "By aid of the Seer Stone, sentences would appear and were read by the Prophet and written by Martin ... but if not written correctly it remained until corrected, so that the translation was just as it was engraven on the plates" (vol. 1, p. 129).

Those who saw Joseph Smith translating gave a contradictory account. Martin Harris, Emma Hale Smith (wife of the prophet), and David Whitmer made statements saying that Joseph Smith would place a stone in a hat and cover his face with the hat, then in the stone would appear the characters from the plates and the English equivalent. Whitmer relates, "I will now give you a description of the manner in which *The Book of Mormon* was translated. Joseph Smith would put the seer stone into a hat, and put his face in the hat . . . a piece of something resembling parchment would appear, and on that appeared the writing" (*An Address to All Believers in Christ,* p. 12).

Millions of people have placed their faith in the work of Joseph Smith. Besides the nonbiblical divination used to produce it, the contents of *The Book of Mormon* contradict the Bible. Every effort of Smith to copy the style of the Bible could not keep it free from error that exposes its fraudulent nature.

There has been no archaeological evidence to support *The Book of Mormon,* even though the Mormon Church has spent untold thousands of dollars and man-hours searching for it. They have produced films and books trying to show parallels between early Central America cultures and *The Book of Mormon,* but to this day there has never been any indisputable discovery.

Thomas Stewart Ferguson, a professor at Brigham Young University, spent twenty-five years of his life researching archaeological evidence for *The Book of Mormon.* At the end of his career he wrote a paper on the result of a life-long project—it was a failure. He finally concluded that *The Book of Mormon* was "fictional," and gave parallel columns showing the text in question and the lack of evidence (see *Ferguson's Manuscript Unveiled,* Utah Lighthouse Ministry, Box 1884, Salt Lake City, Utah 84110).

Doctrine and Covenants

The *Doctrine and Covenants* is a record of 140 revelations since the time of Joseph Smith. This volume contains the distinctive doctrines of Mormonism: including polygamy, the ceasing of polygamy, marriage in heaven, baptism for the dead, many gods, man can become a god, the Father has a body of flesh and bones, and the "Word of Wisdom," including abstinence of meat in summer, tobacco (except for sick cattle), hot drinks, and alcohol (except for washing your body).

Intermingled with these writings are false prophecies and prophecies that were written after the facts were known. An example of the latter is the famous "civil war prophecy" of Joseph Smith. Found in Section 87, it says a war will break out between the Northern States and the Southern States, beginning with a rebellion in South Carolina.

This section was written on December 25, 1832, but there are some curious events surrounding how Smith arrived at the subject matter. United States history books tell us that Congress passed a tariff act on July 14, five months before Smith got his revelation. South Carolina resisted the tariff act and declared it null and void. President Jackson expected trouble and alerted national troops. About a month before Smith's revelation, the governor of South Carolina addressed the Legislature announcing a resistance by force if necessary.

The governor's address was published December 10, 1932, in the *Boston Daily-Advertiser and Patriot*. One of the Mormon leaders, Orson Hyde, was in Boston on December 10, and traveled to Kirtland, Ohio, where Smith was, arriving on December 22. Smith gave his revelation three days later containing the same information in public access and in the newspapers. A prophet of God does not hear the news and repeat it as a prophecy.

Seven sections of the *Doctrine and Covenants* have blatant false prophecies. In the above mentioned "civil war prophecy," there were parts of the prophecy that did not come true, such as Great Britain becoming involved in the war and then Britain will call upon other nations for the war; this did not happen.

Another example of one of Smith's false prophecies is Section 114:1-2, which says, "Verily thus saith the Lord: It is wisdom in my servant David W. Patten... that he perform a mission unto me next spring, in company with others, even twelve including himself." Smith gave this prophecy April 17, 1838, but according to the Mormon *History of the Church*, Patten died a faithful member on October 9, 1838, five months before his mission.

Pearl of Great Price

This volume of Mormon scripture is usually bound together with the *Doctrine and Covenants*. It contains five sections: the *Book of Moses*, the *Book of Abraham, Joseph Smith—Matthew, Joseph Smith—History*, and the *Articles of Faith*. The *Book of Moses* and *Joseph Smith—Matthew* are excerpts from Joseph Smith's retranslation of the Bible in 1831. The *Joseph Smith—History* is the 1839 account of the first vision and the visitation of Moroni. The *Articles of Faith* contain thirteen statements of faith. The *Book of Abraham* is supposed to be a translation of an Egyptian papyri that rewrites Genesis chapter 1 as "the gods" create, instead of God.

Controversy has swirled around the *Book of Abraham* since Smith first introduced it in 1835. Eleven Egyptian mummies, buried with rolls of papyrus, had been willed to Mr. Michael Chandler of New York. Mr.

Chandler toured the countryside charging admission for observers. When he arrived in Kirtland, Ohio, Joseph Smith purchased the mummies from Chandler. Smith began to translate the hieroglyphics of the papyri and "much to our joy found that one of the rolls contained the writings of Abraham, another the writing of Joseph of Egypt" (*History of the Church*, 2:236). The resulting translation of one papyri was accepted as scripture by the Mormons, the *Book of Abraham*.

In 1967 the collection of papyrus that formed the *Book of Abraham* had been rediscovered in the Metropolitan Museum in New York. This gave Egyptologists a fresh look at the work of Joseph Smith, but to the disappointment of the Mormon Church, no Egyptologist confirmed a single word in Smith's translation. Worse than that, the papyri had nothing to do with Abraham, but only contained burial instructions for a common Egyptian funeral.

This shows the fraudulent nature of Joseph Smith's translation. His work is an imposture and it placed false doctrine in the guise of scripture. The gods mentioned in the *Book of Abraham*, Chapters 4 and 5, are just as false as the Egyptian gods in the papyri. He completely disregarded the warning about false prophets in Deuteronomy 13:1-4, by leading his people after other gods.

Mormon Theology

The Mormon Church presents the public image that they are just another Christian church. They wish to be accepted as such, which is shown in the vague meaning of their first Article of Faith: "We believe in God, the Eternal Father, and in His Son, Jesus Christ, and in the Holy Ghost." If these words were isolated from the Mormon context, they would be accepted as orthodox by most Christians. That is the problem with semantics, the final determination depends upon how you define your terms.

The Nature of God in Mormonism

In clarification of the Mormon *Articles of Faith,* Joseph Smith outright denied the doctrine of the Trinity—one God in three Persons. He said, "Many men say there is one God; the Father, the Son, and the Holy Ghost are only one God! I say that this is a strange God anyhow—three in one, and one in three!...He would be a wonderfully big God—He would be a giant or a monster" (*History of the Church,* 6:476). Smith never disavowed this claim.

He stepped away from monotheism and embraced polytheism in these words, "I will preach on the plurality of Gods...I wish to declare I have always and in all congregations when I have preached on the subject of deity, it has been the plurality of Gods" (ibid., 6:474). As previously mentioned, the *Book of Abraham* is polytheistic as well, "And then the Lord said: Let us go down...that is the Gods...and the Spirit of the Gods was brooding upon the face of the waters...And the Gods called the light day...and the Gods ordered the expanse" (Abraham 4:1-7).

The true God we read of in the Bible is eternal, from everlasting to everlasting. Dr. Norman Geisler argues for the existence of a necessary Being, God:

> We offer the claim that theism is the only adequate world view. All others are self-defeating or actually unaffirmable. Only theism is actually undeniable. It offers an argument with undeniable premises that lead inescapably to existence of an infinitely perfect and powerful Being beyond this world (*Christian Apologetics,* Grand Rapids, MI: Baker Book House, 1976, p. 258).

Cultures that teach polytheism lack this truth. When one god follows another god in succession, then you must give an account for where the gods come from.

Joseph Smith answered this by saying God is an exalted man: "God himself was once as we are now and is an exalted man" (*History of the Church*, 6:305). Mormon scripture adds to this: "The Father has a body of flesh and bones as tangible as man's" (*Doctrine and Covenants*, 130:22). Elsewhere, Smith elaborates upon this by teaching that the Father once lived on another planet and worshiped a god before him: "John discovered that God the Father of Jesus Christ had a Father, you may suppose that he had a Father also" (*History of the Church*, 6:476).

It is not uncommon to find goddesses in polytheistic religions. The Mormon Church also adds this to their theory and worship. In the hymn book of the Mormon Church, two stanzas of the song *O My Father* is devoted to veneration of their heavenly Mother. Mormon apostle James Talmage wrote of her in his book *Articles of Faith*: "We are expressly told that God is the Father of our spirits . . . we must know that a Mother of spirits is an existent personality" (Salt Lake City: Deseret Books, p. 443).

Jesus in Mormonism

The gods and goddesses in Mormon theology have the power to procreate spirit-children in heaven. The Mormons refer to this as the preexistence of spirits. The Father of this planet had children with his goddess wife, of which Jesus was the firstborn. The sixth prophet of the Mormon Church, Joseph F. Smith, said, "Among the spirit children of Elohim the firstborn was and is Jehovah, or Jesus Christ, to whom all others are juniors" (*Gospel Doctrine*, p. 70).

In the preexistence all the spirit children are one large family. The second child born in Mormonism is

Lucifer. Mormons take no shock in calling Jesus a spirit-brother to Lucifer. One Mormon writer said, "The appointment of Jesus to be the savior of the world was contested by one of the other sons of God. He was Lucifer, Son of the morning . . . this spirit-brother of Jesus desperately tried to become the savior of mankind" (Milton Hunter, *Gospel Through the Ages*, Salt Lake City: Stevens and Wallis, 1945, p. 15).

When the appropriate time came for Jesus to come to earth, the Mormons teach that the heavenly Father came to earth (as an exalted man) and had sexual union with Mary to produce a body for Jesus. Brigham Young said, "When the virgin Mary conceived the child Jesus, the Father had begotten him in his own likeness. He was not begotten by the Holy Ghost" (*Journal of Discourses*, 1:50). Again, he said, "The Father came himself and favored that tabernacle instead of letting any other man do it" (ibid., 4:218). Brigham Young's words make the conception and birth of Jesus Christ a farce and worldly act.

The concept of gods with wives in heaven did not escape Jesus in Mormon theology. To the Latter-day Saints, Jesus is one of many gods in the universe. Apostle Orson Pratt claimed Jesus was married to three women: "It will be borne in mind that once on a time, there was a marriage, in Cana of Galilee: And on a careful reading of that transaction, it will be discovered that no less a person than Jesus Christ was married on that occasion. If he was never married, his intimacy with Mary, Martha and the other Mary . . . must have been highly unbecoming and improper to say the best of it" (*Journal of Discourses*, 2:82).

The Holy Spirit in Mormonism

The doctrine of the Holy Spirit seems to be undergoing change in Mormonism. Originally Joseph Smith taught there was a difference between the Holy Ghost and the Holy Spirit. He was not aware of the fact that the words Holy Ghost are an archaic Elizabethan English phraseology for Holy Spirit. Nevertheless, in Joseph Smith's *Lectures on Faith* (originally published in 1835 in the *Book of Commandments*) he asked a series of questions (pp. 55,58):

> Q: Do the Father and Son possess the same mind?
>
> A: They do . . .
>
> Q: What is this mind?
>
> A: The Holy Spirit.

Brigham Young also preached a false doctrine on the Holy Spirit when he said, "Jesus Christ was not begotten by the Holy Ghost" (*Journal of Discourses*, 1:51). Furthermore, Heber C. Kimball, a member of Young's First Presidency, said the Holy Ghost was born in heaven as a man: "The Holy Ghost is a man, he is one of the sons of our Father and our God" (ibid., 5:179).

Man Evolves to God in Mormonism

Man is an evolving being in Mormonism. He began as an eternal intelligence and then was born as a spirit-child: "Man is a spirit clothed with a tabernacle. The intelligence part of which was never created or made, but existed eternally—man was also in the beginning with God" (Joseph Fielding Smith, *Progress of Man*).

Beginning with Joseph Smith, the Latter-day Saints have taught through the years that man has the potential of becoming a god. Smith said it this way, "Here, then, is eternal life—to know the only wise and true God; and you have got to learn how to be gods yourselves . . . the same as all gods have done before you" (*History of the Church*, 6:306). He also wrote a revelation in the *Doctrine and Covenants* that promises godhood in the resurrection to the faithful Mormon: "Then shall they be gods, because the shall have no end, therefore they shall be from everlasting to everlasting... Then they shall be gods because they have all power" (132:19,20).

Atonement and Salvation

The atonement of Christ is only able to cover some sins in Mormonism. Brigham Young said, "There are sins that men commit for which they cannot receive forgiveness in this world... they would be perfectly willing to have their blood spilt upon the ground" (*Journal of Discourses*, 4:53).

The atonement of Christ in Mormonism provided a general salvation for everyone, this is the resurrection of the just and the unjust. Their third *Article of Faith* states: "We believe that through the atonement of Christ, all mankind may be saved, by obedience to the laws and ordinances of the Gospel." Thus, all people who have not committed unforgivable sins will go to heaven—the first level of heaven in Mormon theology, the "telestial" sphere. People who generally tried to do well and did not obey Mormon ordinances go to the second level, the "terrestrial" sphere. Faithful Latter-day Saints who obeyed all the laws and ordinances of the Gospel will go to the "celestial" sphere, the third and highest level.

The Mormons have a doctrine of baptism of the living on behalf of the dead (by proxy) that allows the dead to be counted as a Mormon. Baptism for the dead is one of the functions of the Mormon temple. It is based upon a misreading of 1 Corinthians 15:29 where Paul spoke about someone outside of himself and the church, "Why are they then baptized for the dead?" (KJV) Obviously it is not a Christian practice because Paul carefully said "they" did it instead of "we" or "I."

Mormon works determine what level one gets in the hereafter. Even if that earthly work is baptism for the dead, it still determines one's destiny in Mormonism. It would do us well to remember what Paul said about salvation and works in Titus 3:5: "Not by works of righteousness which we have done, but according to His mercy He saved us" (KJV).

Biblical Analysis of Latter-day Saint Doctrine

There are two areas of Mormon theology that if dealt with properly, their whole system of theology falls. The Mormon view of gods hinges upon two things: It is polytheistic and it requires preexistence of souls. In refutation of this, if the Bible denies either or both of these, then all other points are secondary. Example: If we show monotheism is biblical, then it also destroys all concepts of gods and goddesses. The establishment of monotheism is not difficult, because the Bible is based upon the existence of one God, all others who claim to be gods are not gods in reality (Galatians 4:8). The following verses are a few that state one God:

> He is God; there is no other besides Him (Deuteronomy 4:35).

> The Lord is our God, the Lord is one! (Deuteronomy 6:4)

> Before Me there was no God formed, and there will be none after Me (Isaiah 43:10).

> There is no other God besides me (Isaiah 45:21).

> There is no God but one (1 Corinthians 8:4).

> You believe that God is one (James 2:19).

The Mormons will typically say they believe in one god. There is a flaw in this. Their "trinity" is three gods who are three persons, born in different times and different places. The biblical Trinity is one God eternally existing as three Persons.

The unity of the Persons and the uniqueness of God is shown in his attributes. Example: There are not "three eternals," there is one God who is eternal and all three Persons share his eternal nature. There are not "three almighties," there is one God who is Almighty and all three Persons share his Almighty nature. This can be said of every attribute of God. There are not "three Lords," there is one God who is Lord and all three Persons share His nature as Lord (One Lord— Ephesians 4:5; The Father is Lord—Matthew 11:25; The Son is Lord—Acts 2:36; The Holy Spirit is Lord—2 Corinthians 3:17). Monotheism is taught even in the doctrine of the Trinity—one God in three Persons.

The preexistence of souls in the Mormon Church is a position rarely held by those outside of Mormonism. The reason is that the Bible does not allow such a concept. Although the Bible does not tell us everything about the soul, it rejects preexistence: Psalm 102:18 shows us that each generation is created, not preexisting. Zechariah 12:1 tells us the spirit is not formed before it is placed in man, which denies its preexistence. Jesus said in John 3:13 that only He has descended from heaven, not billions of souls with Him. He also said in John 8:23 that He is the only one from above and everyone else is from the world. With this we see the preexistence doctrine is false.

Salvation according to the Bible is a free gift from Jesus Christ our Lord. Ephesians 2:8-10 declares:

> For by grace you have been saved through faith; and that not of yourselves, it is the gift of God; not as a result of works, that no one should boast. For we are His workmanship, created in Christ Jesus for good works, which God prepared beforehand, that we should walk in them.

When the people asked Jesus, "What shall we do, that we may do the works of God?" (John 6:28), Jesus replied, "This is the work of God, that you believe in Him whom He has sent" (verse 29). There is no way to earn salvation. One's good works are testimony to the accomplished fact of one's salvation, purchased not by works, but by the blood of Jesus Christ. We are saved through Christ's sacrifice on the cross for our sins, not because of anything we can do ourselves. Hebrews 7:27 says that when Jesus offered Himself for man's sin it was "once for all."

Conclusion

When all the evidence is considered, the Mormon claim to be the restoration of Jesus Christ's church falls to the ground. We have taken up the challenge of Brigham Young who said, "Take up the Bible, compare the religion of the Latter-day Saints with it, and see if it will stand the test" (*Journal of Discourses*, 16:46).

Our conclusion is that when Mormonism is weighed in the balances, it is found wanting.

From the doctrine of God to the prophecies and the extrabiblical revelations, Joseph Smith failed every test of a prophet in the Bible. Galatians 1:8 says: "But even though we, or an angel from heaven, should preach to you a gospel contrary to that which we have preached to you, let him be accursed."

Witnessing Tips

Mormons are individuals for whom Christ died. When you speak with a Mormon about salvation you must bear in mind that he thinks you are already a member of "apostate" Christianity. Do your best to stay on the topic of God and salvation instead of side issues.

As you dialogue, keep the definitions of terms out in the open and perhaps repeat them several times during the course of your discussion. This will help keep the differences clear for the Mormon. It is not out of the ordinary to take a few notes while you talk so that you can refer back to a point.

One well-explained verse that refutes a false doctrine is worth more than rapidly firing ten unexplained verses. Some verses are more clearly presented than others, so look at the context ahead of time and prepare yourself with the verses that establish Christian doctrines the easiest.

5

Jehovah's Witnesses

The Jehovah's Witnesses, officially incorporated as the Watchtower Bible and Tract Society, are the widest published of the western cults. Most households in America and many millions more throughout the free world have been recipients of the door-bell ringing Watchtower representatives at least once if not several times. Their now-famous magazines, *Watchtower* and *Awake!*, had humble beginnings with 6,000 issues, but today they have a combined fifty-five million issues monthly!

What began with a Bible study in Pittsburgh, Pennsylvania, has escalated to a worldwide organization of 60,000 congregations, and more than four million full-time and volunteer workers. In 1990, 9.5 million people attended their Lord's Supper Memorial Service.

No branch of the Catholic or Protestant Church has been spared from the hard-hitting methodology of the Jehovah's Witnesses. They have converted scores of people from every kind of cultural, religious, and national background.

History

The growth of the Jehovah's Witnesses over the past century rivals that of Protestant denominations three times their age. The worldwide operation is directed by the "Governing Body" at their headquarters in Brooklyn, New York. The headquarters houses massive computers and the latest printing technology that keeps them far in advance of Christian publishers and the secular printing industry.

Charles Taze Russell

Charles Taze Russell was born February 16, 1852, near Pittsburgh, Pennsylvania. In 1870, while still in his teens and without formal theological education, Russell organized a Bible class. His only connection with Christianity was membership in the Congregational Church. He convinced his Bible class that he was their "pastor," and he gained followers in a dozen study groups along the Ohio and Pennsylvania border.

It was during these years that he based much of his eschatology (end-times study) upon the teachings of Nelson Barbour, an Adventist and publisher of the *Herald of the Morning*, in Rochester, New York. Barbour taught Russell that Jesus Christ has been invisibly present since 1874. Russell later reinterpreted the dates and predicted the invisible return of Christ for 1914.

In 1879 he founded the magazine *Zion's Watch Tower and Herald of Christ's Presence* in which he published his unique interpretation of the Bible. He organized his new following as Zion's Watch Tower and Tract Society in 1884, while he was still in Pittsburgh. His writings gained a wider distribution in 1886, when the first of six books entitled *The Millennial Dawn* was published (later retitled *Studies in the Scriptures*). A controversial seventh volume was added to the *Studies in the Scriptures* in 1917, a year after Russell's death. It was compiled by Watchtower editors from Russell's unpublished writings and contained his plan for the last days from Ezekiel and the book of Revelation.

By the time of his death on October 31, 1916, Pastor Russell, according to the Watchtower, traveled more than a million miles, gave more than thirty thousand sermons, and wrote books totalling more than fifty thousand pages (*Qualified to be Ministers*, Anon., 1955, p. 310).

Joseph F. Rutherford

A few months after the death of Charles Taze Russell, the society's legal counselor, Joseph Franklin Rutherford, became the second president of the Watchtower Society. Raised by Baptist parents, he began to follow Russell in 1894 and joined Zion's Watch Tower in 1906. He gave them the name "Jehovah's Witnesses," in reference to Isaiah 43:10, "You are my witnesses, declares the Lord," at a convention in Columbus, Ohio, in 1931.

It was under his leadership that Rutherford moved the Society's headquarters from Pittsburgh, Pennsylvania, to Brooklyn, New York. This became the visible representative of God's rulership (theocracy) where all control, power, and decisions generate. The larger operation required more workers, so Bethel was set up to accommodate the means. Bethel is the employment program for the Watchtower, where room and board and $20 weekly spending cash are provided in return for labor by the faithful Witnesses.

Rutherford gave the date of Christ's judgment of Christianity as 1918, meaning that there was one organization designated to represent Jesus on earth, the

Watchtower Society. Rutherford divided the Witnesses into two classes of people: the 144,000 (the "elect," who are born again) and the "great crowd" (the unelect, with everlasting life on earth). Like Russell before him, Rutherford was not ashamed to take credit for his writings, which is evident in the one-hundred books and pamphlets that bear his name. Since the time of Russell and Rutherford all other publications are by anonymous writers.

Nathan Knorr

Rutherford died in 1942 and was succeeded by Nathan H. Knorr, who left the Reformed Church at the age of sixteen to join the Jehovah's Witnesses. It was during Knorr's presidency that the Society grew into the millions, increasing from 115,000 to more than two million members in 207 countries. A training center called the Watchtower Bible School of Gilead was established for educating their future ministers.

In 1950, under Knorr's leadership, the society produced its own English translation of the New Testament entitled *The New World Translation of the Christian Greek Scriptures*. This was later published with their Old Testament version as *The New World Translation of the Holy Scriptures*.

Frederick W. Franz

When Knorr died in 1977, Frederick W. Franz became the new president of the Watchtower and is currently conducting business in Knorr's manner. Franz was the spokesman for the translation committee of the New World Translation and he was the only member of the translation committee who had any knowledge of the biblical languages, although he had no degree backing it up.

Watchtower Bible and Tract Society Structure

It is not hidden from the readers of *Watchtower* magazine that the Governing Body runs the organization on earth. In the December 15, 1971, issue of Watchtower, a flow-chart is presented with Jehovah God at the top, Jesus Christ beneath him, and the Governing Body under Jesus. These are also called the "Faithful and Discreet Slave Class," and all earthly direction is under them. The flow-chart has "Elders in the Congregation" and the "Ministerial Servants" directly under the Governing Body. The organization plays such an important part in the lives of the Jehovah's Witness that it is referred to as their Mother: "We must recognize not only Jehovah God as our Father but his organization as our Mother" (*Watchtower*, May 1, 1957, p. 274).

This Governing Body is considered to be the sole channel of truth for the earth today, "recognition of that governing body and its place in God's theocratic arrangement of things is necessary for submission to the headship of God's Son" (*Watchtower*, December 15, 1972, p. 755). The Bible is read only as outlined by the Watchtower Society: "God has not arranged for that Word to speak independently or to shine forth life giving truths by itself. It is through his organization God provides this light" (*Watchtower*, May 1, 1957, p. 274).

Jesus was supposed to have chosen the Watchtower Society to be His only representative on earth, excluding all Christian denominations: "When Jesus came to God's spiritual temple in 1918 for the purpose of judging men, Christendom was rejected" (*Watchtower*, August 1, 1960). Further on this we find: "Outside the true Christian congregation what alternative organization is there? Only Satan's organization" (*Watchtower*, March 1, 1979, p. 24). The Watchtower

Society openly labels the church as apostate, claiming they alone have the truth: "Recovery from the apostasy waited until the latter part of the nineteenth century" (*Awake!*, February 8, 1960).

The local Kingdom Hall of Jehovah's Witnesses has become popular over the past decade for their unique building program of constructing an edifice in forty-eight hours. The Kingdom Hall is the place where local congregations meet. The services are planned in advance by the headquarters in Brooklyn, even to the point of what song will be sung in what order. The mechanics of every service is the same throughout the world and is directed by the congregation elder. He is under the supervision of a circuit overseer who visits each Kingdom Hall in his district twice annually.

Distribution of the *Watchtower* and *Awake!* magazines door-to-door and on street corners is called "publishing." Publishing is a duty for the most faithful of Witnesses. The topics for discussion are planned in advance with the same opening question being used at each door.

The Lord's Supper Memorial Service is the largest attended service the Jehovah's Witnesses have. It shows the true number of those who believe the message of the Watchtower, but are perhaps inconsistent in attendance. As stated before, in 1990 the Memorial Service drew just more than 9.5 million people worldwide.

Since only the 144,000 may partake of the elements of the bread and wine, most congregations around the world will pass the elements throughout the entire congregation with no one participating. This is due to the shrinking number of living members of the 144,000, of which there are an estimated 5,000 left today.

Biblical Analysis of the Watchtower Structure

The concept that the Jehovah's Witnesses are the

only true representatives of Christianity on earth is foreign to the Bible. Nowhere in the Scriptures do we find a judgment of the organizations on earth to determine the real one. Jesus has always known who His people are, for "he calls his own sheep by name, and leads them out . . . My sheep hear My voice, and I know them, and they follow Me" (John 10:3,27).

Jesus gave two parables in Matthew 13 that set the record straight on how he will separate the true Christians from the false ones. The parables of the tares and wheat and the dragnet of fish show the judgment will be between members in the same "field" and "net," not between organizations.

The Jehovah's Witnesses speak of the church as apostate and they alone have truth. In contrast, the Bible says the church will not fail to exist, "having been built upon the foundation of the apostles and prophets, Christ Jesus Himself being the corner stone" (Ephesians 2:20). The church of Jesus Christ will remain until His coming since the gates of hell cannot penetrate it (Matthew 16:18); and it will be here throughout all ages (Ephesians 3:21).

The Jehovah's Witnesses contradict the Bible with their Memorial Service. In 1 Corinthians 11:26 we find, "For as often as you eat this bread and drink the cup, you proclaim the Lord's death until He comes." Since the Jehovah's Witnesses claim Jesus returned invisibly in 1914, they have denied the statement "till He comes" in this passage. The observance of the Lord's Supper was only until He returns. They attempt to have it both ways: Their books say He returned in 1914, and their Memorial Service says He hasn't returned yet.

Source of Authority

The members are zealous and sincere and claim to accept the Bible as their only authority. However, their theology denies every cardinal belief of historic Christianity including the Trinity, the divinity of Jesus Christ, His bodily resurrection, salvation by grace through faith, and eternal punishment of the wicked.

"Pastor" Russell, not known for his humility, made the following statement: "And be it known that no other system of theology even claims, or has ever attempted to harmonize in itself every statement of the Bible, yet nothing short of this can we claim" (Charles Taze Russell, *Studies in the Scriptures*, 1:348). Even today the Watchtower Society claims to be the only source for truth: "It is God's sole collective channel for the flow of Biblical truth to men on earth" (*The Watchtower*, July 15, 1960, p. 439).

Before he became president of the Watchtower, Frederick W. Franz related how their interpretations come from God:

They are passed to the Holy Spirit who invisibly communicates with Jehovah's Witnesses—and the Publicity Department (*Scottish Daily Express*, November 24, 1954).

There are no "articles of faith" or authoritative doctrinal statements issued by the Watchtower. Their theological views are found in the various publications, including *The Watchtower* and *Awake!*. The doctrine that proceeds from these works is considered authoritative.

The crux of their theology is "reason," as often is seen in the questions they ask during their discussions, "Is it reasonable that we should believe . . . ?" Charles Taze Russell said even the Bible is under the scrutiny of reason: "Let us examine the character of the writings claimed as inspired, to see whether their teachings correspond with the character we have reasonably imputed to God." This does not mean that the Jehovah's Witnesses are reasonable, rational and logical in their conclusions, but they have persuaded a large sector of our society to believe that they are.

The collection of literature published by the *Watchtower* is not always the final answer. They believe that the light gets brighter as they get closer to the truth. This is explained, "Through the columns of *The Watchtower* comes increased light on God's Word as Jehovah makes it known" (*Watchtower*, August 1, 1972, p. 460).

This is how the current president of the organization may overrule the teachings of the former president. Judge Rutherford, in his book *Vindication*, claims that nobody in the past 2,500 years understands the book of Ezekiel as well as he does (that includes Russell!). Whether the former teacher is rejected or respected, the current teachings always have the greater weight.

The Watchtower Magazine

The *Watchtower* magazine gives "spiritual food" from the "faithful and discreet slave," the Governing Body. It is the oldest and most authoritative of any Jehovah's Witness publication: "Since 1879 the *Watchtower* magazine has been used by this collective group to dispense spiritual food regularly to those of this 'little flock' of true Christians" (*Watchtower*, October 1, 1967, p. 590).

Jehovah's Witnesses do not believe that the *Watchtower* magazine replaces the Bible, but it is the only source to interpret the Bible properly: "It is through the columns of the *Watchtower* that Jehovah provides direction and constant Scriptural counsel to his people" (*Watchtower*, May 1, 1964, p. 277). This statement also says that Jehovah is the real source of *Watchtower* articles.

Awake! Magazine and Other Publications

The five services held by the local Kingdom Hall are the public talk, the Watchtower study, the book study, the Theocratic Ministry School, and the Service Meeting. The public talks are similar to church services, except an elder gives a talk instead of a pastor preaching. Following this Sunday morning service is the *Watchtower* study, where a *Watchtower* article is read and the questions are asked that accompany the article. In the mid-week book study, which is informally held in a home, a prescribed book is read by the members. The other two services are instructional meetings and preparation for "publishing"; they are centered on the New World Translation, *Awake!* magazine, and a newsletter called *Our Kingdom Ministry*.

Since the Watchtower Society is "his sole visible channel, through whom alone spiritual instruction was to come" (*Watchtower*, October 10, 1967, p. 590), any of their official publications are Jehovah's message for today. They acknowledge the importance of other publications, "the resolutions adopted by conventions of God's anointed people, booklets, magazine, and the books published by them, contain the message of God's truth and are from the almighty God, Jehovah, and provided by him through Christ Jesus and his under officers" (*Watchtower*, May 1, 1938, p. 143).

Studies in the Scriptures

Charles Taze Russell began publishing his books on Bible study in 1886 as the *Millennial Dawn* series. These, later named *Studies in the Scriptures*, became the springboard for doctrine in the emerging church. Six of the volumes were published during Russell's lifetime and the seventh postmortem. The combined sales of volume one, *The Plan of the Ages*, including all splinter-group sales, was estimated at ten million by 1966.

Pastor Russell's self-assured attitude about his opinions gave his followers a dependency upon his writings. He wrote:

If the six volumes of *Scripture Studies* are practically the Bible, topically arranged with Bible proof texts given, we might not improperly name the volumes "the Bible in an arranged form," that is to say, they are not mere comments on the Bible, but they are practically the Bible itself. Furthermore, not only do we find that people cannot see the divine plan in studying the Bible by itself, but we see, also, that if anyone lays the *Scripture Studies* aside, even after he has used them, after he has become familiar with them, after he has read them for ten years—if he then lays them aside and ignores them and goes to the Bible alone, though he has understood his Bible for ten years, our experience shows that within two years he goes into darkness. On the other hand, if he had merely read the *Scripture Studies* with their references and had not read a page of the Bible as such, he would be in the light at the end of two years, because he would have the light of the Scriptures (Charles Taze Russell, *The Watchtower*, September 15, 1910, p. 298).

This building block of Watchtower theology cannot be overlooked as a nonessential. The same denial of Christian doctrines found in Russell's *Studies of the Scriptures* is also found in current Watchtower publications.

Prophets and Leaders

Although the Jehovah's Witnesses do not openly claim to have a prophet, they have defined the organization as such in *Watchtower* articles: "This 'prophet' was not one man, but was a body of men and women. It was the small group of footstep followers of Jesus Christ . . . Today they are known as Jehovah's Christian Witnesses" (*Watchtower*, April 1, 1972, p. 197). Continuing, they said, "The prophet whom Jehovah has raised up has been, not an individual as in the case of Jeremiah, but a class" (*Watchtower*, October 1, 1982, p. 27). The leadership at Brooklyn's headquarters does the prophesying: "The facts substantiate that the remnant of Christ's anointed disciples have been doing that prophesying to all the nations" (*Holy Spirit*, Brooklyn: WTB&TS, 1976, p. 148). Even the interpretation of biblical prophecies are considered the voice of God: "The interpretation of prophecy, therefore, is not from man, but is from Jehovah . . . it is his truth, and not man's" (*Watchtower*, May 1, 1938, p. 143).

False Prophecies

We cannot find one clear prediction from the Watchtower Society that has ever come true. The dates they give for events of the future are not true to the facts. We will give a few examples of dates projected as false prophecies:

- **1874**—"The Millennial Day, the Day of the Lord's rest, following the six thousand years of evil which ended in 1874" (*Studies in the Scriptures*, 7:301).

- **1914**—"The 'battle of the great day of God Almighty' (Revelation 16:14.), which will end in A.D. 1914 with the complete overthrow of earth's present rulership" (ibid., 2:101).

- **1915**—The end of the time of the gentiles, referred to in the text above, was reprinted with a new date, "which will end in A.D. 1915 with the complete overthrow of earth's present rulership" (ibid., 1914 ed.).

- **1918**—The end of the time of the gentiles was recalculated with new dates in the seventh volume of *Studies*, "and in the light of the foregoing Scriptures, *prove* that the Spring of 1918 will bring upon Christendom a spasm of anguish greater ever than that experienced in the Fall of 1914. Reexamine the table of the Parallel Dispensations in *Studies in the Scriptures*, Vol. 2, pages 246 and 247; change the 37 to 40, 70 to 73 and 1914 to 1918, and we believe it is correct and will be fulfilled 'with great power and glory'" (ibid., 7:62).

- **1920**—"The fleshy apostates from Christianity—shall be utterly desolated, 'even all of it.' Not one vestige of it shall survive the ravages of world-wide all-embracing anarchy, in the fall of 1920" (ibid., 7:542).

- **1925**—"Based upon the argument heretofore set forth . . . that 1925 shall mark the resurrection of the faithful worthies of old . . . we must reach the positive and indisputable conclusion that millions now living will never die" (*Millions Now Living Will Never Die*, Rutherford, 1920, p. 97).

- **1942**—"Those faithful men of old may be expected back from the dead any day now . . . In this expectation the house at San Diego, California . . . was built, in 1930, and named 'Beth-Sarim' . . . It is now held in trust for the occupancy of those princes on their return" (*The New World*, Rutherford, 1942, p. 104).

- **1975**—"In view of the short period of time left, we want to do this [pioneer work] as often as circumstances permit. Just think, brothers, there are only about 90 months left [until Oct. 1975] before 6,000 years of man's existence on earth is completed" (*Kingdom Ministry*, March 1968, p. 4).

- **1980**—"It is possible that A.D. 1980 marks the regathering of all fleshy Israel from their captivity in death. It is just 70 years beyond 1910, the date when Pastor Russell gave his great witness to the Jewish people" (*Studies in the Scripture*, 7:62).

The New World Translation of the Holy Scriptures

In 1961, the Watchtower Bible and Tract Society published the *New World Translation of the Holy Scriptures* (NWT). The rationale for this new translation was given when the New Testament was published in 1950:

> No uninspired translator or committee of translators can claim any direct command from the Most High God to engage in translating the divine Word into another language . . . In presenting this translation of the Christian Greek Scriptures our confidence has been in the help of the great Author of The Book. Our primary desire has been to seek, not the approval of men, but that of God, by rendering the truth of his inspired Word as purely and as consistently as our consecrated powers make possible. There is not benefit in self-deception. More than that, those who provide a translation for the spiritual instruction of others come under a special responsibility as teachers before the divine Judge. Hence our appreciation of the need of carefulness . . . We offer no paraphrase of the Scriptures. Our endeavor all through has been to give as literal a translation as possible, where the modern English idiom allows and where a literal rendition does not for any clumsiness hide the thought (Foreword to the *New World Translation of the Christian Greek Scriptures*, 1950, pp. 7-8).

The translators of the New World Translation have not achieved their goal. Their work is a highly biased attempt to justify some of their non-biblical doctrines. In terms of scholarship, the New World Translation leaves much to be desired.

Dr. Edmund Gruss gives us five reasons for rejecting the New World Translation as valid:

1. *The use of paraphrasing in contradiction to the*

stated purpose. Dr. Gruss gives the example of the Greek word *en* as found several times in John 15. The clear words and intention of Jesus saying the Christian is "in Me" (*en emoi*) is paraphrased by the NWT as "in union with me." The relationship of the Christian being *in* Christ was replaced by us working *along side of* Christ.

2. *The unwarranted insertion of words not found in the Greek.* There are several verses where the NWT has inserted words to change the meaning. There is absolutely no foundation for this in the Greek manuscripts or the grammar. Verses such as John 1:1, Colossians 1:16,17, Philippians 1:23 and Hebrews 9:27 serve as examples.

In John 1:1 the meaning was changed by the insertion of the indefinite article "a" before the word *God*: "In [the] beginning the Word was, and the Word was with God, and the Word was a god" (NWT). The obvious attempt here is to destroy the true deity of Jesus. No matter what arguments Jehovah's Witnesses advance in support of adding the indefinite article to John 1:1, the result will always be polytheism, two gods.

In Colossians 1:16,17 the word "other" was inserted, even though in brackets, to change the meaning, "because by means of him all [other] things were created . . . All [other] things have been created through him and for him. Also, he is before all [other] things and by means of him all [other] things were made to exist" (NWT). The purpose for this insertion is to make Jesus a created thing along with other created things.

In Titus 2:13 the preposition "of" was inserted a second time to cast deity away from Jesus, "while we wait for the happy hope and glorious manifestation of the great God and of our Savior Christ Jesus" (NWT)

3. *Erroneous rendering of Greek words.* These purposed mistranslations are to make passages in

accordance with Jehovah's Witness theology. John 8:58 shows the eternal nature of Jesus with his words, "Before Abraham was born, I am;" but the NWT changed the verse to, "Before Abraham came into existence, I have been." This rendering exchanges Christ's eternal person for a preexistent and created being. When they were challenged by Christians on this they made up nonexistent grammar rules in a desperate attempt to justify it. It is inescapable, though, that Jesus spoke in the present tense, "I am." Their denial of the deity of Jesus is seen again in Colossians 2:9, where the word *Godhead* is mistranslated as "divine quality."

4. *Deceptive and misleading footnotes and appendix.* One factor we find consistently in the appendix of the *New World Translation* is its overall persistence in denial of major Christian doctrines. Some of the topics are soul sleep, denial of Christ's deity, denial of the cross, and denial of eternal punishment.

5. *Arbitrary use and non-use of capitals when dealing with the divine name.* This is seen in the NWT use of "god" for Jesus (John 1:1,18). The Holy Spirit is never referred to as a person nor as God, but only as "holy spirit" (Matthew 28:19), "the helper" (John 14:16), and "the spirit of truth" (John 15:26).

Biblical Analysis of Watchtower Authority and the New World Translation

Russell was wrong to assess God's Word by "what we reasonably impute to God." God gave us reasoning abilities, but we are to recognize our limitations. Our thoughts are not God's thoughts and our ways are not His ways (Isaiah 55:8), which makes our reasoning a faulty vehicle to test the Word of God. Our thinking is not the test for God's Word; His Word is the test for our thinking.

In our study of the cults, Charles Taze Russell is

the only person who has the audacity to say that if one lays aside his writings and goes to the Bible alone, he will go into utter darkness. The Watchtower Bible and Tract Society has set itself up in the position of being the oracle of God, yet when the predictions are tested by time, they all have failed. This is by no means what the Bible declares as a prophet. Jeremiah spoke strongly against the prophets who prophesy falsely: " 'Behold, I am against the prophets,' declares the LORD, 'who use their tongues and declare, "The Lord declares" ' " (23:31). The failed predictions of the Watchtower leaders condemn them with the false prophets of Deuteronomy 18:20-22, where Moses told us not to fear or respect them.

God does not make mistakes in his communication to man. The apostle Paul built a case over the difference between the singular and plural use of "seed" and "seeds" in Galatians 3:16. He relied upon the accuracy of the Hebrew text which shows that it was trustworthy.

When a group like the Watchtower Bible and Tract Society changes and alters what God has said, then they have a lower respect for the Word of God than Paul did. We must make our stand with the apostle Paul that God has given us a reliable means of understanding Him through His written Word. Perhaps Solomon realized this too when he said, "Add thou not unto his words, lest he reprove thee, and thou be found a liar" (Proverbs 30:6, KJV).

Watchtower Theology

The basis for the theology of the Watchtower Bible and Tract Society is older than the Society itself. It can be traced to the fourth century in the teachings of Arius of Alexandria, who taught that Jesus Christ was created and not eternal God. Arianism has surfaced over the centuries but has gained no greater stronghold in the world than through the modern Arians of our time, the Jehovah's Witnesses.

On the Trinity

Rutherford said, "Definition: the doctrine, in brief, is that there are three gods in one: God the Father, God the Son, and God the Holy Ghost, all three equal in power, substance and eternity" (*Let God Be True*, New York: Watchtower, 1946, p.81). Notice here how Judge Rutherford misstated the doctrine of the Trinity as three Gods instead of one God in three Persons. Rutherford continued, "Satan is the originator of the 'trinity' doctrine" (ibid., p. 82). The history of the Jehovah's Witnesses is filled with statements by their leaders, in all publications stating their rejection of the doctrine of the Trinity.

On the Deity of Christ

Russell's notion that even Scripture should be tested by reason is continued by Watchtower today, "that the Father is greater and older than the Son is reasonable, easy to understand and is what the Bible teaches" (*From Paradise Lost to Paradise Regained*, p. 164). Stating that Jesus Christ is younger than the Father leads to their doctrine that Jesus Christ is not God and is a created being. In fact, they teach that He is Michael, the archangel: "Scriptural evidence indicates that the name Michael applied to God's son before He left heaven to become Jesus Christ and also after His return . . . Michael is actually the Son of God" (*Aid to Bible Understanding*, p. 1152).

In their notes concerning John 1:1 of the 1950 edition of the New World translation, they denied the deity of Jesus Christ and called Him a lesser God: "The Word, or Logos, is not God or the God, but is the Son of God, and hence is a god" (p. 775).

On the Holy Spirit

The Watchtower denies the person and deity of the Holy Spirit: "The holy spirit is not a person and is therefore not one of the gods of the trinity" (Rutherford, *Reconciliation,* New York: Watchtower, p. 115). In their effort to describe the Holy Spirit they were careful not to attribute any personal characteristics to Him. The closest metaphor they could find was a radar beam: "It is not a blind, uncontrolled force such as the forces of 'nature'; lightening, hurricanes and the like, but . . . is at all times under His control . . . and therefore may be likened to a radar beam" (*The Watchtower,* July 15, 1957, pp. 431-433).

On the Atonement

The atonement in the collection of Watchtower material has a different bearing upon the individual Jehovah's Witness than what the true atonement does for Christians in the Bible. The atonement is viewed by Watchtower representatives as a ransom and only a ransom. Although the word *ransom* is used within the New Testament, it is not used in the same sense that the Watchtower uses it. The Watchtower representatives call it a "corresponding ransom." What they mean by "corresponding ransom" is:

It was the perfect man Adam that had sinned, and so had lost for his offspring human perfection and its privileges. Jesus must likewise be humanly perfect, to correspond with the sinless Adam in Eden. In that way He could offer a ransom that exactly corresponded in value with what the sinner Adam lost for his descendants. This requirement of divine justice did not allow for Jesus to be more than a perfect man (*Things in Which it is Impossible for God to Lie,* Brooklyn: Watchtower, 1965, p. 232).

What is missing from the Watchtower concept of

the atonement is Christ's "substitutionary atonement" for our sins, and that the justice of God was fully satisfied in the atonement of Jesus. The Watchtower denies that "the ransom" was the justice of God for the sins of man. The justice of God for Adam's fall was death to the human race, according to them, "Justice was satisfied in mankind's suffering death, the just penalty of sin. So the ransom is an expression of God's mercy, His undeserved kindness toward mankind" (Rutherford, *Let God Be True*, Brooklyn: Watchtower, 1946, p. 115).

Since Adam, in their view, lost perfect human life with its rights and earthly prospects, the redemption by Jesus Christ was nothing more than a ransom paid to Jehovah God to recover the rights and prospects again for the human race: "That which is redeemed or bought back is that which was lost, namely, perfect human life, with its rights and earthly prospects" (ibid., p. 114).

On the Bodily Resurrection of Jesus Christ

The Jehovah's Witnesses have denied the bodily resurrection of Jesus Christ since the days of Russell, who said, "Whether it was dissolved into gasses or whether it is still preserved somewhere as the grand memorial of God's love, of Christ's obedience, and of our redemption, no one knows" (*Studies in the Scriptures*, volume 2, p. 129). There are other theories in the Watchtower society of what became of the physical body of Jesus, "The scriptures answer: it was disposed of by Jehovah God, dissolved into its constituent elements or atoms" (*The Watchtower*, September 1, 1953, p. 518).

Rutherford continued his denial of the bodily resurrection, "so the king Christ Jesus was put to death in the flesh and was raised an invisible spirit creature" (*Let God Be True*, p. 122). When Jesus appeared to His disciples following His death and resurrection, the

Watchtower claims that He materialized His body so that they would believe, but it is not the same body that hung on the tree. They relate it this way, "Jesus' resurrection was not of the same body: He merely materialized flesh and blood to be seen and believed" (*Make Sure of All Things*, Brooklyn: Watchtower, 1953, p. 314). Judge Rutherford added, "He was re-created as a divine spirit creature" (*Let God Be True*, p. 116).

On Salvation

Charles Taze Russell began teaching that works are necessary for salvation in his first volume of *Studies in the Scriptures*: "They must be recovered from blindness as well as from death, that they, each for himself, may have a full chance to prove by obedience or disobedience, their worthiness of life eternal" (volume I, p. 158). The Watchtower volume called *Aid to Bible Understanding* presents works for salvation, "More is required of true Christians than mere confession of faith. It is necessary that belief be demonstrated by works . . . those who become Christians repent . . . and submit to water baptism" (*Aid to Bible Understanding*, Brooklyn: Watchtower, 1971, p. 316). The *Watchtower* magazine gives the requirements for salvation:

> Four requirements: Jesus Christ identified a first requirement . . . taking in knowledge . . . of God's purposes regarding the earth and of Christ's role as earth's new king . . . many have found the second requirement more difficult. It is to obey God's laws, yes, . . . a third requirement is that we be associated with God's channel, His organization . . . the fourth requirement is connected with loyalty. God requires that perspective subjects of His kingdom support His government while loyally advocating His kingdom rule to others . . . (*The Watchtower*, February 15, 1983, p. 12).

Again, the Watchtower society declared:

Jehovah God will justify, declare righteous, on the basis of their own merit, all perfected humans who have withstood that final, decisive test of mankind. He will adopt and acknowledge them as His sons through Jesus Christ (*Life Everlasting*, Brooklyn: Watchtower, 1966, p. 400).

Another teaching of the Watchtower Society is that only 144,000 will be born again. The born again class ceased having additional members in the 1930s. The second class in the Watchtower Society is "the other sheep" or "Jonadabs" who are not looking forward to heavenly existence but look forward to eternal life in a paradise on earth. Judge Rutherford wrote, "An unnumbered crowd of faithful persons now working as Jehovah's Witnesses are sometimes called His 'other sheep' or 'Jonadabs.' They do not expect to go to heaven. They have been promised everlasting life on earth" (*Let God Be True*, p. 231).

Biblical Analysis of Watchtower Teachings

In addition to our section on the Trinity in Chapter 3, we find that it is highly important to demonstrate that Jesus is Jehovah. This may be done in a number of ways, but first we will take care of this question: Is Jehovah one person or three persons? We believe a study of Scripture will reveal that there is but one Jehovah in three persons. One Jehovah is well established in Deuteronomy 6:4: "Hear O Israel! The Lord is our God, the Lord is one!" The word *Lord* in this text is the word *Jehovah* or *Yahweh* in the Hebrew text. There is but one Jehovah.

In addition, we find that Jehovah is referred to as the person of the Father in Psalm 103:13 and Isaiah 63:16. Jehovah is also directly referred to as Jesus Christ when we cross-reference Old Testament quotes about Jehovah with New Testament fulfillments in Jesus.

Isaiah 35:4-6 says that "God will come" and He will open the eyes of the blind, unstop the ears of the deaf and heal the lame. Jesus quoted this verse Himself about His own mission in Matthew 11:5 when the disciples of John the Baptist came to Him and asked if He were the coming one, or were they to look for another? Jesus' answer was, "The blind receive sight and the lame walk, the lepers are cleansed and the deaf hear and the dead are raised up, and the poor have the gospel preached to them." This is a direct quote from Isaiah 35:4-6 showing that Jesus attests of His own nature as Jehovah incarnate.

We have another statement found in the Old Testament concerning Jehovah which is fulfilled in Jesus in the New Testament. Zechariah 12:10 clearly states that Jehovah shall be pierced for our sins, and this verse, as quoted in John 19:37, was fulfilled when Jesus was pierced for our sins upon the cross. Jesus is truly Jehovah.

Joel 2:32 contains an important passage about the redemption of Israel that was familiar to most Jews during the days of Christ. It says, "Whoever calls on the name of the LORD [Jehovah] will be delivered." This verse was quoted on two occasions in the New Testament in fulfillment of the work of Jesus Christ. Luke quotes it from Peter's sermon in Acts 2:20-21 and Paul quotes it in Romans 10:9-13. Truly the New Testament believers saw Jesus as Jehovah who would deliver and save them.

A verse that is most familiar to many Christians today concerning Jesus Christ is actually a quotation out of the Old Testament that the apostle Paul used in Philippians 2:10. It says, "That at the name of Jesus every knee should bow, of those who are in heaven, and on earth, and under the earth, and that every tongue should confess that Jesus Christ is Lord, to the glory of God the Father." This text originated in Isaiah 45:23 and was directly applied to Jesus. When we look to Isaiah's account, we see that it was none other than Jehovah to whom every knee should bow and every tongue confess.

We have already mentioned Peter's sermon in Acts 2, but Peter again attests to Jesus as Jehovah in 1 Peter 2:8. In this passage about Jesus, he calls Him, "a stone of stumbling and a rock of offense." Peter got this statement about Jesus from Isaiah 8:13,14. In Isaiah's recording of these words, we find that it is Jehovah who is the stone of stumbling and rock of offense. Truly Peter declared, on more than one occasion, that Jesus is Jehovah from the Old Testament.

Finally, we find another statement from Jesus about Himself. In Revelation 2:23 we have the message of the angel to the church of Thyatira where Jesus said this about Himself, "And I will kill her children with pestilence; and all the churches will know that I am He who searches the minds and the hearts; and I will give to each one of you according to your deeds." Jesus applied Jeremiah 17:10 to himself, which says that Jehovah is the one who searches the hearts and minds and gives rewards according to our deeds.

Cross references of Old Testament quotations with New Testament fulfillments are easily missed by the untrained eye. But to the first-century Jewish believers, it was inescapable that the New Testament writers declared Jesus was Jehovah through application of Old Testament passages to His person, nature and work.

We find the third person of the Trinity, the Holy Spirit, is referred to by New Testament writers in the same way. That is, He is Jehovah. Hebrews 3:7-9 clearly states that the Holy Spirit originated the words in the ensuing quotation. When we look at the quotation in the Old Testament, we find its origin in Psalm 95:7-11.

In the Old Testament they are Jehovah's words; in the New Testament they are the Holy Spirit's words. The Holy Spirit spoke as Jehovah.

Similarly, Hebrews 10:15,16 attributes a quotation from the Old Testament to the Holy Spirit. When we look at the quotation in the Old Testament (Jeremiah 31:33,34), we find that it is none other than Jehovah speaking. In the New Testament the Holy Spirit is claimed as the originator of the words, showing the Holy Spirit and Jehovah are one Being.

Acts 28:25 is a parallel example: "The Holy Spirit rightly spoke through Isaiah the prophet to your fathers." Following this is a quotation from Isaiah 6:8-10, where the originator of the quote is Jehovah. Paul could only attribute the words to the Holy Spirit if he believed that the Holy Spirit is equally Jehovah with the Father and the Son.

In this brief outline, we can see clearly that the Bible teaches there is one Jehovah God who is the Father, the Son and the Holy Spirit, three divine Persons.

Centering our attention upon Jesus again, we can look at parallels of exclusive attributes between Jehovah and Jesus, showing that the two essentially are one. In these exclusive attributes, we will focus upon the words that make these attributes unique to Jesus as Jehovah. Isaiah 42:8 serves as an example. It says that Jehovah alone has the glory and will not share it with another. Let's compare John 17:5, where Jesus said, "And now, glorify thou me together with Thyself, Father, with the glory which I had with Thee before the world was." If the glory belonged only to Jehovah, Jesus, by necessity, would have to be Jehovah because He claimed to have the glory before the world was.

Another exclusive attribute of God is light. John 1:9 says that Jesus Christ is "the true light" that came into the world. Throughout the Old Testament Jehovah is referred to as the light on several occasions, such as Psalm 27:1 and Isaiah 60:20. We would not conclude that Jesus is "the" true light and that Jehovah is another true light. One does not cancel out the other, so we conclude that Jesus and Jehovah share the attribute of true light.

Revelation 17:14 shows exclusiveness when it says that Jesus Christ is Lord of Lords and King of Kings. This does not mean that Jehovah is no longer Lord and King. What it does mean is Jesus Christ claims to be King and Lord as Jehovah. In the Old Testament we find Jehovah is our King (Jeremiah 10:10 and Psalm 47:7). We also find Jehovah is our Lord (Deuteronomy 10:17). Since the Bible teaches that there is but one Lord (Ephesians 4:5) then we find Jesus is Jehovah, Jesus is Lord and King.

Isaiah 43:11 gives a different exclusive characteristic about Jehovah: "I, even I, am the LORD; and there is no savior besides Me." There is no savior besides Jehovah, but the New Testament openly and frequently declares Jesus as our Savior, as we find in Acts 4:12 and 1 John 4:14.

Jehovah's Witnesses, and others who deny the deity of Jesus Christ, usually have two misunderstandings concerning His eternal nature. One, they will confuse the Persons of the Trinity; or two, they confuse the humanity of Christ with His deity.

In the former situation the argument is usually framed as: Jesus is not God because the Father is not the Son. The problem with this statement is that nobody in the Christian church says the Father is the Son. We say the Father and the Son and the Holy Spirit are three Persons of the one God, but not three Persons as one Person. We do not confuse the Persons of the Trinity.

In the latter situation, where Christ's deity is confused with His humanity, they mistake verses like John 14:28, "The Father is greater than I" to mean that Jesus is not equal to the Father. But this verse refers to the voluntary subordination of Jesus during His earthly life when He willingly placed Himself in subordination to the Father. It says nothing about His nature, only His temporary rank on earth. Thus, the quote "greater than" refers to His position rather than His person.

Jehovah's Witnesses also attempt to show that Jesus Christ was created (as Michael the archangel). There are three main passages the Jehovah's Witnesses use to claim Jesus Christ was created. Beginning with the Old Testament, Proverbs 8:22-25 says: "The LORD possessed me at the beginning of His way . . . when there were no depths I was brought forth . . . before the hills I was brought forth." The words *brought forth* in this passage make the Jehovah's Witness think that Jesus had a day in which He was created as Michael the archangel. The context of the passage denies such a proposition. Proverbs 8 is speaking about wisdom in contrast to creation and merely states that wisdom is older than all creation. By necessity, God's wisdom is as eternal as He is, since there has never been a time when God has lacked wisdom.

Colossians 1:15 is another passage that Jehovah's Witnesses use in their attempt to say Jesus was created. It says, "And He is the image of the invisible God, the first-born of all creation." The Watchtower takes this to mean He was the "first one created." However, the passage itself states that Jesus is the creator of all things (verses 16,17), not a created being.

The description first-born refers to His preeminent position, not that He is Jehovah's "first creation." The term first-born can mean one of two things: the first one born or he who has first position. The way we know that Colossians 1:15 puts Jesus in the rank of first position is the context. Verse 18 confirms the context where He is also called "first-born from the dead"—that in all things He might have preeminence. "First-born" cannot be read aside from the context of first place or preeminence.

An illustration of the contrast between firstborn meaning the right of first place and the one who is literally born first is found in Exodus 4:22,23. Israel, as a nation, is called God's "first-born," but God spoke to Moses in verse 23 and told him that He would slay even the firstborn son of Pharaoh meaning the "first one born" of Pharaoh. Colossians 1:15 is telling us that Jesus, being the firstborn of all creation, is the originator of all creation. We see that He made all things, whether visible or invisible, whether in heaven or earth, which portrays Him as the origin of creation.

Another passage we will examine where Watchtower representatives attempt to destroy the eternal nature of Jesus Christ is Revelation 3:14, where Jesus is called "the Beginning of the creation of God." The word *beginning*, in the Greek New Testament, is the word *arche* which means the source or origin of the creation of God. Bruce Metzger points out if the passage were to teach that Jesus Christ was created "by God," it would have required the preposition *hupo* rather than *tou theou* which means "of God" (Bruce Metzger, *Theology Today*, 1953, pp.79-80).

The Watchtower has taken away the power of the blood atonement as Christ's vicarious sacrifice for our sins by making it only a ransom to buy back our perfect human life, earthly rights and prospects. The atonement of Jesus Christ is far more than a ransom. The atonement is clearly a result of God's love for us (Romans 5:8): "But God demonstrates His own love toward us, in that while we were yet sinners, Christ died for us." According to the Scripture, the atonement was necessary. Hebrews 9:22: "And without shedding of blood there is no forgiveness." Doing much more than just giving us right, the Scriptures say the atonement actually cancels out our condemnation. Romans 8:1 says, "There is therefore now no condemnation for those who are in Christ Jesus." Even more so, it is the "propitiation" changing the wrath of God into mercy (Romans 3:25, Hebrews 2:17 and 1 John 2:2). It is the very blood of the lamb which has purchased us and the church (1 Peter 1:18,19 and Acts 20:28).

The bodily resurrection of Jesus Christ, which is rejected by the Watchtower Society, is so central to the beliefs of Christianity that Paul said if the resurrection had not happened, then all our faith is in vain and all our preaching is in vain (1 Corinthians 15:14). Jesus did not materialize a fake body or a counterfeit body in order to deceive the disciples. Rather, He told the disciples the truth when He said, "Touch Me and see, for a spirit does not have flesh and bones as you see that I have" (Luke 24:39).

When Jesus showed His hands and His feet to Thomas in John 20:27, He offered the evidence of His bodily resurrection saying, "Reach here your finger, and see My hands; and reach here your hand, and put it into My side; and be not unbelieving, but believing." When it comes to the Jehovah's Witnesses, our recommendation is the same as what Jesus gave to Thomas, do not be unbelieving, but believing.

Conclusion

A close examination of the Watchtower has demonstrated that it is not what it claims to be: the "sole collective channel for the flow of biblical truth." It is guilty of false prophecy, anti-biblical theology, and misrepresentation of the truth.

We heartily recommend to Jehovah's Witnesses

that they act on the following instruction from the Watchtower: "We need to examine, not only what we personally believe, but also what is taught by any religious organization with which we may be associated. Are its teachings in full harmony with God's Word, or are they based on the traditions of men? If we are lovers of the Truth, there is nothing to fear from such an examination" (*The Truth That Leads to Eternal Life*, 1968, p. 13).

Such an examination will show the shortcomings of the manmade Watchtower and the all-sufficient perfection of Jesus Christ, our "great God and Saviour" (Titus 2:13).

Witnessing Tips

When Jehovah's Witnesses approach the household of Christians, it becomes a time to put our teaching into practice. This is easily said, but for most Christians, not a welcomed situation. This is why it is important to look at the Jehovah's Witnesses as you would anyone else in need of salvation. Try to stay away from the temptation to use your encounter as a battlefield over who can quote the most Scripture.

Pray and allow the Holy Spirit to guide you in a discussion on one or two topics. Look up each Scripture as they are cited and make sure there is an understanding of it before you go on to the next verse. Keep looking for the opportunity to share what God has done in your life personally and continue to let the Jehovah's Witness know he can have the same.

6

Christian Science

The Church of Christ, Scientist (Christian Science) is properly numbered among the western cults because it claims to be genuine Christianity. Its distinctive rejection of pantheism and reincarnation separates it from the New Age groups. The church made this distinction early in its history, "when it is necessary to show the great gulf between Christian Science and Theosophy, hypnotism, or spiritualism, do it, but without hard words" (*Church of Christ, Scientist, Manual*, p. 415).

History

The founder of Christian Science was born Mary Ann Morse Baker, in Bow, New Hampshire in 1821, to Mark and Abigail Baker. Her parents were members of the Congregationalist Church which upheld a strict doctrine of predestination that left young Mary unsettled:

The doctrine of unconditional election or predestination, greatly troubled me: for I was unwilling to be saved, if my brothers and sisters were to be numbered among those who were doomed to perpetual banishment from God (Mary Baker Eddy, *Retrospection and Introspection*, 13:5-9).

Her life later became characterized by the rejection of doctrines that are central to the Christian faith.

Mary Ann Morse Baker's life was beset by early troubles, being left a widow after seven months of marriage to George W. Glover. Mrs. Glover, at the age of twenty-three, bore a son from her first husband and named him George. She shouldered single parenting and hardships for ten years before marrying her second husband, Dr. Daniel Patterson.

She divorced Dr. Patterson in 1866 on the grounds of desertion. His dental practice was inconsistent and itinerant in neighboring towns. It was during this marriage that Mary Baker Patterson enjoined the search for spiritual enlightenment. She reassumed the name Mrs. Glover after her divorce from Patterson and published her first book under that name in 1875.

Her third marriage was to Asa G. Eddy in 1877, who was one of her students and the first healing "practitioner" for the church. She outlived her third husband who died of heart disease in 1882.

Christian Science Discovered

In 1866, while married to Dr. Patterson, Mary Baker discovered the principle of Christian Science after a serious fall allegedly brought her near death. Her account of the severity of the injuries was contradicted by the attending physician. Nevertheless, the principles "discovered" during this time became the basis of Christian Science. In 1875, her work *Science and Health* was published with the additional *Key to the Scriptures* added in 1883. For this work she claimed divine revelation:

> I should blush to write of *Science and Health With Key to the Scriptures* as I have, were it of human origin, and were I, apart from God its author. But I was only a scribe echoing the harmonies of Heaven in divine metaphysics, I cannot be super-modest in my estimate of the Christian Science Textbook (*The First Church of Christ, Scientist, and Miscellany*, Boston: Trusties Publishers, 1941, p. 115).

In 1879 in Charlestown, Massachusetts, the Church of Christ, Scientist was organized and was then changed in 1892 to the First Church of Christ, Scientist. The Church Manual was published in 1895 establishing the procedures of governing the church.

Phineas Quimby

In a sermon delivered in June of 1890, Mrs. Eddy again made the claim to divine revelation: "Christian Science is irrevocable—unpierced by bold conjecture's sharp point, by bald philosophy, or by man's inventions. It is divinely true, and every hour in time and in eternity will witness more steadfastly to its practical truth" (Mary Baker Eddy, *Seven Messages to the Mother Church*, pp. 20-21). There is strong evidence to the contrary; that Mrs. Eddy's "divine revelation" is not original to her, but is a plagiarism of Phineas Quimby's writings and ideas.

Phineas Quimby was a self-professed healer who applied hypnosis and the power of suggestion in affecting his cures. He called his word, "The science of the Christ" and "Christian Science." Mrs. Eddy became an enthusiastic follower of Quimby in 1862 after her back injury was healed by him. She wrote letters to the Portland (Maine) *Evening Courier*, praising Quimby and comparing him to Jesus Christ.

Upon his death she eulogized Quimby in a poem,

titling it, "Lines on the Death of Dr. P. P. Quimby, who healed with the truth that Christ taught in contradistinction to all Isms." Eventually she attempted to separate any connection between herself and Quimby when charges of borrowing his ideas surfaced. However, the facts are otherwise.

In 1921, Horatio Dresser published *The Quimby Manuscripts*, which when compared with Mrs. Eddy's writings, revealed many parallels leading some to comment, "As far as thought is concerned, *Science and Health* is practically all Quimby" (Ernest Sutherland Bates and John V. Dittermore, *Mary Baker Eddy: The Truth and The Tradition*, 1932, p. 156).

Mrs. Eddy received the principles of Christian Science from some place other than the God of the Bible. Since her teachings contradict the teachings of God as revealed in the Bible, they are thereby condemned by the Bible and she is therefore a false teacher.

Sole Channel of Truth

The Church of Christ, Scientist teaches that primitive Christianity was lost only to be rediscovered. *The Christian Science Church Manual* states their purpose as "to commemorate the word and works of our master, which should reinstate primitive Christianity and its lost element of healing" (*The Church Manual*, eighty-ninth ed., p. 17).

Mrs. Eddy's claims are clear: The revelation she received while near death was divine. She also claims exclusive truth: "Is there more than one school of Christian Science? ... There can, therefore, be but one method in its teaching" (*Science and Health*, 112:3-5). Needless to say, the one method is her method.

In furthering her claim as the sole collective channel for truth, she said that Jesus left his church to wander blindly until she discovered Christian Science:

"Our Master . . . practiced Christian healing . . . but left no definite rule for demonstrating this Principle of healing and preventing disease. This rule remained to be discovered by Christian Science" (*Science and Health,* 147:24-29).

Mrs. Eddy assures her followers that they are practicing the same rules Jesus practiced:

> Late in the nineteenth century I demonstrated the divine rules of Christian Science. They were submitted to the broadest practical test, and everywhere, when honestly applied under circumstances where demonstration was humanly possible, this science showed that truth had lost none of its divine and healing efficacy, even though centuries had passed away since Jesus practiced these rules on the hills of Judaea and in the valleys of Galilee (*Science and Health,* 147:6-13).

The Death of Mrs. Eddy

Although she taught that death is "an illusion, a lie of life" (*Science and Health,* 584:9), Mrs. Eddy passed away December 3, 1910. Today there is a self-perpetuating board of directors which governs the church.

There is no way to get an accurate number of Christian Scientists today since *The Church Manual* says, "Christian Scientists shall not report for publication the number of the members of the Mother Church, nor that of the branch churches" (Article VIII, p. 48). Observers estimate membership at 420,000 with about 3,000 congregations worldwide.

Biblical Analysis of Christian Science Discovery

The healing of the sick in Christianity has not been ignored throughout the history of the church. There are testimonies in every age where faithful saints prayed to God for healing and were spared. The difference between this and what Mrs. Eddy wrote of is the level of importance. The strength of Christianity is not found in what God does to our physical body but what He does to our soul when we are regenerated through the renewing of the Holy Spirit (Titus 3:5). Christian Science emphasizes the wrong end of the spectrum. It cherishes the well-being of the body above that of the soul.

The lack of balance in Mrs. Eddy's view of healing is also found in her lack of biblical examples of Christians who were not healed. Paul had physical infirmities (Galatians 4:13). Paul left his companion Trophimus sick at Miletus (2 Timothy 4:20), and he prescribed wine for Timothy's stomach and frequent illness (1 Timothy 5:23). There is ample evidence that God heals in the Bible, but the seldom discussed passages cited above show us that He does it according to His plan for our lives.

The unfolding gospel plan of the Bible concerns our eternal destiny—"that the world through Him might be saved" (John 3:17). God's primary consideration in sending Jesus as our Savior was to save us from eternal condemnation in hell (John 3:16). Healing, as well as other benefits in answer to prayer, may come to the believer, but even then it is by God's mercy (Philippians 2:27).

Mrs. Eddy did not rediscover a rule for healing that was lost from the first century. Her concept has two glowing errors: 1. It challenges the authenticity and reliability of the Bible; and 2. It renders Jesus' words meaningless when He promised to send the Holy Spirit who would bring all things to the disciples' remembrance (John 14:26). There are no teachings of Jesus essential to our salvation that are missing from the Bible.

Authoritative Sources

Christian Science, like many other cults, claims further revelation that goes "beyond the Bible"—that is to say, new divine truth previously unrevealed.

On page 107, in her work *Science and Health*, Mrs. Eddy quotes the apostle Paul:

> But I certify you, brethren, that the Gospel which was preached of me is not after man. For I neither received it of man, neither was I taught it, but by the revelation of Jesus Christ.

She follows the quotation with the claim that hers is the final revelation:

> In the year 1866, I discovered the Christ Science or divine laws of Life, Truth, and Love and named my discovery Christian Science. God has been graciously preparing me during many years for the reception of this final revelation of the absolute divine Principle of scientific mental healing (*Science and Health*, 107:1-6).

Mrs. Eddy claimed that she derived her teachings from the Bible, which she considered her final authority. However, in practice, and as we have just seen above, she also claimed that her revelations were better and "higher" than the Bible. Where the Bible contradicted her beliefs, she felt free to dismiss its authority: "The Bible has been my only authority. I have no other guide in 'The straight and narrow way' of Truth" (*Science and Health*, 126:29-31).

Although she claimed that the Bible was her guide, her view of Scripture was something less than desirable: "The material record of the Bible ... is no more important to our well-being than the history of Europe and America" (Mary Baker Eddy, *Miscellaneous Writings, 1833-1896*, 1921, p. 170).

The fact is, the teachings of Christian Science are in

direct contradiction to the Bible. The real authority in Christian Science is not the Bible, but the writings of Mrs. Eddy. She has this to say about her own work:

> It is the voice of Truth to this age (*Science and Health*, 456:27,28).

> The revealed Truth uncontaminated by human hypothesis (ibid., 457:1-2).

> No human pen nor tongue taught me the Science contained in this book, SCIENCE AND HEALTH; and neither tongue nor pen can overthrow it (ibid., 110:16-19).

She concludes:

> I won my way to absolute conclusions through divine revelation, reason, and demonstration. The Revelation of Truth in the understanding came to me gradually and apparently through Divine Power (ibid., 109:20-23).

Biblical Analysis of Authority Sources

Christian Science does what so many of the cults do; it has a second authority which supersedes the Bible as the final authority in solving doctrinal matters. The writings of Mrs. Eddy constitute the final word as far as Christian Scientists are concerned, with the Bible relegated to a secondary status, although she paid lip service homage to the Bible.

Merely making the assertion that truths are missing from the Bible does not make it so. She failed to show any early manuscript of the Old Testament or the New Testament that contained her truths.

The final revelation of God to man is found in Jesus Christ. Hebrews 1:2 tells us "in these last days He has spoken by His Son." Since Mrs. Eddy cannot show her teachings are from the New Testament manuscripts, then we cannot trust them to be from Jesus.

The Theology of Christian Science

Even though Christian Science claims to be a re-statement of primitive, pure Christianity, it denies everything that is considered sacred to God's Word.

God

Mrs. Eddy defined God as, "The great I Am; the all-knowing, all-seeing, all-acting, all-wise, all-loving, and eternal; Principle; Mind; Soul; Spirit; Life; Truth; Love; all Substance; Intelligence (*Science and Health*, 587:5-8).

Elsewhere she calls God "Divine Principle, Life, Truth, Love, Soul, Spirit, Mind" (ibid., 115:13-14).

When she refers to God as Mind, she is not saying He is a big brain up in the sky. Mind, in metaphysical writings, refers to an impersonal, everywhere present spirit that contains all available knowledge. The fact remains that this concept is a denial of the Personal God in the Bible. Mrs. Eddy denied the Trinity, since that also involves the personal nature of God: "The theory of three persons in one God ... suggests polytheism, rather than the one ever-present I AM" (ibid., p. 256).

Jesus Christ

The Christian Science view of the person of Christ is wholly unbiblical:

Christ is the ideal truth that comes to heal sickness and sin through Christian Science, and attributes all power to God. Jesus is the name of the man who, more than all other men, has presented Christ, the true idea of God ... Jesus is the human man, and Christ is the divine idea; hence the duality of Jesus the Christ (*Science and Health*, 473:9-16).

Mrs. Eddy attempts to make a distinction between

"Jesus" and "the Christ" as if they were two separate entities. "The spiritual Christ was infallible," she wrote. "Jesus as material manhood, was not Christ" (*Miscellaneous Writings*, p. 334).

Since Jesus Christ are two different entities in Christian Science, the doctrine that Jesus Christ is God is rejected: "The Christian believes that Christ is God . . . Jesus Christ is not God" (*Science and Health*, 361:1,2,12).

Unnecessary Atonement of Jesus

In Christian Science there exists no evil:

> Here also is found the path of the basal statement, the cardinal point in Christian Science, that matter and evil (including all in harmony, sin, disease, death) are unreal (*Miscellaneous Writings*, 27:9-12).

According to Christian Science, "Christ came to destroy the belief of sin" (*Science and Health*, 473:6,7). It is further emphasized that "evil is but an illusion, and it has no real basis. Evil is a false belief, God is not its author" (*Science and Health*, 480:23,24).

Since evil is an illusion, the idea of the death of Christ on the cross for our sins is unnecessary:

> The material blood of Jesus was no more efficacious to cleanse from sin when it was shed upon "the accursed tree" than when it was flowing in his veins as he went daily about his Father's business *Science and Health*, 25:6-8).

Salvation

Concerning salvation, Mrs. Eddy said: "Life, Truth, and Love understood and demonstrated as supreme over all; sin, sickness and death destroyed" (*Science and Health*, p. 593:20-22). Since to the Christian Scientist there is no such thing as sin, salvation in the biblical sense is totally unnecessary. The teachings concerning salvation in Mrs. Eddy's writings are both ambiguous and inconsistent. She stated over and over again that sin is just an illusion (*Miscellaneous Writings*, 27:11-12; *Science and Health*, 71:2, 287:22,23, 480:23,24, etc.).

On the other hand, she states, as quoted above, that salvation is "sin, sickness and death destroyed." If sin is only an illusion, having no real existence, how can it be destroyed? Putting it another way, do you destroy something that does not exist? Since there is no harmonious teaching in Christian Science concerning salvation, it is difficult to evaluate it objectively.

Biblical Analysis of Doctrines

The God of the Bible is infinite (Psalm 139:7-16), yet personal (Isaiah 45:20-25). The God of the Bible and the God of Christian Science are not the same. The apostle Paul declared the true God:

> The God who made the world and all things in it, since He is Lord of heaven and earth, does not dwell in temples made with hands, neither is He served by human hands, as though He needed anything, since He Himself gives to all life and breath and all things (Acts 17:24,25).

In direct contradiction to Mrs. Eddy's denial of the Trinity, the Bible clearly teaches the doctrine of the Holy Trinity. We do not believe in polytheism, or more than one God. We believe that in the nature of the one true God (Isaiah 43:10), there exists three eternal and distinct persons (Luke 3:22): the Father (2 Peter 1:17); the Word or Son (John 1:1,14); and the Holy Spirit (Acts 5:3,4). These three persons are the one God (Matthew 28:19).

The distinction Mrs. Eddy makes between Jesus as a man and the "Christ" as a principle is not possible because Jesus Christ is one person. Jesus is His name meaning "Yahweh is Salvation"; Christ, His title, meaning "The Anointed One." The attempted distinction that Christian Scientists make between the two shows a complete lack of understanding of the Scriptures, such as Luke 2:11, 1 John 2:22, and 1 John 5:1.

The reality of salvation is shown in our Savior's vicarious atonement. The Bible teaches that evil is real (1 John 5:19) and that we would be without salvation if Jesus Christ had not died on the cross for our sins (Hebrews 9:22). As Christians we can rejoice in the good news that Jesus Christ "gave Himself for our sins, that He might deliver us out of this present evil age, according to the will of our God and Father, to whom be the glory forevermore. Amen" (Galatians 1:4,5).

Christian Science Healing

In a section entitled "Fruitage" in *Science and Health*, the following claim is made:

> Thousands of letters could be presented in testimony of the healing efficacy of Christian Science and particularly concerning the vast number of people who have been reformed and healed through the perusal or study of this book (*Science and Health*, p. 600).

Followed by this claim are approximately one hundred pages of testimonials of healing of every conceivable disease by those who have embraced the principles of Christian Science. The obvious question arises: Can Christian Science heal? While many of the healings in Christian Science can be explained without appealing to the miraculous, there are some accounts of seemingly true healings.

If this be the case, then it would be an example of the "signs and false wonders" the apostle Paul spoke about (2 Thessalonians 2:9). Satan is the great counterfeiter and his attempt to duplicate the works of God and the miracle of healing is no exception. We all want to be healthy, but not at the cost of abandoning Christ.

Conclusion

Christian Science is neither Christian nor scientific because every important doctrine of historic Christianity is rejected by Christian Science. The claim of divine revelation by Mrs. Eddy is contradicted by the facts that clearly attest she does not represent the God of the Bible. Although she speaks in the name of Jesus, her teachings conflict with His in every respect.

Fortunately, Jesus warned us ahead of time about people like Mrs. Eddy: "Beware of the false prophets, who come to you in sheep's clothing, but inwardly are ravenous wolves. You will know them by their fruits" (Matthew 7:15,16).

Witnessing Tips

The people involved in Christian Science are usually well-read and intelligent people. They take great offense when someone outside the group accuses them of one belief or another. We find it much more advantageous to ask questions on particular issues and allow the Christian Scientist to explain his views. Then, once a commitment has been made on belief, these views may be compared with the Bible.

When the Bible is read by Christian Scientists it is rarely read in its entirety. Most verses are only partially quoted and read in light of Mary Baker Eddy's "discovery." We have seen many Christian Scientists come to find genuine faith in Jesus Christ when a Christian challenges them to read the Gospel of John. Meet with the Christian Scientist regularly as he reads it and ask questions about what he has learned. In this way you can share a powerful witness about the person, nature and work of Jesus Christ.

7

The
Unity School
of
Christianity

A mong the western cults, the Unity School of Christianity is perhaps the most difficult to classify. It has several parallels to the New Age Movement (which causes an overlapping of beliefs by its ministers), yet it maintains a distinctiveness that is uncommon to New Agers, namely panentheism and a final resurrection following twenty incarnations.

Panentheism (Greek: *pan*, "everything"; *en*, "in"; *theos*, "god") is the belief that God includes and permeates the material world, but He also transcends it and is not limited by it. This theory was advanced by recent philosophers (K. Krause, A. Whitehead) and should not be confused with pantheism (Greek: *pan*, "everything"; *theos*, "god"), that the material world is god, as found in classical Hinduism. For a refutation to panentheism see *Christian Apologetics* by Norman Geisler (Grand Rapids, MI: Baker Book House, 1976, pp. 193-212).

History

The Unity School of Christianity was founded by Charles and Myrtle Fillmore. Charles Sherlock Fillmore was born near St. Cloud, Minnesota in 1854. He married Mary Caroline Page (or "Myrtle") in 1881.

The early years of their marriage recorded many financial ups and downs until they finally established a modest real estate office in Kansas City, Missouri. Myrtle's family had a history of tuberculosis and she was eventually stricken ill with the dreaded disease. She also contracted malaria and was given, by her doctor, only six months to live. She abandoned her Methodist background and sought answers to her health problems through metaphysical groups.

In 1886, the Fillmores went to a lecture which was to change their lives dramatically. The speaker, E. B. Weeks, said to the crowd that night, "I am a child of God and therefore I do not inherit sickness." Myrtle believed the statement and continued to recite it over and over again. Eventually she was healed.

At first, Charles, who was raised an Episcopalian, refused to accept his wife's new technique but he was willing to investigate it, along with other religions. After an extensive study of the science of mind and Eastern religions, including Hinduism and Buddhism, he decided to try his wife's meditation technique. He practiced reciting affirmations, and soon his withered leg was healed. He joined Myrtle in founding a new religious system, later called the Unity School of Christianity.

Borrowing heavily from Christian Science and New Thought (a nineteenth-century metaphysical healing movement developed from the system of mental healer Phineas Quimby), the Fillmores added their own interpretations, including the Eastern concept of reincarnation.

Structure of Unity

Fillmore published a magazine under several names: *Modern Thought* (1889), *Christian Science Thought* (1890), *Thought* (1891), and eventually took the name *Unity* in 1895. It was organized as a religious movement in 1914 which he called Unity School of Christianity. They broke ties with other New Thought organizations and published criticisms of spiritualism, hypnotism, mesmerism, and astrology. Today they renounce New Age practices of channelling, palm reading and using crystals.

Myrtle Fillmore died in 1931 whereupon Charles married Cora Dedrick, his private secretary. Charles Fillmore died in 1948. The leadership of Unity was taken over by the Fillmores' two sons, Lowell and Rickert, and subsequently experienced a rapid growth. Today, Unity is run by the great-granddaughter of Charles and Myrtle Fillmore, Connie Fillmore, who oversees some two million adherents worldwide. Its headquarters is located at Unity Village, in Lee's Summit, Missouri, a suburb of Kansas City.

The three magazines published by the organization are *Unity*, *Daily Word*, and *Wee Wisdom*. They mail sixty million pieces of literature annually and have 600 centers and groups worldwide.

Unity embraces the early heresy of gnosticism, believing it to be the true teaching of Jesus. Frank Giudici, a Bible teacher at Unity's Ministerial School, told one author, "We're Gnostic." He continued, "The Gnostic says you're saved through knowledge . . . We're Gnostic in that we believe you're saved when you understand that Christ indwells you" (*Misguiding Lights*, ed. by Steven M. Miller, Kansas City, MO: Beacon Hill Press, 1991, p. 67).

Unity also boasts of a prayer tower in which 150 to 200 devout members pray twenty-four hours a day for requests that are sent in. The "prayers" are mostly in-vocations of positive thinking. "Silent Unity," as it is called, repeats positive affirmations to produce health and wealth for its followers. In silent meditation they wait for intuition or guidance about which affirmation to apply to the situation. "I Am that I Am," reads one affirmation, "I Am Spirit. I Am life. I Am the Christ. I know no evil. I deny all sin and sickness. I have all power. I am God manifest in the flesh."

Biblical Analysis of Unity's Structure

The basic world view of Unity is that of gnos-ticism. Gnosticism is a theological term referring to a system of belief that qualitatively separates the spirit from the material. It also believes knowledge is secret and only obtainable by a select few. Gnostics generally believe that what is spiritual is good and what is material is bad. They teach that God is impersonal spirit and the "christ" is not a person but an eternal principle. Jesus, then, was a man on whom the "christ principle" came, and any other man can obtain the same level through knowledge.

The differences between Christianity and gnos-ticism are many. Simply put, we are saved by *who* we know, not *what* we know! Christianity is an objective faith and we place faith in the person, nature and work of Jesus Christ.

In the New Testament period a Gnostic teacher named Cerenthus became a source of trouble at Ephesus, where the apostle John lived. Cerenthus denied Jesus is the Christ, he denied the reality of sin and evil, he denied the deity of Jesus Christ, he denied the effectiveness of Jesus' atonement, and he denied sal-vation by grace, saying salvation came through "gnosis" (special knowledge).

Each of these teachings are fully assumed by Unity

today, but they were completely denied by the apostle John in his first epistle. John counters the Gnostics by presenting true knowledge, not in esoteric gnosis, but in Jesus Christ. He uses the word "know" twenty-eight times in 1 John to show that we have a solid faith in the gospel message: "We know we are in Him . . . you know He is righteous . . . you know He was manifest . . . we know we are of the truth . . . you may know you have eternal life."

John turns the table on the Gnostics and affirms everything they deny. We know Jesus is the Christ (1 John 2:22), we are sinners before God (1:10), Jesus is God (5:20), His blood cleanses us from sin (1:7), and we are saved by His grace when we believe upon the name of the Son of God (5:13).

Making positive affirmations will not create a new environment nor will it move the hand of God. One may search the entire Bible in vain for positive affirmations as God's way of responding to our needs. What we find instead is the prayers of faith (James 5:13-16). We need to seek God's will (James 4:15) and pray without ceasing (1 Thessalonians 5:17; Ephesians 6:18). In this way we can trust God to answer according to His plan for our life and not by our selfish demands and affirmations.

Authoritative Sources

Unity has several writers whose works they consider authoritative. H. Emile Cady, Eric Butterworth, James D. Freeman and Frank B. Whitney are familiar names to Unity students, in addition to the Fillmores.

It was thirty years before Charles Fillmore drafted a statement of faith which was qualified with the following:

We are hereby giving warning that we shall not be

bound to this tentative statement of what Unity believes. We may change our mind tomorrow on some of the points, and if we do, we shall feel free to make a new statement (James Dillet Freeman, *What Is Unity?*, Lee's Summit, Missouri, n.d., p. 5).

The Bible is revered as a divinely inspired source in Unity, but not infallible. Eric Butterworth, past president of the Unity Ministers Association, said, "One of the greatest limitations to understanding the Bible is to insist on it infallibility" (*Unity: A Quest for Truth*, New York: Speller and Sons Publishers, 1956, p. 23).

Charles Fillmore rejected the literal interpretation of God's Word and accused Christians of reading "the Bible in the letter instead of the spirit" (*Metaphysical Bible Dictionary*, Lee's Summit, MO: Unity School of Christianity, 1931, p. 2). He sought the spiritual meaning (mostly allegorical) behind what is said, "By metaphysics we refer to the inner or esoteric meaning of the name defined" (ibid.).

Fillmore believed that all religions had some truth but Christianity was superior. He claimed to be in direct communication with God: "I received revelations . . . I do not remember that I asked who the author of my guidance was; I took for granted that it was Spirit" (J. D. Freeman, *The Household of Faith*, Lee's Summit, MO: Unity, 1951, p. 41). He also claimed his system was the most logical: "Logic is necessary, you must trust logic" (ibid.).

Biblical Analysis of Authoritative Sources

Certainly God expects us to be logical, but the lack of logic in Mr. Fillmore's system is apparent in his inconsistent application of the Bible. Looking for a metaphysical meaning behind the hundreds of biblical words redefined in his *Metaphysical Bible Dictionary* reveals his lack of logic and his inconsistencies. If God does not mean what He says and we need Mr. Fillmore's book to reveal the true meaning, then the god of Mr. Fillmore is less dependable than Fillmore's own mind! Mr. Fillmore drives us to the conclusion that his words are more literal than God's. But why should we take the *Metaphysical Bible Dictionary* definition literally? Fillmore provides no reason why God's Word is not literal and his word is.

We learn our rules for biblical interpretation in evangelical Christianity from Jesus and the apostles. They never allegorized or spiritualized any part of the Old Testament. The historical matters of the Old Testament were repeated by Jesus with the confidence of accuracy. He spoke of the creation of Adam and Eve (Matthew 19:4), and He mentions Able (Matthew 23:35), Sodom and Gomorrah (Matthew 10:15), Abraham (John 8:56), Moses (Luke 24:44) and Jonah (Matthew 12:39) as literal figures in literal historical settings.

It is a dangerous movement that bases its beliefs on a man who does not know for certain where his revelations came from. Fillmore said he assumed it was the Spirit, but that assumption is too vague for the Bible. The Bible specifically demonstrates that a man's words must agree with what the Bible already states (Isaiah 8:20; 2 Corinthians 11:4). The only way new revelation can agree with the former revelation is if the former revelation is literally true. Fillmore could not even agree with the Bible on that point, let alone have the same message.

The Beliefs of the Unity School of Christianity

Understanding metaphysics is not always easy, since it is clothed in esoteric language that usually requires a special understanding. If a Christian dialogues with a member of Unity, for example, both parties may be using the same word but thinking different things.

Every time heaven or hell is mentioned, the Unity member will think of a "state of mind" while the Christian will think of a place of eternal destiny. As we carefully outline their beliefs, please note the redefined terms in Unity.

God in Unity

God the Father, Son, and Holy Spirit are depersonalized in an utter destruction of the Trinity. Fillmore said, "The Father is Principle, the Son is that Principle revealed in creative plan, the Holy Spirit is the executive power of both Father and Son carrying out the creative plan" (*Metaphysical Bible Dictionary*, p. 629). The Father, Son, and Holy Spirit are not real persons in Unity: "The truth is, then, that God is Principle, Law, Being, Mind, Spirit, All-God" (*Science of Being*, Kansas City, MO: Unity, 1912, p. 16).

Since personal attributes and titles have no real significance, God can freely be neuter, "it," or addressed as a female: "We believe that creative Mind, God, is masculine and feminine . . . Almighty Father-Mother" (*Unity's Statement of Faith*, 16,30). One Unity publication states, "God is all and all is God" (*Unity*, August 1974, p. 40).

Fillmore also said, "God is not loving . . . God does not love anybody or anything. God is the love in everybody and everything. God is love" (*Jesus Christ Heals*, Unity School of Christianity, 1944, p. 31).

Jesus in Unity

In an outright rejection of the uniqueness of Jesus as God in the flesh, Fillmore claimed that "the Son of God" lived in Jesus the same as the "Son of God, the Anointed in us . . . this Christ lives within us that lived in Jesus" (*Unity Treasure Chest*, p. 49,51).

According to their teachings, God is a Principle, or

Mind, and Christ is the "real self in all men." Jesus happened to be the first man to fully manifest this "Christ," but Jesus is not the only embodiment of the Christ Principle: "Unity teaches the goal of life is to do the same thing Jesus did and discover the Divine Mind . . . true, spiritual, higher self" (*Metaphysical Bible Dictionary*, p. 150).

Unity's reincarnated Jesus was on a journey of self-salvation. Mr. Fillmore called the former incarnations of Jesus "His days in school" (*Unity* magazine, Vol. 14, 1901, p. 149). Jesus could have been known under any name "in the many religious systems. The Krishna of the Hindu is the same as the Christos of the Greeks and the Messiah of the Hebrews" (*Science of Being*, p. 22).

Atonement and Salvation in Unity

In Unity, sin is an illusion to be denied. Mr. Fillmore said joy comes when "the mind has been cleansed by denial of sin" (ibid., p. 35). "The atonement has not taken sin," he wrote, "the red blood of the flesh does not carry the power to cleanse your conscience from dead works" (*Metaphysical Bible Dictionary*, p. 79,129).

Salvation by grace through faith in Jesus is not available in Unity. They choose to repeat affirmations to deny sin: "I am not a sinner. I never did sin. I cannot sin" (*Unity* magazine, 1936). The work in this affirmation is supposed to free one from reincarnation and resurrect the body, as Jesus did His, "through the mind we may resurrect ourselves from the dead" (*Science of Being*, p. 146).

Biblical Analysis of Unity Beliefs

The Fillmores and other Unity writers confuse the attributes of God with God Himself. God is more than attributes such as love. He is personal (Exodus 3:14). He

is not to be equated with the impersonal "substance behind creation" for He has a separate existence apart
from creation (Isaiah 44:1-28; Romans 1:18-25).

The New Testament maintains that Jesus is different from us by the fact that He is God by His very
nature: "In the beginning was the Word, and the Word
was with God, and the Word was God" (John 1:1). No
one else can be the Son of God as Jesus Christ is the Son
of God (John 5:18-23). He alone is the "image of the invisible God" (Colossians 1:15), the "radiance of His
glory and the exact representation of His nature"
(Hebrews 1:3).

On the subject of sin, Unity is in direct contradiction to the Bible that acknowledges sin as a reality, "For
all have sinned and fall short of the glory of God"
(Romans 3:23). Furthermore, "The wages of sin is death,
but the free gift of God is eternal life in Christ Jesus our
Lord" (Romans 6:23). If a person does not come to
Christ for salvation, he will be lost in his sin: "For unless you believe that I am He, you shall die in your
sins" (John 8:24).

Reincarnation teaches that only through many
lifetimes can one rid himself of the debt for all of his
sins. However, the Bible teaches that through Jesus
Christ we can be rid of all of our sins at one time (1 John
1:8-10). His purpose for dying on the cross was as a
sacrifice for our sins (Acts 3:18,19).

Jesus Christ is the only Savior we ever need because "He abides forever, holds His priesthood
permanently. Hence, also, He is able to save forever
those who draw near to God through Him, since He always lives to make intercession for them" (Hebrews
7:24,25). We have the promise of God Himself that our
salvation has been guaranteed through faith in the
sacrifice of Jesus Christ on the cross (1 Peter 1:2-6).

Conclusion

The Unity School of Christianity has no biblical authority to use the name Christian to describe its organization, for it is decidedly not Christian. Unfortunately, many Christians read the publications of Unity without realizing it is a non-Christian cult denying the basic beliefs of Christianity.

In the first publication that proceeded from the Fillmores, the non-Christian basis was revealed when they said, "We see the good in all religions and we want everyone to feel free to find the Truth for himself wherever he may be led to find it" (*Modern Thought,* 1889, p. 42). In contrast to this, Jesus of Nazareth said, "I am the way, and the truth, and the life; no one comes to the Father, but through Me" (John 14:6).

It is clear that Unity and Christianity are opposed to each other on the basic issues with no possible way of reconciling Unity as being part of Christianity.

Witnessing Tips

The Unity School of Christianity seems to place emphasis upon subjective experience. Love is spoken of often and highly respected. When a Christian encounters a Unity member, or any cultist for that matter, his love should be genuine for the lost soul. With gentleness and reverence is how 2 Peter 3:15 portrays our attitude in giving answers to those outside of the Christian church. Many good witnessing opportunities have been stifled by a sarcastic comment or a lack of tact in witnessing. If your love is genuine, it will be observed by those you encounter. The person whom you are witnessing to may not accept Jesus as Lord and Savior at that moment, but your love may open the door for another opportunity.

8

The
Unification Church ("Moonies")

W e have placed the Unification Church among the western cults even though it has earmarks of eastern and New Age cults. Our reason for this is its claim to be the true Christian church. The Bible and Jesus Christ play central roles in its theology whereas the eastern and New Age cults deny this centrality.

History

The founder and leader of the Unification Church is Sun Myung Moon who was born in North Korea on January 6, 1920. His family converted to Christianity when he was ten and became members of the Presbyterian Church.

At age sixteen young Moon experienced a vision while in prayer on a Korean mountainside. Moon claims that Jesus Christ appeared to him and admonished him to carry out the task that Christ had failed to complete. Jesus supposedly told Moon that he was the only one who could do it. After much repeated asking by Jesus, Moon finally accepted the challenge.

Moon spent the next few years of his life preparing for the great spiritual battle ahead. The years between his "conversion" experience and his coming to America are shrouded in much controversy. For documentation on those intervening years we recommend *The Moon Is Not the Son* by James Bjornstad (Minneapolis: Dimension Books/Bethany House Press, 1976).

Moon Comes to America

After achieving success with his new religion in the Far East, especially South Korea, Moon came to America at the end of 1971 and his cult began to flourish. Today they claim some two million members worldwide.

The Claims of Sun Myung Moon

Sun Myung Moon has made it clear that he believes himself to be the messiah for this age. He has been the center of controversy among conservative and evangelical Christians because of his claim that the Second Coming of Christ was to be in Korea between 1917 and 1930. His birth date, January 6, 1920, falls conveniently between these.

Moon rarely makes the direct public statement that he is the messiah. At a conference hosted by the Unification Church in San Francisco, California, Sun Myung Moon went on record saying that he is the messiah:

> According to an Evangelical Press News Service report, Moon said the world needs to find its "true parent" to free itself of Satan's dominion. "This person is the messiah," he said. "To help fulfill this very purpose I have been called upon by God . . . so that I can live with the heart of true parents to love races of all colors in the

world" (*Pentecostal Evangel* magazine, December 9, 1990, p. 28).

Sun Myung Moon's followers have long held the position that he is their messiah:

> Rev. Moon is Messiah, Lord of the Second Advent . . . If only they can understand the fall of man they can understand that Father is Messiah . . . Rev. Moon found this. The man who found this must be sinless. Then he must be qualified to be the Messiah (Dr. Sudo, *120-day Training Manual*, Unification Church, 1975, pp. 160,222,400).

Moon has also said, "No heroes in the past, no saints or holy men in the past, like Jesus or Confucius, have excelled us" (*Master Speaks*, March 11, 1973, p. 3).

Even though Moon's doctrines are opposed to Christianity, he claims that it was Jesus who revealed them to him:

> You may again want to ask me, "With what authority do you weigh these things?" I spoke with Jesus Christ in the spirit world. And I spoke also with John the Baptist. This is my authority. If you cannot at this time determine that my words are the truth, you will surely discover that they are in the course of time. These are hidden truths presented to you as a new revelation. You have heard me speak the Bible. If you believe the Bible, you must believe what I am saying (Rev. Moon, *Christianity in Crisis*, p. 98).

Like all cult leaders, Moon claims exclusive knowledge: "We are the only people who truly understand the heart of Jesus, and the hope of Jesus" (Rev. Moon, *The Way of the World*, p. 20).

To his followers there appears to be no question about it; Moon is the messiah. He is reportedly seen in spirit-form by his followers when they close their prayers in the name of "True Parents." Moon has stated, "God is now throwing Christianity away and is now establishing a new religion, and this new religion is the Unification Church . . . With our right foot, we step on Christianity and we subjugate Christianity" (*Master Speaks*, Paris Address, April 2, 1972, pp. 3,5).

Biblical Analysis of Moon's Vision

Visions are found in the Bible as one of the "many ways" God has spoken "long ago to the fathers in the prophets" (Hebrews 1:1). We do not deny this. There is a danger, however, in accepting a vision as being from God without testing it against the solid standard of the written Word. In the Old Testament, visions were subjected to the test of Scripture (Deuteronomy 13:1-4).

In Jeremiah 23:16, God sharply rebukes those who say they have had a vision and give false messages: "They speak a vision of their own imagination, not from the mouth of the Lord." We can see from this that God always provides a test for those who claim to have dreams and visions. Sun Myung Moon has failed the test of Scripture, since his vision of Jesus is contrary to what Jesus said in the New Testament.

Source of Authority

In the Unification Church the writings and teachings of Moon take precedence over the Bible:

> It may be displeasing to religious believers, especially to Christians, to learn that a new expression of truth must appear. They believe that the Bible, which they now have, is perfect and absolute in itself (*Divine Principle*, 2nd ed., 1973, p. 9).

Moon further stated, "The New Testament Words of Jesus and the Holy Spirit will lose their light . . . [this] means that the period of their mission has elapsed with the coming of the new age" (*Divine Principle*, p. 118).

The basic work containing the supposed revelations given to Moon is entitled the *Divine Principle*.

The Unification Church uses the Bible throughout their writings, whether it is a sermon of Moon (known as *Master Speaks*) or one of their books. In one of Moon's sermons, however, he reveals his plan to eventually eliminate the Bible when it has served his purpose: "Until our mission with the Christian Church is over, we must quote the Bible and use it to explain the Divine Principle. After we received the inheritance of the Christian Church, we will be free to teach without the Bible" (*Master Speaks*, April 1967, Number 7, p. 1).

The Divine Principle

For the members of the Unification Church, the *Divine Principle* is the ultimate authoritative work, superseding even the Bible. The *Divine Principle* is known as the "completed testament" because it supposedly contains the present truth for this age which heretofore had never been revealed. It is not actually written by Moon himself, but it is his teachings translated into English by his students.

The *Divine Principle* is a complete reinterpretation of the Bible through the Oriental philosophy of Taoism. Everything, according to this theory, has yang and yin as its basis (positive and negative, masculine and feminine). This dualism in the universe begins with God and filters down throughout creation. Everything God does is viewed as the "give-and-take relationship" of yang and yin. Thus, within God's nature there is a harmonious give and take with his negative and positive aspects (Father and Holy Spirit).

Creation is also in a give-and-take relationship with God and with all other created things. When creation is out of harmony, there is no give and take with God. There is also no harmonious give and take with the other objects of creation. This is what the *Divine Principle* calls the problem of our corrupt world. Their mission is to restore God's harmonious dualism with creation.

A major problem with this system, before we analyze it with the Bible, is that their concept of God leaves Him with the potential of imperfection. He is not fully perfect until all creation is back in harmony with Him and itself. While some Unification literature reflects their belief that God has "perfect intellect, emotion and will" (*Unification Seminary Affirmation*, October 14, 1976), still Mr. Moon says that God has incompleteness. He teaches that God needs creation for his own self-fulfillment (*Outline of the Principle, Level 4*, p. 22). According to Moon, God needs to be "saved" and has no love without man:

> Are we here for the cosmos or God? How can you save God if He is already omniscient and omnipotent, unchanging and unique? It is because of love, which God does not have, that even you can save God. God cannot love by Himself because He needs an object; He needs you (*Master Speaks*, May 1, 1978, p. 4).

Denying God's perfect sovereignty, Moon says:

> Because you know God so well you can say, "God, You are almighty and omnipresent, but no matter how great You are, You need me because without Your object You cannot be subject [give and take]. I am Your partner and without me you are not perfect" ... When God is struck by your true love He is rendered helpless ... The situation of God existing alone without man is unthinkable. Subject and object cannot exist without each other. If man did not exist then God would vanish (*Master Speaks*, May 27, 1977, p. 6).

Biblical Analysis of Divine Principle

The *Divine Principle* interprets God and the Bible

through the give-and-take relationship of Taoism. Biblically, Mr. Moon has led his followers astray after another god (Deuteronomy 13:1-4). The first thing we should take note of in refutation to Moon's dualistic god is how the God of Israel is eternal and unchanging (Deuteronomy 33:27; Psalm 90:2; Malachi 3:6; Acts 17:25; James 1:17).

Since the true God is unchanging, He does not need man or any created thing for self-fulfillment. If God did need self-fulfillment, then He is changeable, which is contrary to Scripture. If God could vanish, as Mr. Moon says, then again, He would be changeable. God is perfect, according to the Bible, and lacks nothing. Mr. Moon's god is not perfect because he needs man to keep him from vanishing.

The assertions of Moon are at complete odds with the Bible. The Scriptures testify that the Word of God will not be done away with, but is eternal: "The grass withers, the flower fades, but the word of our God stands forever" (Isaiah 40:8). Jesus said, "Heaven and earth will pass away, but My words shall not pass away" (Matthew 24:35). The idea that the words of Jesus will somehow lose their light is totally foreign to the teaching of the Bible.

Moreover, the Bible records the strongest condemnation for those who would add to what the Scriptures have revealed: "Do not add to His words lest He reprove you, and you be proved a liar" (Proverbs 30:6). Furthermore, the Scriptures make it plain that the faith has been "once for all delivered to the saints" (Jude 3). Any so-called revelation that contradicts that which was previously revealed is guilty of adding to the Word of God and should be discarded. The *Divine Principle* is in this category.

Unification Doctrine

It is difficult for Moon to justify his dualistic interpretation when it contradicts so many parts of the Bible.

God in Unification Theology

Mr. Moon directly attacks the biblical doctrine of the Trinity, which is one God in three distinct Persons. According to Moon there are several "trinities" and the trinity of the Father, Son, and Holy Spirit began sometime after the crucifixion of Christ. He says the original trinity was Adam, Eve, and God. After the fall of man the trinity changed to Adam, Eve, and Satan.

Moon also has a New Trinity which will soon be revealed as God, the Third Adam, and the Third Eve. The Third Adam and Third Eve, referred to as True Parents, are none other than Mr. and Mrs. Sun Myung Moon (*Divine Principle*, pp. 218-219, and *Outline, Level 4*, pp. 98-99). This new trinity is called the spiritual and physical trinity, but in the meantime the Moonies have to settle for the lesser, spiritual-only trinity of Father, Son, and Holy Spirit.

Moon's dualistic god is defined as, "God's essential positivity and essential negativity are the attributes of His essential character and essential form...Here we have the positivity and negativity of God, 'masculinity' and 'femininity,' respectively" (*Divine Principle*, p. 24).

Moon describes the form of God in unusual terms: " 'Good spirits' is the collective name for God, good spirit men on His side, and angels" (ibid., p. 87). He said, "God is in the shape of man" (*Master Speaks*, 5:5). And, "God either projected the full value of Himself in His object, or He created nothing at all . . . So man is the visible form of God, and God is the invisible form of man. Subject and object are one in essence. God and man are one. Man is incarnate God" (*New Hope*, p. 5).

Jesus Christ in Unification Theology

Moon has a non-biblical view of the person of Jesus Christ by denying the unique deity of Jesus Christ:

> It is plain that Jesus is not God Himself (*Divine Principle*, p. 258).

> But after his crucifixion, Christianity made Jesus into God. This is why a gap between God and man has never been bridged. Jesus is a man in whom God is incarnate, but he is not God Himself (*New Hope*, pp. 12-13).

Moon tells his followers that they cannot only equal Jesus, they can also excel Him: "You can compare yourself with Jesus Christ, and feel you can be greater than Jesus Himself" (*Master Speaks*, June 30, 1974, p. 4).

Jesus, according to Moon, was a failure: "Abraham was the father of faith, Moses was a man of faith, Jesus was the Son of man, trying to carry out his mission at the cost of his life. But they are, in a way, failures" (*Master Speaks*, March 31, 1973, p. 1).

The will of God was a failure in the mission of Jesus: "When this will was again a failure, due to the disbelief of the people" (*Divine Principle*, p. 196).

The Death and Resurrection of Christ

Rev. Moon denies the power of the cross: "We, therefore, must realize that Jesus did not come to die on the cross" (*Divine Principle*, p. 144).

The Scriptures teach "that God was in Christ reconciling the world to Himself" (2 Corinthians 5:19). But Moon declares, "the physical body of Jesus was invaded by Satan through the cross" (*Divine Principle*, p. 148).

He utterly denies salvation through the atonement:

> We must realize that through the crucifixion on the

cross, God and Jesus lost everything . . . There was no redemption; there was no salvation; and there was no beginning of Christianity. So there on the cross, salvation was not given (*The Way of the World*, p. 13).

Moon spiritualized the bodily resurrection of Christ: "Jesus after the resurrection was not the same Jesus who had lived with his disciples before his crucifixion. He was no longer a man seen through physical eyes, because be was a being transcendent of time and space" (*Divine Principle*, p. 360).

The Fall of Man and the New Adam

According to the *Divine Principle*, until now no one has correctly understood the Genesis account of the fall of man. The *Divine Principle* teaches there were two falls (dualism), one physical and one spiritual. Moreover, both falls were sexual in nature. Eve supposedly had an illicit sexual relationship with Lucifer causing the spiritual fall. Afterward, her sexual relationship with spiritually immature Adam resulted in the physical fall (cf., *Divine Principle*, p. 72).

Since there was a dual aspect of the fall there also needs to be a dual aspect of redemption, necessitating both physical and spiritual salvation. Jesus formed the second Adam and the Holy Spirit formed the second Eve. Jesus was to find the perfect bride and marry her to produce sinless offspring, thereby producing a sinless race and saving man dually—physically and spiritually.

John the Baptist lost faith and failed to clear the way for Jesus. This caused the Jewish people to abandon Jesus and crucify him. The crucifixion was not God's first will since it only saved mankind halfway (spiritually).

A new plan must be initiated with a Third Adam and a Third Eve to save mankind physically and produce sinless offspring. It is taught by Moon that Jesus did not predict his second coming, but the coming of a different "lord" who would be the Third Adam: "Jesus promised the Lord would come and fulfill the will without fail" (*Divine Principle*, p. 196).

The Holy Spirit in Unification Theology

Moon says the Holy Spirit is the female aspect of God: "There are many who receive revelations indicating that the Holy Spirit is a female Spirit; this is because she came as the True Mother, that is, the second Eve" (ibid., 215). This temporary second Eve will move over when the new trinity is established and the Holy Spirit will be replaced by Mrs. Moon, the Third Eve (*Outline, Level 4*, p. 99).

Salvation in Unification Theology

Man's dual fall required a dual salvation: "If Jesus had not been crucified, what would have happened? He would have accomplished the providence of salvation both spiritually and physically" (*Divine Principle*, p. 147). Moon further elaborates, "God's salvation of man is simply to restore man to the original state of goodness . . . So salvation is equivalent to restoration. God is going to restore the Kingdom of Hell to the Kingdom of Heaven" (*New Future*, p. 77).

Biblical Analysis of Unification Theology

The Bible does not specifically address every evil doctrine of man. Each false teaching is refuted by God's Word in a general way if the doctrine does not align with His truth. Since Moon's dualistic god (yang and yin) is not the biblical Trinity (Father, Son, and Holy Spirit) then we must opt for the biblical view in rejection of Moon's view. Within the Word of God we find three eternal Persons as God, the Trinity. Moon's dualistic god is refuted by a clear presentation of the Trinity.

In the following verses we find the unique attributes of God applied equally, without reservation, to all three Persons of the Father, Son, and Holy Spirit. All three Persons are Eternal (Deuteronomy 33:27; John 1:1-14; Hebrews 13:8; Hebrews 9:14). All three Persons are omnipotent (Jeremiah 32:17; Matthew 28:18; 1 Corinthians 1:24; Luke 1:35-37). All three Persons are omniscient (Psalm 139:1-6; John 16:30; 1 Corinthians 1:24; Isaiah 40:13). All three Persons are omnipresent (Jeremiah 23:24; Matthew 18:20; Psalm 139:7-10).

In speaking of the work of Christ, the writer to the Hebrews said, "For by one offering He has perfected for all time those who are sanctified" (Hebrews 10:14). The Scriptures testify that the work of Christ on the cross is complete, sufficient to secure the salvation of the individual. Jesus accomplished all that was necessary for the full salvation of mankind. He was not a failure.

The Bible plainly states that Jesus Christ came to this earth for the specific purpose of dying for the sins of the world: "Just as the Son of Man did not come to be served, but to serve, and to give His life a ransom for many" (Matthew 20:28).

The Bible portrays two comings of one messiah—Jesus! The first advent was fulfilled when Jesus of Nazareth was born to the virgin Mary: "Now after Jesus was born in Bethlehem of Judea in the days of Herod the king, behold, magi from the east arrived in Jerusalem, saying, 'Where is He who has been born King of the Jews?' " (Matthew 2:1,2).

The Bible speaks over and over again of the second coming of the same Christ, which will be a visible, bodily, return from heaven: "Men of Galilee, why do you stand looking into the sky? This Jesus, who has been taken up from you into heaven, will come in just the same way as you have watched Him go into heaven" (Acts 1:11); and "Behold, He is coming with the clouds, and every eye will see Him" (Revelation 1:7).

There is no biblical teaching that the messiah will be born physically a second time to accomplish an unfinished physical salvation. Jesus accomplished both physical and spiritual salvation at His first coming by His work on the cross and His physical resurrection. He is the only Savior. There is no need for another messiah since Jesus gave us "physical salvation" through his resurrection (Romans 8:23). Because He was raised we shall also be raised from the dead (1 Corinthians 15:21-22). Our future resurrection is the ultimate in physical redemption (John 5:28,29; Philippians 3:21; 2 Corinthians 3:18).

What the Moonies are hoping for has already been accomplished by Jesus: "And there is salvation in no one else; for there is no other name under heaven that has been given among men, by which we must be saved" (Acts 4:12). Another messiah is both unbiblical and unnecessary.

Conclusion

Although the Unification Church makes astounding claims for itself, the facts speak otherwise. The teaching of the *Divine Principle* is at odds with the Bible at all of its central points and therefore cannot be a completion of God's revelation.

Moon has no messianic credentials and must be considered as a false prophet, of which Jesus warned: "Beware of the false prophets, who come to you in sheep's clothing, but inwardly are ravenous wolves. You will know them by their fruits" (Matthew 7:15,16).

Witnessing Tips

Contrary to adverse publicity during the 1970s, few Moonies are "brainwashed." If a person can leave a cult by seeing the internal contradictions on his own, then the person is thinking for himself, at least to the point of separation. This has happened over the past decade to the Moonies in large numbers.

Whether the "brainwashing" stories are true or not, this is not what determines our witness. We believe in the power of the Holy Spirit to convict and convince the unbeliever (John 16:8-13). Many Moonies have been won to the Lord through evangelizing them as we would any others. "Greater is He who is in you than he who is in the world" (1 John 4:4b).

The point to emphasize when encountering a Moonie is what they are waiting for we have already obtained. We are completely saved, both spiritually and physically, through Jesus Christ. Verses on the bodily resurrection are good to use (1 Corinthians 15). The same messiah who ascended is the same one who will return. They reinterpret every verse that mentions Christ returning, since they consider "christ" to be a vague term. Turn to the verses that specifically mention Jesus returning by name. This eliminates any possibility of vagueness since Moon does not call himself Jesus (John 14:3; Acts 1:11; Philippians 3:20,21; 1 Thessalonians 4:14; Titus 2:13; Revelation 22:20).

9

The
Unitarian Universalist Church

The Unitarian Universalist is the merging of two groups in 1957, the Unitarian Church and the Universalist Church, to form a larger organization that fits the description of a western cult. In fact, the former groups are two of the oldest cults now merged as one.

Tolerance, free-thinking and open-mindedness toward all other beliefs leaves the Unitarian Universalist non-aggressive in mission work: "By deliberate choice we send no missionaries over the face of the earth to convert others to our way of believing ... other religions have as much to teach us as we have to teach them" (Jack Mendelsohn, *Why I Am a Unitarian*, p. 147).

We cannot allow this non-aggressive pattern to dull our senses about the growing body of Unitarians today. Most older universities in our larger cities have a Unitarian Church gracing the perimeter of their campuses. In recent years the Unitarian Universalist Church has been growing due to their participation in peace rallies and liberal political concerns.

History

The Unitarian movement can be traced to the anti-Trinitarians of the Reformation era. They had formally established congregations in eastern Europe and England in the sixteenth and seventeenth centuries. Unitarianism was born in America through the preaching of Jonathan Mayhew (1720—1766) and William Channing (1780—1842). Mayhew was pastor of the West Church in Boston from 1747 until his death. This gave him nearly twenty years to gain a wide audience in the already wavering liberal Christians of the area.

The Episcopalian King's Chapel in Boston was the first American congregation to vote on adopting a Unitarian position in 1796. Unitarian ministers were already serving in other churches without the church voting for a change. The thrust of the movement was anti-Trinitarian, anti-Calvinistic, and anti-Creedal in favor of "the Fatherhood of God and the brotherhood of man." Many public debates took place during the nineteenth century between Unitarians and conservative ministers. Harvard University, once a stalwart of sound theology, became a center for Unitarian professors. The movement spread through Dartmouth and other universities that were originally established to spread the gospel.

The Universalist Church that merged with the Unitarian Church is rooted in the belief that none will be doomed in hell for eternity and all will eventually gain salvation, regardless of their religion or lack thereof. Both churches were of the most liberal persuasion in their reading and interpretation of the Bible. Their kindredness left nothing to prevent them from merging into the second largest Arian (Jesus was created and is not God) group in America, trailing behind the Jehovah's Witnesses.

Authoritative Sources

One should walk cautiously when approaching a Unitarian with an assumption of what he believes. They emphasize free-thinking and no creed to the point that, once encountered, a Unitarian may deny what his church has in print. After all, that is what his free-thinking is about. Nevertheless, creed or not, there are authoritative statements from which we may draw an overview of their beliefs.

The paradox of the Unitarian Universalist Church rests in its attempt to balance its denial of biblical authority while being born of "Christian" origin. Some of its leaders may profess agnosticism or atheism toward God. The Congregational Churches have been the most effected by its growth as many of their congregations have become Unitarian. A number of liberal churches have also embraced the teachings of Unitarianism.

Jack Mendelsohn wrote, "I am willing to call myself a Christian only if in the next breath I am permitted to say in varying degrees I am also a Jew, a Hindu, a Moslem, a Buddhist, a Stoic, and an admirer of Akhenaten, Zoroaster, Confusius, Law-Tse and Socrates" (ibid., p. 68). He also denied the Bible has any special significance: "Bibles and creeds are the creations of men" (ibid., p. 38). And he believes the Bible is "replete with inaccuracies, inconsistencies, and errors" (ibid., p. 125).

Unitarian Universalist Beliefs

Unitarians say they have no creed. A more accurate statement is they have no officially binding creed. In practicality anyone who says the words "I

believe . . . " has a creed, since the word creed is from
the Latin word *credo*, meaning "I believe." Unitarianism
has recurrent themes in its publications that reveal a
trend for belief.

God in Unitarian Thought

Unitarianism is known for its anti-Trinitarian position, which comes forth in more than one writing:

> Unitarians and Universalists reject the doctrine of the
> Trinity, the Deity of Christ, the belief in supernatural
> Miracles, the concept of election as the means of salva-
> tion, the concept of Hell as a place to which the dead go
> to be punished (George N. Marshall, *Unitarians and
> Universalists Believe*, Unitarian Universalist Association,
> n.d., p. 2).

When the Unitarian movement began, it opposed
the Trinity. Today, however, Unitarianism has shifted
to a wider "tolerance" of belief; they "may call themselves agnostics, humanists or even atheists. Moral
values, they believe, do not require a supernatural
Being for their inspiration or fulfillment" (John Nicholis
Booth, *Introducing Unitarian Universalism*, Pamphlet
Commission, Unitarian Universalist Association, eighth
printing, 1965, p. 159).

Jesus Christ in Unitarian Thought

Look magazine published interviews with official
representatives from religions across America in 1955.
The representative for the Unitarian Church said this:

> Unitarians do not believe that Jesus is the messiah
> either of Jewish hope or of Christian fantasy. They do not
> believe he is "God incarnate" or the second Person of the
> "Trinity" or the final arbiter at the end of time who "shall
> come to judge the quick and the dead" (*Look* magazine,
> March 8, 1955).

In a denial of the apostle Paul's doctrine, Mr. Mendelsohn said, "Most Unitarians believe that on the basis of the evidence available to us, Jesus, at most, thought of himself as the Jewish Messiah. It was later followers and interpreters, like the apostle Paul, who transformed Jesus into a Christian Savior atoning to God for the sins of mankind" (*Why I Am a Unitarian*, p. 43).

Sin and Salvation in Unitarian Thought

Sin is denied as the problem of the human race:

Unitarian Universalism is the religion of faith in man. When man sins he is blocking the perfectibility of his own conscience, for spirit is being degraded by the external act. Man is not fundamentally sinful. No man stands condemned. Given the freedom to guide himself according to the best that religion can teach, motivated by his own properly developed conscience, man can gain ultimate victory over himself (*Introducing Unitarian Universalism*, p. 17).

Some Unitarians believe it is offensive to call man a sinner: "God sent his only begotten son into the world, to die for sinful men. Such doctrine Unitarians find offensive, unbiblical, even immoral" (*Look* magazine, March 8, 1955, p. 78).

Unitarian Universalists deny the literal existence of heaven and hell, saying "Unitarians emphatically repudiate such beliefs" (ibid., p. 80). It is their contention that everyone will eventually stand righteous before God on their own merit. This makes salvation somewhat of a nebulous term in Unitarian thinking. What they are working for is a peaceful society on earth:

They hold that as man develops a society where moral values and spiritual insights are treasured, man will find the road to peace, justice and brotherhood. God's help is not likely to come to those who cast all their burdens on the Lord. There is practical wisdom in the saying: "God helps those who help themselves" (ibid., p. 78).

Biblical Analysis of Unitarian Universalism

There is no doubt that the name for God in the Old Testament was represented in the tetragrammaton YHWH, Yahweh, or more popularly, Jehovah. Since the Unitarian Universalists accuse the early Christians of making Jesus into God, we will use Old Testament verses to demonstrate that Yahweh said He would come to his own people. Even most liberal theologians will admit that Yahweh was the term used of Israel for the True God, excluding all false gods. In showing the coming of the Lord (Yahweh) we must conclude that the New Testament apostles, including Paul, did not mistake the identity of Jesus when they called Him God.

Psalm 96:13 says, "Before the Lord [Yahweh], for He is coming; For He is coming to judge the earth" (Psalm 98:9 repeats this). In the New Testament we see the Judge who came was none other than Jesus (John 5:22). Truly Yahweh came as our Judge, He came as Jesus: "For judgment I came into this world" (John 9:39).

Isaiah 35:4 is one of the clearest verses that tells us the Lord (Yahweh) will come to His people: "Say to those with anxious heart, 'Take courage, fear not. Behold, your God will come with vengeance; the recompense of God will come, but He will save you.' " Verse 5 tells us what will occur when God comes to His people: "Then the eyes of the blind will be opened, and the ears of the deaf will be unstopped."

In Matthew 11:5 Jesus used this verse to answer the disciples of John the Baptist when they asked (in verse 3), "Are You the Expected One, or shall we look for someone else?" His answer was, "The blind receive sight and the lame walk, the lepers are cleansed and the deaf hear, and the dead are raised up, and the poor have the gospel preached to them." There is no question that Jesus is the "Expected One," but when we look to the Old Testament, the one coming in Isaiah 35:5 is the Lord, Yahweh!

There are other verses that speak of the coming one as Yahweh. Isaiah 40:10,11 speaks of the Lord coming with might and He shall shepherd His people. Most Bibles correctly cross-reference the coming Shepherd with John 10:11, where Jesus said He is the good Shepherd. Certainly Jesus is the Shepherd who was prophesied by Isaiah and He is called Yahweh in Isaiah 40:10. An interesting parallel on Yahweh coming to Israel is Isaiah 59:20, "the Redeemer" and Isaiah 66:15.

Another passage that speaks of Yahweh coming is Zechariah 2:10, " 'Sing for joy and be glad, O daughter of Zion; for behold I am coming and I will dwell in your midst,' declares the Lord." Zechariah is also the prophet who spoke so clearly about the manner of the messiah's death, claiming it would be Yahweh who would be pierced: "They will look on Me whom they have pierced" (Zechariah 12:10). Zechariah's profound prophecy of Yahweh becoming pierced could only take place in the crucifixion of Jesus Christ.

Unitarianism denies the authority of God's Word and what it says about Jesus, the atonement, heaven, hell, and salvation. Their arguments against the Bible are not new. They search through its pages to find what they consider "inaccuracies, inconsistencies and errors," instead of looking for the message of salvation from the Author of Life. For further reading on the subject of answering criticisms of the Bible, we refer our readers to: *Evidence That Demands a Verdict* (Volumes 1 and 2) by Josh McDowell; and *Answers to Skeptic's Questions* by Josh McDowell and Don Stewart.

Unitarian Universalists speak about the love of God. For them to accept the love of God as literal from the Bible, but not the justice of God, is to fragment the nature of God. Jesus spoke of a literal hell as a place of eternal punishment (Mark 9:43-48; Luke 16:19-31). They have built a contradictory authority structure if they can accept any part of the Bible they like and discard anything they find unpleasant. They place the authority of the Bible under their emotional desires, which should be reversed. We should accept what God says as truth over what our emotions say.

Their structure for a peaceful society is built upon the "goodness of man." It will never come to pass, since the Bible (and all history) shows us that "there is none righteous, not even one" (Romans 3:10). Jesus is the only one who was born without sin. The rest of the human race is born in sin (Psalm 51:5). The Unitarians will never be able to produce a sinless person because "all have sinned and fall short of the glory of God" (Romans 3:23). Our sins separate us from God (Isaiah 59:2) which makes their utopian society a vain dream without the help of the only wise God (1 Timothy 1:17). Punishment is certain for sin (Proverbs 11:21) since none can hide from God (Amos 9:2). The very fact that the Unitarians are attempting to work for world peace shows they feel that the evils of man must be dealt with justly. God is the only fair, true and righteous judge of the souls of men (Psalm 93:13; John 5:22).

Conclusion

The Unitarian Universalist Church has been publishing liberal views of the Bible and theology since the time of the Reformation. They are basically a church founded on man, built around man, and has man as its only hope. What a destitute situation for any group of people. It is this kind of hopelessness that caused God to care enough about the human race to send us our only Savior, Jesus. It is to their own destruction that the Unitarian Universalist Church has forsaken the only Savior who can help them or humanity. It is for this reason that our conclusion is they are a non-Christian cult.

Witnessing Tips

The ministers of the Unitarian Universalist Church are graduates from liberal seminaries. They have years of listening to a one-sided tale about higher-criticism of the Bible. It is not impossible to reach them or their congregation members with well planned defenses for the reliability of the Bible. Be prepared to do your homework, because they will send you home with more questions than what you have answers for on your first encounter. Patiently present the truth of God's Word to them and let God call them to repentance (2 Timothy 2:24-26).

10

The Way International

The Way International, taking its name from Acts 9:2, is a western cult after the teachings of Arianism, like the Jehovah's Witnesses, Christadelphians, and Unitarians that preceded them. It also has incorporated elements of the health and prosperity message from E. W. Kenyon. Since their founder's death, The Way has been disturbed by inside power struggles and splinter groups.

History

The Way International, which began in 1958, has its headquarters in New Knoxville, Ohio. It was founded by Victor Paul Wierwille (1916—1985), a former Evangelical and Reformed minister, and is currently led by its president, Craig Martindale, a former Baptist.

The Way calls itself a "biblical research ministry." They do not claim a formal membership, but they have published the number of followers who have taken the *Power for Abundant Living* course, which has topped 150,000 participants. The number of new people taking the course has declined since Wierwille's death and the active members have split into various camps of thinking.

The Way publishes an attractive magazine and ten books by Victor Paul Wierwille that contain the foundational teachings for members. Their missionary program, Word Over the World (WOW), has sent zealots to more than fifty nations. They own two colleges, one in Rome City, Indiana, and the other in Emporia, Kansas.

Like so many cult leaders before him, Victor Paul Wierwille claimed that God gave him a special revelation and spoke to him audibly. God was supposed to have told him that the Christian church is wrong and Wierwille was to teach the Word of God as it has not been taught since the first century.

Beliefs of The Way International

Mr. Wierwille had several catchy slogans he used repeatedly in his *Power for Abundant Living* course, telling his students to "put away their extra books and go only to the Bible," and "The Word of God is the Will of God." He would continue, "The Word of God fits together like a hand in a glove," and, "The Word of God is mathematically precise and scientifically accurate." How can such good sounding statements be bad for The Way? The problem is that Mr. Wierwille did not heed his own advice. The very books written by Wierwille that tell the students to put away extra books is an extra book itself. He had convinced his followers that his writings were exempt from false interpretations of the Bible.

Wierwille on God

Mr. Wierwille used to teach solid biblical doctrine when he was with the Evangelical and Reformed Church. We have compared the first edition of his book *Receiving the Holy Spirit Today* to the current edition published by The Way and have discovered drastic changes. He once taught the Trinity, but later denied it. He once taught the Holy Spirit was third Person of the Trinity, but later denied it.

In a book published ten years before his death, he denied the Trinity: "That defines the doctrine of the trinity, and this I do not believe the Bible teaches" (*Jesus Christ Is Not God*, New Knoxville, OH: American Christian Press, 1975, p. 5). In the same work, he said, "If the Bible had taught that there is a Christian trinity, I would have happily accepted it" (ibid., p. 3). The fact is he once taught it and later abandoned it for a false concept.

Wierwille on Jesus

Wierwille gives his opinion of those who teach the deity of Jesus:

> Those who teach that Jesus Christ is God and God is Jesus Christ will never stand approved in "rightly dividing" God's word, for there is only one God, and Thou shalt have no other gods.

> The Bible clearly teaches that Jesus Christ was a man conceived by the Holy Spirit, God, whose life was without blemish and without spot, a lamb from the flock, thereby being the perfect sacrifice. Thus he became our redeemer (ibid., p. 79).

> They [the Father and the Son] are not "co-eternal, without beginning or end, and co-equal" (ibid., p. 3).

Wierwille on the Holy Spirit

Mr. Wierwille came up with a new theory that the

words Holy Spirit (*pneuma hagion*) in the Greek New Testament could be subdivided into two entities. The first Holy Spirit is another name for the Father (like Bob is for Robert). This Holy Spirit is always capitalized and is called Holy Spirit the Giver. The second holy spirit is the gift from the Giver. Since God is Holy and God is Spirit, then He gives what He is, holy spirit. This second holy spirit is never capitalized and is the human spirit.

This is based upon Wierwille's view of the fall of man. He believes that Adam lost his human spirit through sinning. Adam is called an "animal man" by Wierwille, possessing only a body and soul, but no spirit. God waited until the day of Pentecost to give man a spirit again, the holy spirit. This holy spirit is not God, nor third person of the Trinity, but is a gift from God: "The giver is God the Spirit. His gift is spirit. Failure to recognize the difference between the giver and His gift has caused no end of confusion in the Holy Spirit field of study" (Victor Paul Wierwille, *Receiving the Holy Spirit Today*, p. 3). This second holy spirit is a created spirit (ibid., p. 276).

Wierwille on Salvation

Wierwille believes salvation is receiving the created holy spirit (the gift) from the Father (Holy Spirit the Giver). The proof that one has salvation, or the created holy spirit, is he will speak in tongues: "The only visible and audible proof that a man has been born again and filled with the gift from the Holy Spirit is *always* that he speaks in a tongue or tongues" (ibid., p. 148).

Wierwille also teaches a sinless perfection doctrine that says after a person is converted his spirit can never sin: "Do we sin in the spirit? No, but in body and soul we fall" (*Power for Abundant Living*, p. 313).

Biblical Analysis of The Way

One of the strongest arguments for deity is worship. The very word *worship* connotes divinity. Wierwille himself states, "There has always been one sin which God did not and will not tolerate and that is worshipping any god other than God the Creator."

Here Wierwille is in agreement with Scripture: Worship the Lord your God and serve Him only. The Old Testament reference is Deuteronomy 6:13 and Exodus 20:2-6. What is found in the New Testament is that Jesus Christ clearly receives worship, and approves of homage paid to him.

In Matthew 14:22-33, Christ clearly accepts the disciples' worship after the storm. The blind man in John 9 worships Christ. The triumphal entry in the Gospels is one of the clearest examples of Christ receiving worship, yet is often overlooked. God the Father commands all his angels to worship the son in Hebrews 1:6. In all these passages the same word for worship is used.

The problem with Wierwille's position on God is that he misunderstands the doctrine of the Trinity. Simply stated, there is one God and this one God is three distinct Persons, the Father, the Son, and the Holy Spirit, and these three Persons are equal to the one God. We do not believe in three gods but rather one God who is three Persons. It is the clear teaching of Scripture and the historic belief of the Christian church.

The Scriptures teach there is only one God: "For there is one God, and one mediator also between God and men, the man Christ Jesus" (1 Timothy 2:5). The Scriptures also teach that there is a Person called the Father who is designated God: "Paul, an apostle (not sent from men, nor through the agency of man, but through Jesus Christ, and God the Father, who raised Him from the dead)" (Galatians 1:1).

The Bible speaks of a second Person, called the Son, who is personally distinct from the Father but who is also called God: "In the beginning was the Word . . . and the Word became flesh, and dwelt among us" (John 1:1,14); "For this cause therefore the Jews were seeking all the more to kill Him, because He not only was breaking the Sabbath, but also was calling God His own Father, making Himself equal with God" (John 5:18).

Moreover the Bible talks about a third Person who is distinct from both the Father and the Son who is also called God: "But Peter said, 'Ananias, why has Satan filled your heart to lie to the Holy Spirit . . . You have not lied to men, but to God' " (Acts 5:3,4).

Thus the Father is called God, the Son is also referred to as God and the Holy Spirit is called God. The Bible clearly teaches that only one God exists. Therefore, the Father, the Son and the Holy Spirit are co-equal as the one God. This is the biblical doctrine of the Trinity.

Additional support for the Trinity comes from the divinely inspired word-choice in the Old Testament. In the famous Jewish *Shema* of Deuteronomy 6:4, the backbone of historic Judaic teaching, it reads, "Hear, O Israel! The LORD is our God, the LORD is one."

The passage says, "God is one." But what does this mean? The word for "one" here is *echod*, the exact same word used for "one" in Genesis 1:5 where it reads, "And there was evening and there was morning, one day." Also the same as the word "one" in Genesis 2:24, "They shall become one flesh."

All of these usages refer to a plurality in oneness. There is light and darkness in the one day. There is husband and wife in one flesh. Here *echod* is used to show oneness in a compound sense.

The power of this argument is driven home by

another Hebrew term for perfect unity or solitary-one. The word is *yachid*. It is often translated as "only." The word can be found in Genesis 22:2, Judges 11:34 and Jeremiah 6:26.

Mr. Wierwille confused the Persons of the Father and the Holy Spirit in saying they are the same Person. Any verse of Scripture that shows the distinction of the Father and the Holy Spirit refutes his claim. Matthew 28:19 is one such case where each Person "the Father, and the Son, and the Holy Spirit" is separated by the conjunction "and" (*kai*), which shows their distinction, and each carries the definite article "the," again showing distinction.

What the apostles received at the day of Pentecost was not a second-rate created spirit, but was God the Holy Spirit, third Person of the Trinity. Few people in The Way have stopped to realize that they do not have God indwelling them, they have a "created" holy spirit, something unheard of in biblical theology.

Specifically on the deity of Jesus Christ, it is impressive to people in The Way when they see the teaching of "theophanies" in the Bible. A theophany is an appearance of God (Greek: *theos*, "God;" *epiphany*, "to appear"). Some theologians prefer to call these Christophanies, an appearance of Christ. Several good books on theology will have sections devoted to theophanies, but for a quick reference it is found in the cyclopedic index of the *Open Bible* and the annotation of Genesis 12:7 in the *New Schofield Reference Bible*. Nevertheless, the student of the Bible must come to grips with the clear teaching that God appeared to many of the people in the Old Testament before Jesus was born through Mary.

There were several occasions when God appeared in a visible manifestation to men in the Old Testament. Sometimes He would be appear as an angel and at

other times as a man, or in a burning bush. On a few occasions the form of the appearance was not described
(as in Isaiah 6:1-5), so we leave it open to stay away
from speculation.

The Gospel of John records that no man has seen
the Father (John 1:18; 6:46). If the Father was not seen in
the Old Testament, who was it that appeared to the
Patriarchs? We believe it was the second Person of the
Trinity before He was born unto Mary.

Jesus indicates this in John 8:56-58 where He discussed Abraham with the Jews. *Jameson, Fausett, and
Brown's Commentary* on this points to something deeper
in the discussion; that is, Jesus claimed a special
relationship with Abraham which drew the Jew's retort,
"You are not yet fifty years old, and have You seen
Abraham?" (John 8:57) There are three times that
Abraham saw a theophany, an appearance of God, in
the Old Testament: Genesis 12:7; 17:1; 18:1. If we know
that no man has seen the Father (John 1:18; 6:46), then it
had to be the Son who appeared.

Another passage in John's Gospel where Jesus was
seen by an Old Testament prophet is found in John
12:37-41. The appearance of the Son of God to Isaiah
was so strong in this passage that the *New International
Version* translated the Greek pronoun "him" (*autos*) as
the "dynamic equivalent" noun "Jesus" in verse 41:
"Isaiah said this because he saw Jesus' glory." The
question naturally follows, when did Isaiah see the
glory of Jesus? Isaiah 6:1-10 has the answer. When one
compares the two passages, it is obvious that Isaiah 6:10
is the verse quoted in John 12:40.

Paul was also familiar with the concept that Jesus
appeared as God in the Old Testament. He refers to
Him as the rock that followed Israel through the desert
(1 Corinthians 10:4). This is especially significant since
there was no strange god with Israel (Deuteronomy

32:12). The context of Jude 3,4 also confirms the presence of the Son of God in the Old Testament as our "only Master and Lord, Jesus Christ," who saved the people out of Egypt (see NAS, NIV).

Some of the appearances of God in the Old Testament are: Genesis 12:7; 17:1; 18:1; 26:2; 26:24; 35:9; Exodus 3:2-6; 6:3; 24:9-11; 33:18; Isaiah 6:1-5. These theophanies are preincarnate appearances of Jesus Christ the Son. The testimony of Scripture is:

1. God appeared in the Old Testament.

2. The Father appeared to no man.

3. Several New Testament passages tell us that Jesus was known in the Old Testament.

Wierwille's doctrine of salvation says there must be a verbal confession of faith in Christ followed by the proof of speaking in tongues. However, the Scriptures attest that simple belief in Jesus Christ is sufficient for salvation: "He who believes in the Son has eternal life" (John 3:36). Belief in the name of Jesus is also our assurance for salvation, "These things I have written to you who believe in the name of the Son of God, in order that you may know that you have eternal life" (1 John 5:13).

The teaching that you can sin in the flesh and it will not effect the spirit is falsified by Paul in 2 Corinthians 7:1. The apostle John said, speaking to the believer, "If we say that we have no sin, we are deceiving ourselves, and the truth is not in us ... If we say that we have not sinned, we make Him a liar, and His word is not in us" (1 John 1:8,10). Until the believer is changed from corruptible to incorruptible he will wrestle with sin, but we always have an advocate with the Father, Jesus the righteous (1 John 2:1).

Conclusion

Victor Paul Wierwille's claim that he is teaching the Scriptures as they had not been known since the first century is a distortion of the facts. Wierwille's teachings are authoritarian and are at odds with Holy Scripture. The teachings deny basic Christian beliefs, such as the doctrine of Jesus Christ, the virgin birth, the Holy Spirit, the Trinity and salvation. The inescapable conclusion is that The Way International is a non-Christian cult and must be treated as such.

Witnessing Tips

When discussing salvation with a person in The Way, try to use a modern translation of the Bible. A Greek interlinear translation would be most helpful and a *Strong's Concordance* with the Hebrew and Greek dictionaries is useful. It is not hard to get a person in The Way International to sit down and discuss doctrines, but he will want to teach you instead of your teaching him, so set up a time table to keep it fair.

The best subject to deal with is the deity of Jesus Christ. Let the person know the only reason you believe Jesus is God incarnate is because the Word of God tells you so. Stick to the major issue and do not get distracted by clever-sounding jargon. The person in The Way may say, "Nowhere in the Bible does it directly say, 'Jesus Christ is God.' " (Although these four words are not found in this exact order, there is ample evidence of Jesus being called God.) You may wish to point out, "Nowhere in the Bible does it say, 'Jesus Christ is not God,' as does the unscriptural title of Mr. Wierwille's book."

Introduction

to

Eastern Cults

The groups that properly belong to the category of eastern cults are those rooted in oriental philosophy. Whether it is an outgrowth of Confucianism, Taoism, Hinduism, Buddhism, Jainism, or Shintoism, each eastern cult will claim that they alone portray the true eastern philosophy. Some will gain entrance into western society through blending terminology and redefining terms.

The eastern cults we will examine usually say they are compatible with Christianity. They do not claim to be the true Christian church like the western cults. Since all cults are factions of world religions, some eastern cults will claim that they are the only true group following their persuasion.

The eastern cults do not believe the Bible to be an authoritative work of God even though they make reference to it to please western converts. The eastern cults view Jesus as a good man, prophet, guru or seeker of

181

truth, but by no means do they exalt Him as the only true God in human flesh, the messiah and exclusive savior of mankind.

Eastern cults deny the personal nature of God. They usually speak of God as the "One" who transcends personhood. In their view a personality limits God. Contrary to this, the Bible speaks of God's tri-personal nature (Father, Son, and Holy Spirit) and shows how His personal qualities make his love, grace, and communication a real experience for the Christian. We find it difficult to say "I love you" to a God who cannot respond as a person; we also find His words of love (John 3:16; Romans 5:8) meaningless if He is not a personal Being. His actions are proof of His person, or His actions mean nothing at all.

11

Transcendental Meditation

Transcendental Meditation (TM) is an eastern cult that disguises itself in western terminology and a scientific veneer. It was proven to be Hinduism under a modern name in a New Jersey federal court (Malnak v. Maharishi, October 19, 1976) and thereafter banned as a course in public schools, where it had previously been offered since 1974.

History

The founder of TM, Mahesh Prasad Warma, later known as Maharishi Mahesh Yogi, was born in India around 1910. After graduating from Allahabad University in 1942 with a degree in physics, Mahesh became the disciple of the Indian religious leader Guru Dev. It was Guru Dev who instructed Maharishi to devise a meditation technique from the Vedas (part of the Hindu scripture). The title Maharishi Mahesh Yogi is from *Maha,* meaning great; *rishi,* meaning seer or saint.

Mahesh is his family name. Yogi is a master of yoga meditation techniques.

The Maharishi (as he is referred to) was devoted to fulfilling the plan of Guru Dev in bringing his teachings to the world. In 1958 Maharishi founded the Spiritual Regeneration Movement in India. He came to America the following year and set up his organization while spreading the gospel of Guru Dev. Today, several million people in the United States and around the world have been taught the Maharishi's meditation techniques, said to be nonreligious, although thoroughly Hindu.

The Claims of TM

How would you like to have your health improved, your self-image and productivity increased, and your intelligence and creativity heightened without stress or tension?

According to its advertisements, these are some of the ways TM will benefit individuals. Allegedly all this can be done within any religious or nonreligious system since TM supposedly has no religious basis. Moreover, TM has developed some very admirable goals to accomplish this in the lives of people by setting up centers worldwide.

Under a World Plan, 350 teaching centers of the Science of Creative Intelligence have been founded in the largest cities throughout the United States and the world. In fact, resolutions drawn up by the Maharishi and promoting TM have been adopted by legislatures throughout the country.

The Maharishi University, located in Fairfield, Iowa, has advanced classes for devotees of TM. One astounding claim was that the most advanced students, called Siddhis, had the powers of levitation and telepathy. These practices, all but new, have been claimed for centuries past and aptly revealed as trickery by investigating scientists (cf., K. T. Behanan, *Yoga: A Scientific Evaluation*, New York, 1937).

TM, however is not a neutral discipline that can be practiced without harm to the individual. In actuality, TM is a Hindu meditation technique that attempts to unite the mediator with Brahman, the Hindu concept of God.

The Religious Nature of TM

Despite claims to the contrary, TM is religious in nature. The authoritative sources come directly from Hindu scriptures. Those who are initiated into TM are initiated during a ritual where the Puja, a Sanskrit hymn of worship, is recited. It mentions twenty-four gods of Hinduism and says the initiate will bow down twenty-seven times during the ceremony. The initiate, not knowing the Sanskrit language, is unaware of the invocation to these gods. It is still no less an act of worship on the initiate's part. (An English translation of the Puja is available from Jude 3 Missions, P. O. Box 1901, Orange, CA 92668.)

From the translation of the Puja, the religious nature of TM can clearly be seen. In 1977, a New Jersey federal court barred the teaching of TM in the schools of that state, the presiding judge concluding:

> The teaching of SCI/TM and the Puja are religious in nature; no other inference is permissible or reasonable . . . although defendants have submitted well over 1500 pages of briefs, affidavits and deposition testimony in opposing plaintiffs' motion for summary judgment, defendants have failed to raise the slightest doubt as to the facts or as to the religious nature of the teaching of the Science of Creative Intelligence and the Puja. The teachings of SCI/TM courses in New Jersey violates the establishment clause of the First Amendment, and its

teaching must be enjoined (United States District Court, District of New Jersey, Civil Action No. 76-341).

The claim of the Maharishi and his followers as to the non-religious basis of TM has no basis in fact.

Maharishi may have tried to hide the religious nature of TM from the public, but his followers are aware of his statements: "Transcendental Meditation is a path to God" (*Meditations of the Maharishi Mahesh Yogi*, New York: Bantam Books, 1968, p. 59). He calls it, "the fulfillment of every religion, the simple practice of transcendental deep meditation" (*Transcendental Meditation*, p. 253).

Is It Harmless?

"The TM program has no adverse side effects and can promote what pills cannot—natural psychological growth" (Harold Bloomfield, mediator and psychiatrist, *Discovering Inner Energy and Overcoming Stress*, p. 149).

There are, however, some authorities that would disagree with Bloomfield's statement:

> That the dangers of meditation are considerable among the immature appear to be overlooked by these [TM] enthusiasts who regard meditation as a universal panacea (Una Kroll, M.D., *London Times*, June 30, 1973).

> As a person enters or is in an ASC [altered state of consciousness], he often experiences fear of losing his grip on reality, and losing his self-control (Arnold M. Ludwig, *Altered States of Consciousness*, Charles Tart, ed., p. 16).

A revealing article from the *Journal of the American Medical Association* said it had been "hoodwinked by followers of Hindu guru Maharishi Mahesh Yogi." The reference was to an article in the *Journal* (May 1991) entitled "Maharishi Ayur-Veda: Insights Into Ancient Medicine," in which was hidden false information and unfounded claims. The American Medical Association sharply rebuked TM for deception, "An investigation of the movement's marketing practices reveals what appears to be a widespread pattern of misinformation, deception and manipulation of lay and scientific news media," and called it, "the latest of the Maharishi's schemes to boost declining numbers of people taking TM courses" (*Los Angeles Times*, October 7, 1991, p. B:3).

The Religious Beliefs of TM

We have already observed that TM is religious in nature, based upon Hinduism; consequently their theology is in direct contrast to Christianity.

God

The Maharishi's view of God reflects a denial of the infinite, personal God revealed in Scripture. He writes, "God is found in two phases of reality: as a supreme being of absolute, eternal nature and as a personal God at the highest level of phenomenal creation" (Maharishi Mahesh Yogi, *Science of Being and Art of Living*, rev. ed., 1967, p. 271).

This "supreme being" is identified with nature: "Everything in creation is the manifestation of the unmanifested absolute impersonal being, the omnipresent God" (Maharishi Mahesh Yogi, *Transcendental Meditation*, p. 266); "This impersonal God is that being which dwells in the heart of everyone" (ibid, p. 269).

Man is also identified with God: "Each individual is, in his true nature, the impersonal God" (Maharishi Mahesh Yogi, *Science of Being and Art of Living*, rev. ed., 1967, p. 276). This same God is controlling evolution: "God, the supreme almighty being, in whose person the process of evolution finds its fulfillment, is on the top level of creation" (Maharishi Mahesh Yogi, *Transcendental Meditation*, p. 270). "He [God] maintains the entire field of evolution and the different lives of innumerable beings in the whole cosmos" (ibid, p. 271).

Jesus Christ

The Maharishi does not have much to say about Jesus, but when he does he contradicts the Bible on the purpose of Christ's atonement:

> Due to not understanding the life of Christ and not understanding the message of Christ, I don't think Christ ever suffered or Christ could suffer . . . It's a pity that Christ is talked of in terms of suffering . . . Those who count upon the suffering, it is a wrong interpretation of the life of Christ and the message of Christ . . . How could suffering be associated with the One who has been all joy, all bliss, who claims all that? It's only the misunderstanding of the life of Christ (*Meditations of Maharishi Mahesh Yogi*, pp. 123-124).

Jesus is understood by the Maharishi and his followers as an enlightened man, but not the savior of mankind. They believe that all people have God within them, so Jesus does not stand out as uniquely God incarnate.

Sin and Salvation

Maharishi, like other cult leaders, tells his followers that his way is the only way:

> Only when a man has become permanently established in the eternal freedom of absolute Being is he "freed from all sins." The Brahmabindu Upanishad declares that a huge mountain of sins extending for miles is destroyed by Union brought about through Transcendental Meditation, without which there is no way out (*Commentary on Bhagavad-Gita*, p. 299).

On page 203 he claims that TM is "the only way out of the field of sin." From his *Meditations of*

Maharishi, he adds, "Very easily a sinner come out of the field of sin and becomes a virtuous man," by practicing TM (p. 119).

Release from reincarnation and union with the absolute Being is the result the TMers are seeking. Maharishi promises godhood to his successful followers: "Be still and know that you are God, and when you know that you are God you will begin to live Godhood" (*Meditations of Maharishi Mahesh Yogi*, p. 178).

Biblical Analysis of Transcendental Meditation

Maharishi's view of God and man is not in accord with the Bible. Scripture teaches that God is infinite (Psalm 90:2) while man is finite (Hebrew 9:27). Man can never become God or attain Godhood for he is part of God's creation (Hosea 11:9). Man is a creature (Genesis 1:26). God is the creator (Genesis 1:27). Although man is part of God's creation, he is not to be identified with God (Numbers 23:19). God, the creator, is a Being separate from His creation (Psalm 50:21). God is by nature eternal, whereas God's creation is temporal (it came into being at a particular time). Man, the finite, will never become God, the infinite.

The Maharishi misunderstands the purpose of Christ's coming, which was to die for the sins of the world: "The next day he saw Jesus coming to him, and said, 'Behold, the Lamb of God who takes away the sin of the world!' " (John 1:29), and "Just as the Son of Man did not come to be served, but to serve, and to give His life a ransom for many" (Matthew 20:28). Jesus Christ, contrary to the teaching of the Maharishi, suffered on the cross for our sins so we might receive forgiveness from God for our sins. His suffering was real.

Conclusion

Transcendental Meditation (The Science of Creative Intelligence), though claiming to be a method of relaxation and personal growth without harmful side effects, can be a danger to the individual both emotionally and spiritually. Although some degree of success in relaxation can be achieved by practicing TM, the dangers far outweigh the benefits. There is a Christian alternative to TM and that consists of meditation on God's Word, the only source of real peace. No one said it better than the psalmist:

> Blessed is the man that walketh not in the counsel of the ungodly, nor standeth in the way of sinners, nor sitteth in the seat of the scornful. But his delight is in the law of the LORD; and in his law doth he meditate day and night. And he shall be like a tree planted by the rivers of water, that bringeth forth his fruit in his season; his leaf also shall not wither; and whatsoever he doeth shall prosper. The ungodly are not so: but are like the chaff which the wind driveth away. Therefore the ungodly shall not stand in the judgment, nor sinners in the congregation of the righteous. For the LORD knoweth the way of the righteous: but the way of the ungodly shall perish (Psalm 1:1-6, KJV).

Witnessing Tips

When confronting a person who practices Transcendental Meditation, we must not forget the dedication they have applied to their life. The devotees spend twenty minutes each morning and again each evening in meditation, which is usually more time than the average Christian spends in prayer and Bible study.

The TMer will try to match his meditation time with your prayer time. He will try to match his experience of enlightment with your experience of salvation. What he cannot match is two things: 1. The objective truth of the Word of God; and 2. Your assurance of salvation.

The bodily resurrection of Jesus Christ placed Christianity in the context of objective verification. Its truth does not rely upon personal belief because it was true before your birth and will continue as truth after you are gone. This is not the same with Transcendental Meditation. The only way it is "true" is if it is experienced. There is no objective reality to it. Furthermore, the truth-claims it has have been rebutted by independent sources.

The assurance of salvation in Christianity should not be taken lightly. We are confident in our faith because of the objective reality of our faith coupled with the internal witness of the Holy Spirit. First John 5:13 says, "These things I have written to you who believe in the name of the Son of God, in order that you may know that you have eternal life." We have an assurance of salvation.

Ask the TMer how he knows he will make it beyond his system of reincarnation. Ask him what proof does he have that even Maharishi can make it. There is no assurance. If he points back to the writings of Maharishi, then he is guilty of circular reasoning. He cannot use Maharishi to prove Maharishi is correct.

There is no objective truth in TM. What is worse is how those who are supposed to be free from sin in TM are still practicing deception as quoted in the *Journal for the American Medical Association*. It appears that those with the most enlightment in TM continue the same sins as an unenlightened person. TM does not work.

12

ISKCON/
Hare Krishna

The International Society for Krishna Consciousness (ISKCON), somewhat loosely referred to as the Hare Krishna Movement, is an eastern cult after the tradition of Hinduism. They claim to be the true followers of Krishna, believing that other Hindu groups have emphasized the wrong Hindu god. Jesus is called the son of Krishna and the Bible is only quoted when it supports their teaching. They have become less aggressive in converting new members since the death of their founder.

History

The origin of the Hare Krishnas dates back to the fifteenth century A.D., when Chaitanya Mahaprabhu developed The Doctrines of Krishnaism from the Hindu sect of Vishnuism.

Simply stated, Vishnuism believed Vishnu, the Supreme God, manifested himself at one time as Krishna. Chaitanya Mahaprabhu taught the reverse: Krishna was the chief God who had revealed himself at one time as Vishnu. The doctrinal system of Krishnaism is Hinduistic, while worshipping Krishna acknowledges universal monism. This system believes every individual must go through a series of successive lives (reincarnation) to rid himself of the debt of his actions (karma).

Krishnaism was one of the early attempts to make philosophical Hinduism appealing to the masses. While pure Hinduism's god is impersonal and unknowable, Krishnaism (and other sects) personalize god and promote worship of and interaction with the personalized aspects of god, such as Krishna.

In 1965 Krishnaism came to America by means of Abhay Charan De Bhaktivedanta Swami Prabhupada, an aged Indian exponent of the worship of Krishna. He founded ISKCON and remained its leader until his death in 1977. Presently, ISKCON is ruled by two different groups, one group of eleven men rule over spiritual matters while a board of directors heads the administrative matters. This wealthy organization presently has about 10,000 members in America. Part of ISKCON's wealth comes from soliciting funds and distributing its lavishly illustrated periodical *Back to Godhead.*

The Teachings of ISKCON

ISKCON's beliefs are those of Hinduism and are wholly incompatible with Christianity. This can be observed by a comparison between the statements of ISKCON on matters of belief with those of the Bible.

God

ISKCON assumes traditional monistic pantheism

as is found in several Hindu sects, saying all the gods are forms of the Absolute One they call Krishna:

In the beginning of the creation, there was only the Supreme Personality Narayana. There was no Brahma, no Shiva, no fire, no moon, no stars in the sky, no sun. There was only Krishna, who creates all and enjoys all.

All the lists of the incarnations of Godhead are either plenary expansions or parts of the plenary expansions of the Lord, but Lord Sri Krsna [alternate spelling of Krishna] is the original Personality of Godhead Himself (Srimad Bhagavatam 1:3,28, Bhaktivedanta Book Trust, n.d.).

This indicates that ISKCON devotees believe that Krishna is the "life" of all living things, "the living entity, being the fragmental part and parcel of the Supreme Lord, is qualitatively one" (*Bhagavad-Gita As It Is*, translated by A. C. Probhupada, New York: Bhaktivedanta Book Trust, 1970, p. 704).

Jesus Christ

ISKCON denies the eternal person of Jesus as God by making Him one of the demi-god manifestations of Krishna. In this sense Jesus is only one of "the millions of incarnations" of Krishna (ibid., p. 261). "Jesus is the son, and Krishna is the Father, and Jesus is Krishna's son" (*Jesus Loves Krsna*, Los Angeles: Bhaktivedanta Book Trust, n.d., p. 26).

In a denial of the uniqueness of Jesus and His mission, Prabhupada said:

God sent Jesus to be the spiritual master of particular people in a particular time and place . . . He did not claim (as others claim today) that He was the only Representative Agent of the Supreme Person ever to walk the earth in the past or future (ibid., p. 44).

It is also believed by those in ISKCON that Jesus

worshiped Krishna. Krishna demands total surrender
of love and devotion: "Abandon all varieties of religion
and just surrender to Me" (*Bhagavad-Gita As It Is*, p.
835).

Salvation

According to ISKCON, salvation must be earned
by performing a series of works. To get rid of the ignorance, one must practice disciplinary devotion by
chanting the name of Krishna, hearing and singing his
praises, meditating upon the divine play and deeds of
Krsna, and engaging in the rites and ceremonies of worship. One must also repeat the name of God to the
count of beads (ibid., p. 326). There is a minimum number of times a person must chant the "Hare Krishna"
mantra. The string of 108 beads reminds the devotee of
each round of chants, "Hare Krishna, Hare Krishna,
Krishna, Krishna, Hare, Hare, Hare Rama, Hare Rama,
Rama, Rama, Hare, Hare." This must be done a minimum of sixteen times on the 108 beads totalling 1,728
chants of the mantra daily.

Self-denial of materialism and sacrifice of water,
rice, flowers and other objects are crucial for salvation
in ISKCON. Note the following quotation:

> All these performers who know the meaning of
> sacrifice become cleansed of sinful reactions, and, having
> tasted the nectar of the remnants of such sacrifices, they
> go to the supreme eternal atmosphere (ibid., p. 81).

The denial of materialism is essential for self-salvation in ISKCON, they say, because it distracts a person
from loving Krishna. The only solution is to divest
oneself of materialism—"That alone will save him from
all the turmoil" (*Bhagavad-Gita As It Is*, p. 287). "In this
age of quarrel and hypocrisy the only means of
deliverance is chanting the holy name of the Lord
[Krishna]. There is no other way" (ibid., p. 320).

Finally, at the end of life, one must have Krishna as the last thing on his mind, or he is doomed to reincarnate as another life form: "Whatever state of being one remembers when he quits his body, that state he will attain without fail" (ibid., p. 416).

Biblical Analysis of ISKCON

The Bible speaks of God as the infinite-personal creator of the universe. He is eternally a separate entity from His creation. Romans 1:20 says that the invisible attributes of God have been clearly seen through what He created. ISKCON has this message backward when it confuses what God is with what God has made. God is not the life of every living thing, which is evident in Ecclesiastes 3:21, where the distinction between the spirit of man and beast is presented. Throughout the Bible, when the life or spiritual nature of man is mentioned, it is always in the context as made or given by God, which shows us it cannot be God Himself (Genesis 2:7; Job 33:4; Ecclesiastes 12:7).

According to Scripture, Jesus Christ is God Almighty who became a man in order to die for the sins of the world (John 3:16). He has been God from all eternity: "In the beginning was the Word, and the Word was with God, and the Word was God" (John 1:1).

The Godhead is not a part of the human race, but Jesus was the fulness of the Godhead in bodily form (Colossians 2:9). Nothing was missing from Jesus. "Fulness" in this verse means every quality and attribute of God was in Jesus.

The Bible teaches that all of us have sinned against the holy God and are therefore in need of a Savior: "For all have sinned and fall short of the glory of God" (Romans 3:23); "For the wages of sin is death, but the free gift of God is eternal life in Christ Jesus our Lord" (Romans 6:23). The only remedy for sin is through the

shed blood of Jesus Christ on Calvary's tree. Our work
cannot purchase the precious blood of Jesus, neither can
silver or gold give us a place in heaven (1 Peter 1:18,19).
Neither will the Father be impressed if we chant the
same thing over and over 1,728 times: "And when you
are praying, do not use meaningless repetition, as the
Gentiles do, for they suppose that they will be heard for
their many words" (Matthew 6:7).

Prabhupada should have read the Bible more carefully before he made the statement that Jesus never
claimed to be the only representative for God. Jesus
said it very clearly in John 10:8: "All who came before
Me are thieves and robbers, but the sheep did not hear
them." Jesus also said, "Many will come in My name,
saying, 'I am the Christ,' and will mislead many...
Then if anyone says to you, 'Behold, here is the Christ,'
or 'There He is,' do not believe him" (Matthew 24:4,23).
Jesus singled Himself out as our only way of salvation
by telling us not to believe those before Him or after
Him. This is why Christians place so much emphasis
upon the verse, "I am the way, and the truth, and the
life; no one comes to the Father, but through Me" (John
14:6).

Reincarnation is not biblical because it is appointed unto man once to die and after that is the
judgment (Hebrews 9:27). Robert and Gretchen Passantino have done extensive research in the area of the
cults, and they offer pertinent comments regarding salvation in ISKCON:

> Salvation in Hare Krishna is thoroughly entwined
> with the Hindu concept of karma, or retributive justice.
> This teaching, which requires belief in reincarnation
> and/or transmigration of the soul, says that one's deeds,
> good and bad, are measured and judged either for or
> against him. Only when his good deeds have "atoned"
> for his bad deeds (and he is thus cleansed of this evil

world) can he realize his oneness with Krishna and cease his cycles of rebirth.

The idea of karma and reincarnation is anti-biblical. Is it just or reasonable for a man to suffer in this life or be required to atone for sins in this life that he committed in a previous life that he doesn't even remember? How can suffering for an unknown sin reform the sinner and mature him to the point where he no longer performs that sin? Such so-called justice is cruel and absolutely opposed to the God of the Bible (*Answers to the Cultist at Your Door*, Eugene, OR: Harvest House Publishers, 1981, p. 150).

Conclusion

Since ISKCON has a different God, a different Jesus, and a different way of salvation from what the Bible reveals, it is impossible for there to be any compatibility between the two. They differ on all crucial issues. A person must choose between Krishna and Jesus Christ; no harmony can exist between the sect of Hare Krishna and Christianity.

Witnessing Tips

Most of the time we see the followers of ISKCON in public places raising funds. They have given up the chiffon robes and now wear wigs to cover their shaven heads to look more conventional. They blend in so well with society that virtually the only way to spot them is by the colorful magazines they sell.

If you are in an airport, or a similar place, do not give them a donation, but just ask if you can stand by them for a minute and look at their magazine. While you are scanning its pages pray for the Lord to show you something to begin a discussion (and pray for remembrance of your Bible verses). We have had several good discussions with ISKCON members in this way, and you may find it fruitful too.

13

The
Church
of
Scientology

The Church of Scientology is a group that rightly belongs with the eastern cults. L. Ron Hubbard spoke highly of his own writings, believing his work to be the unfinished work of Buddha. It is not classical Buddhism but it offers a high-tech blending of ideas from the world religions coupled with L. Ron Hubbard's own "discoveries."

History

Layfayette Ronald Hubbard (1911-1986), affectionately known as "Ron" by Scientologists, would have had a legacy in life even without Scientology. Before the days of his religion he was a very popular science fiction writer and his novels are still in print fifty years after they were penned. This is no small feat in the field of writing, but it was only the beginning of L. Ron Hubbard's name gaining international recognition.

There is no certainty among his friends whether he grew tired of writing science fiction in the 1930s and 1940s, or whether his religion was a long-time dream. Nevertheless, Scientology gave him no retirement from writing. They claim he published fifteen million words in science fiction and another twenty-five million words under the name of Scientology.

Time magazine reported that Hubbard spoke before a science fiction writer's convention in 1949 in New Jersey, and said, "Writing for a penny a word is ridiculous. If a man really wanted to make a million dollars, the best way would be to start his own religion" (*Time*, April 5, 1976, p. 57). Scientologists say their founder was joking, but critics say it was a prediction of Scientology. The fact remains that Hubbard released *Dianetics: The Modern Science of Mental Health* a year after this comment, in May, 1950. He wrote his first book on Scientology in 1951 and incorporated the Church of Scientology of California, February 18, 1954.

Dianetics remains an introductory level book for Scientology, according to a published list. It has sales topping fourteen million copies since its first release and is available in twelve foreign languages. Scientology is now a global religion with six million adherents, although active members range between 200,000 and two million (*Time* magazine, February 10, 1986, p. 86).

The history of the Church of Scientology has not always been favorable. The church has been in more court battles than any other new religion. The U. S. Supreme Court declared Scientology a *bona fide* religion which prevented the IRS from revoking its nonprofit status. Its religious status did not prevent raids by the Food and Drug Administration where a counseling aid called an E-meter and a vitamin compound called GUK were confiscated. The CIA kept a running file on Hubbard. The IRS revoked their tax-exempt status in 1959 (later overturned). And it was raided by the FBI in 1977. Some writers have criticized the investigation by government agencies, labeling it persecution. Others believe that Scientology perpretrated wrongdoing that invited the investigation. Either way, the battle between Scientology and government agencies appears to be continuing.

Total innocence cannot be assumed for the church because the evidence recovered from the FBI raid in July 1977 showed that high-ranking Scientologists had master-minded a covert operation to break into several government offices and steal documents from the U. S. Army, U. S. Navy, U. S. Customs, CIA, Federal Trade Commission, IRS, the U. S. Courthouse and others (*People Weekly*, August 14, 1978, p. 23). There was enough evidence to put seven of the top officials of Scientology in prison, including Mary Sue Hubbard, wife of the founder (*Reader's Digest*, May 1980, p. 91).

An Overview of Scientology

Mr. Hubbard was skillful at coining new words in his works. Some of his books have so many new terms that a glossary is published with it. Scientology publishes its own dictionary to help the students wade through the definitions.

The first principle taught to the Scientologist is that you are not your body. According to them, you are a Thetan. A Thetan is a spirit-being (similar to the soul) which has supposedly existed for some 300 trillion years. The Thetan has spent most of those years entering bodies only to die and reenter another life form elsewhere in the universe.

The problem for the Scientologist is that each past life had abberative experiences, called Engrams, which attach themselves to the Thetan like barnacles on a ship. The presence of the Engrams is what makes the individual react so overtly in society. The natural solution is to remove them. This creates a second problem. The only way to remove them is through Scientology "auditing" and technical courses. The auditing is done while the subject holds two tin cans with wires fed to a galvanometer called an E-meter. The needle on the E-meter is observed by a trained Scientologist who helps the person find his Engram tracks.

Auditing can be costly, sometimes into the tens of thousands of dollars. Once the Engrams are totally removed, then the Thetan is pronounced "clear." The benefit of being clear means that the Scientologist can gain control of his life and free him from the endless cycle of birth and rebirth (reincarnation). There are eight advance levels for the Scientolgist after clear. These are called "OT" levels, for Operating Thetan. The OT Scientologist is supposed to have total control of his life and control over Matter, Energy, Space and Time.

Beliefs of Scientology

Scientology claims it clarifies the spiritual nature of man and "does not conflict with other religions or religious practices" (*Volunteer Minister's Handbook*, L. Ron Hubbard, Los Angeles: ASHO, 1968, 1976, p. xiv). Conflict for a Bible-believing Christian means anything contrary to what the Bible says. With the following subjects we will examine Scientology with the Bible to see if it conflicts with Christianity.

The Bible

L. Ron Hubbard believed that his work was the unfinished work of Buddha: "The truth of the matter is that you are studying an extension of the work of Gauthama Siddhartha, begun about 2,500 years ago . . . Buddha predicted that in 2,500 years the entire job would be finished in the West . . . Well, we finished it!

(*Advance*, December 1974, p. 5) He also claimed inspiration from the Vedic Hymns of Hinduism, where "a great deal of our material in Scientology is discovered" (*The Phoenix Lectures*, Los Angeles: ASHO, 1968, p. 12).

The Bible is held in less esteem than other writings. Hubbard believed the Bible had its origin in other religions:

> It is no wonder when we look into the Christian Bibles we find ourselves reading the Egyptian Book of the Dead. Now the parables which are discovered today in the New Testament are earlier discovered, the same parables, elsewhere in many places. One of these was the Egyptian Book of the Dead, which predates the New Testament considerably (ibid., p. 27).

God

Scientologists will say they do not define God. In Christian thinking anytime they deny the God of the Bible they have the wrong definition. Hubbard said this:

> For a long while some people have been cross with me for my lack of co-operation in believing in a Christian Heaven, God and Christ. I have never said I didn't believe in a Big Thetan [spirit] but there was certainly something very corny about Heaven, et al (*Victoria Report*, 1965, p. 151).

In another sense Hubbard wrote of many gods:

> There are gods above all other gods ... there is not argument here against the existence of a Supreme Being or any devaluation intended. It is that amongst the gods, there are many false gods elected to power and position ... Three are gods above other gods, and gods beyond the gods of the universes (*Scientology 0 - 8008*, Los Angeles: ASHO, 1967, p. 73).

We see that Hubbard rejected the Christian teach-

ing of God. He went further by stating that
Christianity's God is found in Hinduism, "The Christian god is actually much better characterized in the
Vedic Hymns than in any subsequent publication, including the Old Testament" (*Phoenix Lectures*, p. 31).

Jesus Christ

What typifies the writings of Hubbard is his matter-of-fact statements with no supporting evidence to
back it up. Of Jesus' crucifixion, he said, "You will find
the cross as a symbol all over the universe, and the
Christ legend as an implant in pre-clears a million years
ago" (*Victoria Report*, p. 150).

Hubbard misunderstands the Hebrew definition
of messiah and portrays Jesus as one of many messiahs:

> Now the Hebrew definition of Messiah is One Who
> Brings Wisdom—a Teacher. Messiah is from 'messenger'
> ... Now here we have a great teacher in Moses. We have
> other Messiahs, then we arrive with Christ (*Phoenix Lec-
> tures*, pp. 27-28).

He tried to relate Jesus to the Hindu Vedas:

> Christ ... was a bringer of information. He never an-
> nounced his sources. He spoke of them as coming from
> God. But they might just as well have come from the god
> talked about in the Hymn to the Dawn Child ... the
> Veda (ibid.).

Sin, Salvation, and Reincarnation

Man is basically good in Scientology. Hubbard
rejected the concept that man was evil, "It is despicable
and utterly beneath contempt to tell a man he must
repent, that he is evil" (*Victoria Report*, p. 150). In his
Volunteer Minister's Handbook he said, "Nobody but the
individual can die for his sins" (p. 349).

Salvation in Scientology is release from reincarnation: "Personal salvation in one lifetime [is] freedom from the cycle of birth and death" (*Scientology: A World Religion*, p. 16). The subject of past lives is covered in detail by Hubbard in his book *A History of Man*. In this book one reads of the journey of the Thetan through various low life forms, including sea creatures, birds, sloths, on its way to manhood. The next stage for man's evolution, according to Hubbard, is "homo-novas," which he describes as "very high and godlike" (ibid, p. 38).

Biblical Analysis of Scientology

The God of the Bible is a personal Being. He exists as three Persons, the Father, the Son, and the Holy Spirit (Matthew 28:19). In the Bible we find that the Father, Son, and Holy Spirit are the one true God (Isaiah 44:8; 48:16). There are no other gods in existence because there is only one God by nature (Galatians 4:8). None existed before Him and none shall exist after Him (Isaiah 43:10).

The word *messiah* is not from the word *messenger*. It is the word for the Anointed One. The word *Christ* is the Greek rendering of messiah. Hubbard was wrong in his definition and in saying that there are many messiahs. Jesus said anyone else who claims to be a messiah is a deceiver and false (Matthew 24:5,11). Never is Jesus called "a" Christ, but always "the" Christ. In 1 John 2:22 we read, "Who is the liar but the one who denies that Jesus is the Christ?"

Mr. Hubbard felt it was beneath contempt to tell someone to repent or say he is evil, but this is exactly what Jesus did (Matthew 7:11). "Jesus began to preach and say, 'Repent' " (Matthew 4:17). Salvation, according to the Bible, is to apply faith in the person and work of Jesus Christ (Romans 10:9,10; Acts 4:10-12). The sacrifice of Jesus Christ cleanses us from our sins if we believe on Him (1 John 1:7; Revelation 1:5).

Reincarnation is a doctrine rejected by Jesus and the inspired Scriptures. Jesus taught that He alone is from above (John 8:23) and that we are from the world. He taught that we die only once (Luke 20:36) and that there is no return to earth after death (Luke 16:27-29). The book of Hebrews says, "And as it is appointed unto men once to die, but after this the judgment" (9:27, KJV). The entire message of the Bible takes its stand in the story of redemption through the blood of Jesus.

Conclusion

Scientology is a religion built on a combination of Hinduism, Buddhism and modern technology. We conclude, after an examination of its statements about God, Jesus, and salvation, that it is a manmade religion. It does not offer a true way of salvation for mankind because it denies the concepts of the Bible.

Witnessing Tips

Scientologists have their own jargon that is published in a dictionary for its members. Do not be surprised when you witness to a Scientologist that you may have to ask for a definition of terms. This is a good idea anyway since it helps to break down communication barriers. Take notes on your discussion as you move through it.

Scientologists can be won to the Lord. What we have found is that they must first recognize the failure of self-salvation and then see the need for Jesus' substitutionary atonement. The story of *The Pilgrim's Progress* by John Bunyon gives a refreshing look at the folly of self-salvation. Once a Scientologist sees that he cannot make it without Jesus then he can shed his excess baggage and run to our Savior's merciful love.

14

Self-Realization Fellowship

Self-Realization Fellowship is one of the older Hindu cults to gain a strong following in America. Centered in mysticism, they do not recruit members; they expect new followers to find them through their literature. The other gurus to step foot on western soil learned from the style of Paramahansa Yogananda (Par-RAM-a-hansa YO-gan-an-da) who was creative in adapting Hinduism to scientific terms and western vocabulary. Hide it as you will, but the Hinduism still remains intact to be analyzed by the Bible.

History

The Self-Realization Fellowship incorporated in Los Angeles, California, in March 1935, and has grown to an international operation. Its founder, Swami Paramahansa Yogananda, came to America in September 1920, by invitation of the American Unitarian Association. He was a featured speaker on October 6,

1920, at the International Congress of Religious Liberals, held in Boston, Massachusetts. His popularity spread from there as he crisscrossed the country for fifteen years giving lectures on Kriya Yoga.

The first base of operation for Paramahansa Yogananda was a building atop Mt. Washington in Los Angeles County. They purchased the estate in 1925 and use it today as the international headquarters for the organization. He returned to India in 1935 to establish the Yogoda Satsanga Society, which sponsored Yogoda centers in India and other countries.

Yogananda journeyed to London and back to America in 1936. He continued to build meditation centers and temples until his death on March 7, 1952. During his thirty-two years of lecturing he initiated more than 100,000 people into Kriya Yoga. His autobiography claims that he initiated several distinguished people, including Mahatma Gandhi and Luther Burbank (the famed horticulturist).

Both the Self-Realization Fellowship and the Yogoda Satsanga Society are directed through the international office in Los Angeles. The current president is Sri Daya Mata. She joined the movement in 1931, after listening to Yogananda lecture in Salt Lake City, Utah. She is their third president and has been in that office since 1955.

Authoritative Sources

Paramahansa Yogananda wrote thirteen books that are considered more authoritative than the Bible. The Hindu scriptures (Upanishads and Veda) would normally become the source for Hindu cults, but Yogananda virtually eliminated the reliance upon anything other than his writings to achieve self-realization. *Autobiography of a Yogi* (Los Angeles: International Publication, 1946) has received the widest circulation and is available in nineteen languages. The Bible and Jesus Christ are only referred to when there is an apparent support for Self-Realization teachings.

The misapplication of the Bible by Yogananda is quickly observed when words are changed to force a foreign meaning upon the text. An example is found on page 371 (ibid.) where he says that John the Baptist and Jesus Christ are Elijah and Elisha reincarnated. He claimed this was predicted in Malachi 4:5, which is quite imaginative, since Elisha is not so much as mentioned in the text. It was a pure invention on the part of Yogananda to force reincarnation into the Bible.

There are different practices of Yoga in Hinduism: Hatha Yoga, Karma Yoga, Mantra Yoga, Bhakti Yoga, Jnana Yoga, and Raja Yoga. Paramahansa Yogananda was taught by his gurus that Kriya Yoga, the most advanced form of Raja Yoga, is the essential practice for spiritual liberation. He defined Kriya Yoga as "union [yoga] with the Infinite through a certain action or rite [Kriya]" (ibid., p. 275). Initiation into Kriya Yoga is a foundational source of authority for the path of self-realization. The Yogi master is one who practices yoga and has disciplined the body and mind so that the soul is "liberated" (p. 261). The Swami is one who achieves union with the "Swa or Self" (ibid.).

Doctrines of Self-Realization Fellowship

Hinduism is based on a pantheistic world view. This comes out clearly in Yogananda's *Autobiography of a Yogi* where he quotes his guru: "All created things—solids, liquids, gasses, electricity, energy, all beings, gods, men, animals, plants, bacteria—are forms of consciousness" (p. 488). The dualistic principle behind this rests on the conviction that there is one Infinite Reality (which the Hindus call Spirit or God). The low vibration of this Reality is what forms all created things.

These are called maya (or an illusion) by the Hindus because their reality is only relative to our perception.
Everything is essentially the one Infinite Spirit.

Even though Yogananda tried to explain Christianity in Hindu terminology, he still denied every core
doctrine of the Bible. Beginning with the Trinity, he
denied the uniqueness of the one God in three Persons
and redefined it as the Hindu words, "Sat, Tat, and
Aum." He said:

> These biblical words refer to the threefold nature of
> God as Father, Son, Holy Ghost (Sat, Tat, Aum in the
> Hindu scriptures). God the Father is the Absolute . . .
> beyond vibratory creation. God the Son is the Christ con-
> sciousness (Brahma . . .) existing within vibratory
> creation . . . the outward manifestation of the om-
> nipresent Christ Consciousness, . . . is Aum, the Word or
> Holy Ghost (p. 169).

He confused the Word (identified as Jesus in John
1:1-14) with the Holy Ghost and he made the Holy
Spirit into the mystical vibration sound OM (Aum). In a
further denial of the personal nature of the Holy Spirit,
he said, "Aum or the Holy Ghost [is] the sole causative
force that upholds the cosmos through vibration" (p.
565). The Holy Spirit is reduced to nothing more than
vibratory sound. Yogananda wrote that the Aum, or
Holy Spirit, had three manifestations: "Each time a man
utters a word he puts into operation one of the three
qualities of Aum" (p. 22).

Yogananda taught that Jesus Christ is not the
anointed one, the only messiah and savior for mankind.
Jesus is pictured as the reincarnated Elisha (p. 371) who
worked out his own salvation through many former incarnations. He gained victory over his three bodies
(physical, astral and causal) giving him infinite union
with the Infinite. He chose to come back to earth as a

prophet (p. 490) to be crucified and take upon him the karma of others (p. 236).

Jesus is not the unique Son of God because there are many yogi-christs (p. 198). He is on the same level as Krishna or a goddess or light (p. 242). While he was on earth Jesus practiced Yoga or similar techniques (p. 275) and his resurrection was only a materialization of atoms, not a real body (p. 347,354).

Yogananda taught the standard Hindu belief that all men are divine (p. 197) and have latent occult powers that come through a third eye in the forehead (p. 299). Man's bad karma is released through reincarnation, which takes most souls one million years to complete (p. 279), but some will be able to reduce this down to three years through Self-Realization Fellowship (p. 279). Works are the way of release from karma and reincarnation (p. 562).

Biblical Analysis of Self-Realization Fellowship

The teachings of Jesus refute the doctrines of Paramahansa Yogananda and the Self-Realization Fellowship. God is a personal Being; in fact, He is tri-personal as the Father, Son, and Holy Spirit. God's personal nature is not an illusion as is seen in Jesus addressing God as "our Father" (Matthew 6:9) in His prayers. There is no question that Jesus is a person and is God in Scripture. This is easily seen in Hebrews 1:8 where the Father addresses the Son as God.

Jesus also spoke of the Holy Spirit existing in the same way He exists. When He said the Father will "give you another Helper" (John 14:16), we find the word for "another" (Greek, *allon*) means "one of the same kind." This shows us that Jesus (our first Comforter or Helper) is equal in nature to the Holy Spirit (our second Helper). They both have distinction as persons in the unity of God's nature.

It should be no surprise to Jesus' disciples that He spoke of the Holy Spirit as a person, for it was taught in 2 Samuel 23:2,3 that the "Spirit of the LORD" is a person ("His word was on my tongue") and He is God ("the God of Israel said"). The blasphemous remarks of Yogananda that the Holy Spirit is a vibratory sound Aum or OM is laid to rest in the scriptural evidence of His person. In addition to this, the unchangeable (immutable) nature of God demonstrates His personal nature is eternal.

Pantheism is destroyed by God's unchangeableness. If He cannot change and is eternal, then He exists eternally separate from matter and created things. The immutability of God is seen in this verse: "For I, the LORD, do not change" (Malachi 3:6).

Another way to disprove the concept of pantheism is to apply biblical passages that show the distinction between God and creation. Isaiah 31:3 gives us such a distinction: "Now the Egyptians are men, and not God, and their horses are flesh and not spirit." The things of the universe are created by the spoken word of God (Genesis 1), not as a part of Himself, "By faith we understand that the worlds were prepared by the word of God, so that what is seen was not made out of things which are visible" (Hebrews 11:3).

God says that created things did not exist before He called them into existence, "[He] calls into being that which does not exist" (Romans 4:17). If pantheism were correct, then God could not have said this. What was created was not made from what was already existing.

Yogananda rejected the blood of Jesus and His bodily resurrection in favor of the law of karma and reincarnation. Man did not previously live in other forms, however, according to the Bible. Jesus said He was the only one from above and all others are from this world (John 8:23). The power of His blood cleanses us from all sin (1 John 1:9) and "cleanses [our] conscience from dead works to serve the living God" (Hebrews 9:14). This cleansing freed us from works for salvation, "But if it is by grace, it is no longer on the basis of works, otherwise grace is no longer grace" (Romans 11:6), so the Hindu law of karma is refuted by the grace of God.

Jesus received His own body back in His resurrection as was witnessed by His apostles (1 Corinthians 15:5-7). His resurrection stands against reincarnation because He guarantees our future resurrection (1 Corinthians 15:20-58). Reincarnation is denied by Paul when he speaks of us receiving the same body, only in a glorified state. Note especially the use of "this" in reference to our present body: "For this perishable must put on the imperishable, and this mortal must put on immortality" (1 Corinthians 15:53).

Conclusion

Self-Realization Fellowship is an eastern cult that rejects all the soul-saving truths of the gospel. It is one of the first Hindu cults to utilize the Bible throughout its works in an attempt to combine Christianity with Hinduism. It was miserably unsuccessful in its attempt.

Witnessing Tips

If you were to visit one of the temples or ashram centers of the Self-Realization Fellowship, you will no doubt find many converts from Christianity. Much emphasis is based on the personal experience. If the person had a "bad" experience in "Christianity" that he has replaced with a "good" experience in Self-Realization Fellowship, then begin to question him about his former connection in Christianity. More than likely it was with a liberal church that based little authority on the Word of God to begin with.

In your questioning, begin to probe for a common-ground discussion about Christianity. Not "every" experience in Christianity was bad, so can he think of anytime he enjoyed Sunday school, church, or youth fellowship? As you find a connection, begin to open up the Bible and show him that he may have been led astray from the Word of God in his former days and his present experience in the Self-Realization Fellowship is a continued stray from the true God. "All we like sheep have gone astray" (Isaiah 53:6, KJV). Show him the futility of his works through Kriya Yoga and tell him about the wonderful assurance of salvation we have through God's grace.

Introduction
to
New Age Cults

In one sense, the New Age cults are a new phenomena in western culture; yet they are not so new. It all depends on how far back one pushes the history of the New Age. The term "New Age," although it had been used by various writers for the past century, did not emerge as a household word until the 1970s. This places the history into the trendy, consciousness-expanding human potential movement of the 1960s and forward.

On the grassroots level, the history spans a century and stems mainly from the writing of Madame Blavatski and the Theosophical Society. Still others rightfully trace the history much further to the transcendentalism of Ralph Waldo Emerson and stepping backwards to gnosticism in the first century.

All of these have a segment of the truth, but one thing that forever separates the New Age from Christianity is its doctrine. Unlike the western cults, the Bible and Jesus Christ do not play central roles in the New Age Movement. They do not claim to be the true Christian church. Unlike the eastern cults, the New Age Movement does not claim to be the restoration of Hinduism, Buddhism, or Taoism. It claims to be a melting pot of all beliefs with the overriding theory of monistic pantheism, that is, "all is one" and sometimes it is said, "all is god." What also distinguishes the New Age Movement from eastern cults is its two-fold agenda of transforming the self and then transforming the world.

In this section we have devoted a lengthy examination of the New Age Movement and then we break it down into chapters on four of the larger New Age cults.

We'd like to acknowledge and thank Kurt Van Gorden for his careful research and writing in this section. We are indebted to him for his excellent work.

15

New Age
Cults

The New Age Movement emerged in the western society from a melting pot of ideas that has been trickling down through the ranks and files. It embraces a number of beliefs foreign to Christianity and the Bible. These beliefs would include such concepts as occultic practices, the human potential movement of the 1960s, the teachings of Theosophy, the teaching of eastern gurus, and the law of karma and reincarnation. Even the writers for *Time* magazine have shown that the New Age Movement is not all that new: "Here we are in the New Age, a combination of spirituality and superstition, fad and farce, about which the only thing that is certain is that it's not new" (*Time*, December 7, 1987, p. 62).

The New Age Movement embraces some eastern ideas and some western. The diversified New Age cults have common elements of belief. These would include such eastern underlying philosophies as pantheism and monism. What is interesting about the New Age Movement is the new twist in terminology applied to old beliefs. An example is found in karma and reincarnation. The varying New Age groups have different cycles for people to go through. Some New Age groups may teach transmigration of the soul; that is, the soul passes from lower life to higher life and perhaps back to lower life again, such as in classical Hinduism. Other groups may teach that the soul can only pass from one human to another human to another human. Still other groups may teach the interplanetary travel of souls on earth or other planets traveling from one place to another in its evolutionary cycles for reincarnation.

Where the New Age Came From

There has been an influx of human potential techniques, self-help books, New Age magazines and courses that are being used by corporations, schools and individuals which are actively a part of a worldwide movement popularly dubbed the New Age. Dr. J. Gordon Melton, professor and founder of the Institute for the study of American Religion (located at the University of California, Santa Barbara), places the history of the New Age Movement into perspective:

> The New Age Movement can best be dated from circa 1971. By that year, Eastern religion and transpersonal psychology (the key new elements needed to create the distinctive New Age synthesis) had achieved a level of popularity, and metaphysical leaders could begin to articulate the New Age vision. The *East-West Journal* became the first national periodical to focus on the issues of the new movement . . . By 1972, the first national network directories were published (*New Age Encyclopedia*, Detroit: Gale Research, 1991, p. xxii).

Every large city now has its own New Age resource newspaper. Its contents highlight articles on

New Age techniques and it is filled with various groups advertising their techniques in competition with other New Age groups. Although they see a diversity of techniques, they always claim a unity in their goal. This shows the eclectic nature of the New Age Movement.

The New Age has been popularized in many facets of our society. Actress Shirley MacLaine has written about her experiences in three major selling New Age books, one of which became material for a movie on her experiences. She speaks about her dabbling in occultic practices, seances, out of body experiences, reincarnation, soul mates and her New Age friends who assisted her while she looked for answers to life through New Age teachings. Judging from the sales of her books, she is not the only one who is searching for reality that can only be found through our Lord Jesus Christ.

The New Age also has been accepted in scientific circles through the writings of Fritjof Capra, a physicist who began to describe his labratory experiences in New Age terms. In his books, *The Tao of Physics* and *The Turning Point*, he attempts to draw parallels between New Age concepts and discoveries in physics.

The New Age has entered classrooms across the country through yoga in physical education classes, meditation as a stress release and through the promotion of Confluent Education of Beverly Galyean.

The New Age is prominent in many Saturday morning cartoon series, showing the cartoon figures meditating, communicating to ascended masters of wisdom, and teaching the monistic world view that all is one. It has not escaped the movie industry, where underlying New Age philosophies become the central theme of movies such as *The Dark Crystal*, a Disney production, and Shirley MacLaine's story, *Out on a Limb*. All of these things serve as examples of the emerging world view called the New Age Movement that is monistic, where all is one. The only reality to the New Ager is the reality within.

We see four key factors why New Age thinking has gained such wide acceptance:

1. The birth of nineteenth-century transcendentalism and mind-science/metaphysical groups.

2. Popularization of occultic practices.

3. Growing interest in oriental philosophies.

4. A widespread condemnation of Christianity.

The Birth of Nineteenth-Century Transcendentalism and Mind-Science Groups

The New Age scientist Fritjof Capra has followed in the footsteps of a nineteenth-century scientist who abandoned his practice to seek after the mystical realms of the spirit world. His name was Emmanuel Swedenborg. Capra claimed to see the atoms of his own body dancing; not just any dance, but the "shiva dance" of Hinduism. Like the claims of his predecessor Emmanuel Swedenborg, Capra's visions are taken as reality. Swedenborg claims to have gone on astral trips of our solar system. A fallacy, as pointed out by Dr. J. Gordon Melton, is that Swedenborg only visited the planets that were known to have existed in his day, which eliminated Uranus, Neptune and Pluto. Had there been truth to his astral tours, we would certainly expect it to contain truth consistent with facts (ibid., p. xxiii).

Transcendentalism, as popularized by Ralph Waldo Emerson (1803-1882), became the accepted practice of many Americans. Emerson, a Unitarian and a graduate of Harvard Divinity School, gave up his Unitarian ministry to pursue broad-minded studies, including the eastern philosophy that his work reflects. It is a noted fact that many early metaphysical groups traced the origin of some of their principles to the transcendentalism of Emerson. Emerson's theory of a universal spirit that permeates the universe was taken in part from Emerson's rendition of Hinduism. He believed that man was at his best when he was in harmony with the universal spirit. The unity school of Christianity, founded by Charles and Myrtle Fillmore, is an example of one early metaphysical group that attributes Emerson with their foundational teachings in combination with Christian Science.

Popularization of Occultic Practices

The occult delves into supernatural powers outside of the God of the Bible. Wide acceptance of the occult entered into mainstream society beginning with the table tappings of the Fox sisters, founders of the Spiritualism movement in upstate New York during the middle 1800s.

During that time, the occult had been taken out of the closet and put into the forefront of society. It became an acceptable thing to do. This resulted in hundreds and thousands of Americans dabbling in the occult under the name of Spiritism. The seeking of supernatural powers and supernatural information outside of the God of the Bible led many to practice the occult in their parlors and in smaller groups through the use of the Ouija board, seances (which Spiritualism embraced), tarot card reading, and tea leaf reading.

From the middle of the nineteenth century until the middle of the twentieth century, the movement in America had grown to three quarters of a million people. Today, it is estimated that there are some four million spiritists in South America alone. Recent experiments in parapsychology have included ESP, telepathy and telekenetics. The popularity of the occult has led millions of people away from the true God they seek answers to life's problems through these supernatural powers. In our own century people like Houdini, Arthur Ford, Ruth Montgomery, Jeanne Dixon and their colleagues promoted seances, mediumship and occultic practices for the general populace.

Growing Interest in Oriental Philosophies

Oriental philosophy began to take on divergent aspects in the western culture. The gurus from the east realized they had to shed the asceticism found in many eastern groups to make their philosophy appealing in the west. Adapting Oriental philosophy to the materialistic west was the key.

The gurus knew that they would only gain converts if they told western society to go ahead and keep western materialism while embracing eastern philosophies. Divergent forms of Hinduism, Buddhism, Zen Buddhism, and Taoism took on new meaning as it was disguised in western terminology and scientific jargon. Whether it be Transcendental Meditation disguising itself under scientific terms or the Taoist interpretation of the Bible by Sung Myung Moon or the abandonment of shaven heads and chiffon robes by the Hare Krishna movement—each one of these had to adapt itself to western culture in order to gain converts. This made Oriental philosophy appealing to western man.

Widespread Condemnation of Christianity

There has been an ever-increasing widespread condemnation of Christianity as a whole. An examination of the *Humanist Manifesto* of 1933 and the *Humanist Manifesto II* of 1973 will reveal that secular humanism could not declare what the naturalistic world view entailed without also attacking the teachings of

Christianity. An example is in the *Humanist Manifesto II* (1973):

> We believe ... that traditional dogmatics, or authoritarian religions that place revelation, God, ritual or creed above human needs and experience do a disservice to the human species ... we find insufficient evidence for belief in the existence of a supernatural God.

Notice how the wording makes attacks upon Christianity. Even though there are millions upon millions of polytheists around the world, the humanists did not feel the need to attack "gods," but the monotheistic God of Christianity. The word "creed," as used in the *Manifesto*, was another attack upon Christianity since the other monotheistic groups of Judaism and Islam do not have formal creeds.

From the 1960s until the present time, the Bible and Christianity have become the scapegoat for groups who wish to change the mode of our society. Many lecturers on evolution have made unprovoked attacks upon the Bible and Christianity. The fallacy with this is that not all those who believe in creation are Christians. There are many who believe in creation who do not hold to the Bible and Christianity. So why is Christianity and the Bible singled out in these lectures on evolution? We see a wide-scale attack on Christianity and a condemnation of the Bible.

Another example is found in debates on abortion. Seldom will a debate take place without an attack of the Bible and Christianity also entering into the discussion. The fallacy again is that not all those who are pro-life believe in the Bible and Christianity, so why the pointed attack?

Other organizations like gay rights activists, the American Civil Liberties Union, and the American Atheists Association have openly and publicly condemned the Bible and Christianity in their efforts to promote their own agenda. Oftentimes this occurs in print, on radio or television without a Christian spokesperson given equal time for rebuttal. Again, we see the wide scale condemnation of Christianity.

These contributing factors have led people to begin looking for alternatives to Christianity. The New Age Movement was there to meet them.

New Age Organizations

We classify organized New Age groups under four topics: religious groups, political groups, socially active groups and prominent representatives. The New Age Movement is an international networking of smaller groups all uniformly working for the same goal. First on their agenda is personal transformation of the individual. This personal or individual transformation takes place through any one of hundreds of techniques of the smaller New Age groups. Second on their agenda is global transformation, which includes world peace, a unified government and one-world religion.

Religious Groups

There are more than 5,000 religious New Age groups. Their underlying world view is based on pantheism (all is god) or monism (all is one). Dr. Walter R. Martin has helped to identify a religious New Age cult without lending to the unbalanced thinking of conspiracy theories or guilt by association:

1. The group is openly committed to furthering the New Age (i.e., Age of Aquarius).

2. The group openly espouses distinctively New Age beliefs such as monism ("all is one"), pantheism ("all is god"), gnosticism (salvation or

spiritual healing come through special experiences of enlightenment), karma and reincarnation, spiritual evolution, ascended masters (equal with Christ), etc.

3. The group openly advocates New Age/occult practices, such as channeling/mediumship, astrology, psychic healing, numerology, magic, various needs for inducing altered states of consciousness (e.g., meditation, chanting, sensory deprivation, hypnosis, etc.), and the use of crystals or pyramids for psychic reasons.

4. The group uses uniquely New Age terminology, such as "create your own reality," "Higher Self," "self-realization," "cosmic consciousness," "universal energy," "chakras," "kundalini," "yin and yang," etc. (*The New Age Cult*, Minneapolis: Bethany House, 1989, pp. 109-110).

Dr. Martin wisely warns us that just because a group may use buzz words that are also found in the New Age Movement, it does not necessarily follow that the group under question is a part of the New Age. The basic question we need to ask: What is their agenda? Is their purpose personal transformation and ultimately global transformation?

Since there are 5,000 New Age religious organizations, it is beyond the scope of this book to list each one of them. Even though each group has variations of the technique used for their personal transformation, their goal is always the same: Transform the person and then transform the world.

Political Groups

The political groups in the New Age Movement work as lobbyists on state and federal levels with the goal of bringing about changes that will benefit the New Age. A group known as the Lucis Trust is located in the United Nations building in New York, New York. Other organizations such as Planetary Citizens are often seen by our society as a harmless group working for world peace. When we look under the veil that shrouds the organization, though, we find that their goal for achieving world peace is actually a one-world government.

Socially Active Groups

Socially active groups are those interest groups trying to bring about massive change by introducing larger numbers of people to New Age teachings, either openly or subtly. Beverly Galyean's Confluent Education, which was federally funded to be introduced into California schools as an experiment, actually taught children that they have a godlike creative consciousness. This experiment produced a rash of yoga, meditation, and conscious expanding instructions in the classrooms.

Corporations in large numbers have hopes of gaining better sales and more productivity through inviting New Age teachers to conduct seminars to white collar and blue collar workers alike. The courses taught were New Age techniques under a more sophisticated name.

The New Age movement has also infiltrated the psychology and medical fields. Hospitals around the country began to offer courses for training nurses how to lay on hands for healing while focusing their attention and concentration upon the destruction of the disease in the person they laid their hands on. These seminars were accredited as further education in the career of the nurses who participated. Holistic health and medicine virtually took over the health food industry. Christian chiropractors from around the country have also reported their colleagues using New Age techniques in their practice.

Prominent Representatives

The prominent representatives are spokespersons for the New Age Movement, introducing the public at large to New Age thinking. One of the most popular New Age promoters is actress Shirley MacLaine. The basic message of her books and her movie is that each one of us are already divine within. We create our own reality, we create our own existence, we are god. She taught the monistic world view that we are all one.

Mr. Benjamin Creme is another representative on the forefront of the New Age Movement. He and the organization he founded, the Tara Center, located in Los Angeles, California, brought the New Age to the doorsteps of the world by purchasing $750,000 worth of advertising in seventeen of the largest newspapers around the world. His April 25, 1982, full-page advertisement read: "The Christ is now here." Mr. Creme claimed that he had received several telepathic communications from the Christ who was living in the Pakistani community of London, England. He claimed that it was his job to tell the world that the Christ had returned. Mr. Creme repeated the advertisement on January 12, 1987, only this time the message had been changed to read: "The Christ is in the world."

Marilyn Ferguson popularized the New Age through her book *The Aquarian Conspiracy*. She outlined the world view for the New Age Movement both politically and religiously, speaking of their goal to have one-world religion and one-world government.

David Spangler has written five best-selling books on the New Age Movement. In his own brand of thinking, he tries to steer people away from using objects in the New Age, such as crystals, pyramids and other

New Age paraphernalia, and tries to head them toward a higher consciousness within.

Helena Petrovna Blavatsky is founder of the Theosophical Society. Theosophy teaches that the foundation of all religions is really the same religion. Man, according to Theosophy and Madame Blavatsky, has three levels of existence: physical body, a mental body, and an astral body. The way man moves to the astral plane is through many reincarnations. Madame Blavatsky claimed to receive her information from Ascended Masters.

The writings of Alice Bailey, who founded the Arcane School, are second only to Madame Blavatsky in spreading the New Age. She received her writing when the Tibetian would channel information through her in the form of automatic writing. Her books unfold the reappearance of the Christ and the plan for the New Age.

Biblical Analysis of the New Age Structure

The New Age concept of world peace, one-world government and one-world religion is contrary to what we find in the Bible. One cannot have true peace with himself until he has made peace with the true and living God of the Bible. The mistake of New Age theology is to look for peace within oneself. The only lasting peace is the peace that comes from God above, which is why Luke 2:14 says, the peace that was promised on earth is only through the true messiah, Jesus Christ. Jesus said in John 14:27, "Peace I leave with you; My peace I give to you; not as the world gives, do I give to you. Let not your heart be troubled, nor let it be fearful."

Worldly peace, according to Jesus, will never last. Only the peace He gives to us will really last. If a person is not looking to the true Jesus, then he will never receive the true peace that Jesus has to offer. Jesus spoke of peace again in John 16:33, "These things I have spoken to you, that in Me you may have peace. In the world you have tribulation, but take courage; I have overcome the world." The contrast that Jesus shows us here is that the world will never have peace. Genuine peace can only come from Him.

Paul makes the comment on peace in 1 Thessalonians 5:3. He says when the world says peace and safety, then sudden destruction comes upon them as labor pains upon a pregnant woman, and they shall not escape. What we find in the New Testament is that there will be moments of peace in the world, and people will become excited about this, but due to our sinful human nature there will always be more evil and destruction. While there is nothing wrong with the desire to have peace, the New Agers' problem is that they are looking to the wrong source.

The impossibility of one-world religion is well presented in Scripture. The only one-world religion will be a false one since no religion is compatible with Jesus Christ and His message. The apostle Paul brings this forth in 2 Corinthians 6:14-16:

> Do not be bound together with unbelievers; for what partnership have righteousness and lawlessness, or what fellowship has light with darkness? Or what harmony has Christ with Belial, or what has a believer in common with an unbeliever? Or what agreement has the temple of God with idols?

Paul's contrast between light and darkness distinctly separates us from the world's religions. Only Christianity holds to the truth of God, and all the world religions have gone the way of darkness, following after man. Jesus brings out the uniqueness of Christianity in John 10:1,8: "Truly, truly, I say to you, he who does not enter by the door into the fold of the sheep, but climbs up some other way, he is a thief and a robber ... All who came before Me are thieves and robbers, but the sheep did not hear them." Jesus singled Himself out as the only way to heaven. All those who had tried to climb up by any other way, which includes the New Age and world religions, is a thief and a robber. This is why Jesus said in John 14:6 that no man can come to the Father but by Him.

Contrary to the desires of the New Age Movement, the only one-world government mentioned in Scripture is that of the anti-Christ in the book of Revelation. It is not the image of world peace, lasting for decades as the New Age tries to portray. Rather, the Bible speaks of hardships, tribulation, persecution, martyrdom, slaying of saints and a consummating battle of Armageddon with the world against Jesus Christ and His saints.

New Age Beliefs

The New Age Movement has many diverse techniques used to transform one's consciousness, self, attitude, outlook on life, and belief systems. Some use esoteric methods such as meditation, silent prayer, channeling, mediumship and chanting in unison. Other New Age groups use exoteric items such as crystals, minerals, homeopathic medicine, pyramids of various sizes and other objects said to have innate powers, whether it be gemstones, magic wands or religious artifacts. Most New Agers believe that any of these techniques can better oneself and some New Agers will use a combination of these techniques.

Since one's experience becomes the source of truth in New Age thinking, you will seldom find New Agers saying that one technique or another has no value at all, even though each New Ager has his favorite. New Age religions do not have a prescribed doctrinal statement.

Over all, we see a uniform agreement among New Age religions. What they agree upon is their dislike for Christianity. They label Christianity as narrow minded, dogmatic and authoritarian. They deny the doctrine of one God in three persons. They deny that Jesus is the Christ. They deny that Jesus Christ is uniquely God in human form. They deny the Holy Spirit as the third person of the Trinity. They deny the blood atonement of Jesus Christ for our salvation. They deny the biblical doctrine of heaven and hell. And they deny salvation by grace through faith in Jesus Christ.

The New Age World View

As for what New Agers *do* believe in, we will first discuss three commonly held beliefs in the world view of the New Age Movement:

1. All is one. All is God.

2. God is impersonal and amoral.

3. The world is not real.

All Is One. All Is God.

Monism and pantheism are central concepts in the New Age world view. Monism teaches that all is one. What is meant by this in New Age thinking is that there is only an apparent distinction between what we perceive with our eyes and what really is. The only distinction between the material and the non-material world is our perception of it. Therefore, a monistic New Ager would say all is one, we're all a part of each other, we're all a part of the same thing, and there is a permeating spirit behind and undergirding all matter.

Pantheism goes one step further than monism by saying that God is the spiritual oneness in all things. God is all there is. The explanation for the world in pantheistic beliefs is that the world is a slow vibration of the substance of God. They would say God is the high vibration of spirit while matter is the low vibration of spirit. New Age writer Benjamin Creme shows us the pantheistic view found in most eastern religions: "You are God. I am God. This microphone is God. This table is God. All is God" (*The Reappearance of Christ and the Masters of Wisdom*, London: Tara Press, 1980, p. 116).

God Is Impersonal and Amoral

One cannot conceive of a personal loving God in any real sense under the monistic or pantheistic world view. New Agers will often ascribe personal characteristics to their idea of God. Impersonal entities cannot love, create, give life or communicate. While New Agers are fond of saying, "God is love," they have not yet surmounted the difficulty of saying that a rock or a table (if it is god) is also love.

Perhaps these difficulties are why some of the writings of Mr. Creme seem to contradict other statements he has made on God: "In a sense there is no such thing as God, God does not exist. And in another sense, there is nothing else but God—only God exists . . . all is God. And because all is God, there is no God" (ibid., p. 110).

Since the monistic world view teaches all is one, evil and good are seen as being different aspects of this same oneness. Furthermore, they are only seen as relative for our existence on earth, so they have no real meaning.

New Ager Fritjof Capra expresses how all things will be absorbed into this oneness: "All boundaries and dualism have been transcended and all individuality dissolves into universal, undifferentiated oneness" (*The Turning Point*, p. 371).

Because God is viewed as only being a universal spirit, He becomes impersonal and amoral.

The World Is Not Real

The monistic and pantheistic world views both hold that the world itself is an illusion, it's not reality. The Hindus refer to it as maya. Matter is real, but it will fade away when all becomes one.

This concept of eastern teaching is often hard for western thinkers to grasp. When New Agers say that the world is not reality, they are not saying that the world does not exist. What they are saying is, the ultimate reality is not the world, but the spirit or oneness that permeates the world. The world and all material existence is a low vibration of the spirit matter that is God.

Most New Agers will say that God created the world out of Himself, as actually a part of His essence, as we saw in our earlier quote by Benjamin Creme. New Age writer Jane Roberts, who channeled for her spirit guide Seth and wrote his communications down through automatic writing, said this: "He is not one individual, but an energy . . . its energy is so unbelievable that it does indeed form all universes; and because its energy is within and behind all universes, systems and fields, it is indeed aware of each sparrow that falls, for it is each sparrow that falls" (*The Seth Material*, Englewood Cliffs, N.J.: Prentice Hall, 1970, pp. 237-238).

The New Age Source of Authority

Subjective experiences of the self becomes the source of authority for New Age people. If you experience it, then it must be real, so they say. New Age teachers shun objective tests for their experience.

Truth Is Within and You Are Divine

New Agers have taught their followers that truth is within, but "truth" has taken on a varied meaning. The word *truth* is being substituted for relative experience, so the result of any New Age experience is subsequently called "truth."

New Age teachers also convince their constituents that they are divine or god within. The conclusion they draw is your experience cannot be false since you are god. In support of the deified human race, New Age actress Shirley MacLaine writes: "Each soul is its own god. You must never worship anyone or anything other than self. For you are god" (*Dancing in the Light,* p. 358). She also supports experience being one's truth: "My own out of body experience . . . served to validate the answers to many questions—the surest knowledge being derived from experience" (ibid., p. 35).

The Nature of Man in the New Age

There are three common points of agreement that most New Age groups have concerning the nature of man. First, in a brash contradiction to the Bible, New Agers will deny the evil nature of mankind and claim that man is "basically good."

Second, New Agers believe that man is divine. New Age thinking borrowed this common statement from eastern religions: "I am not this body." When New Agers speak of the spiritual nature of man, the non-material essence, they account for its existence as being a part of god. Often this is expressed in New Age literature as you are divine or you are a god.

Third, building on their foundation that man is divine and is basically good, New Agers conclude that you create your own existence. By this they mean that you have caused and can cause events to take place in your life out of your will. It's not just the desire to do well in life, but actually creating things and circumstances. Benjamin Creme goes so far as to say that we should "pray to the god within us. He would rather you didn't pray to him, but to god within you, which is also within him" (*The Reappearance of the Christ*, p. 135). Shirley MacLaine, in *It's All in the Playing*, said: "I had created everything I saw, heard, touched, smelled, tasted; everything I loved, hated, revered, abhorred . . . I was my own universe" (New York: Bantam Books, 1985, p. 192).

The New Age view of the nature of man undermines the biblical understanding of Jesus Christ. The New Age denies Jesus' true deity, that He is uniquely God and no other man can be God. The New Age also denies Christ's purpose in dying on the cross for the sins of the world, since it teaches that man is already god, or is basically good.

New Age teachings are patterned after the gnosticism of the first century. Gnostics taught that Jesus was separate from the Christ. They said "Christ" was a spiritual principle that came upon Jesus either during His baptism or birth. Benjamin Creme takes the former position, showing that gnosticism is still prevalent in New Age teachings: "The Christ took over the body of Jesus and manifested through it for the last three years" (*The Reappearance of the Christ*, p. 53). He says again, "When I say 'the coming of the Christ' I do not mean the coming of God . . . the Christ is the master of all the masters, but he is not God and never claimed to be God" (ibid., p. 115).

New Ager Emmet Fox wrote of Jesus:

His teaching is entirely metaphysical . . . a very inconsistent legend was built up by worthy people concerning original sin, vicarious blood atonement, indefinite punishment for finite transgressions. No such theory was taught in the Bible. The "Plan of Salvation" is completely unknown to the Bible as it is to the Koran (*The Sermon on the Mount*, New York: Harper Brothers, 1934, p. 5).

Benjamin Creme attempted to say that all spiritual leaders are the same individual:

At the center of this "Spiritual Hierarchy" stands the World Teacher, the Lord Maitreya, known by Christians as the Christ . . . the Jews await the Messiah, the Buddhists, the fifth Buddha, the Moslems, the imamMahdi, and the Hindus await Krishna. These are all names for one individual (*Advertisement, Tara Center*, April 25, 1982).

While some New Agers seem to have a surface reverence for Christ, most New Agers make no distinction between Him and any other "religious figure."

Moral Consequences in the New Age

All systems of belief that recognize evil and sin in any fashion must deal with the moral consequences of actions done in the human race. The New Agers embrace the eastern philosophies of the law of karma and reincarnation.

The law of karma is the total summation of one's actions during any given state of existence. Reincarnationists who believe in the transmigration of the soul from a lower life to a higher state of existence and perhaps to a lower life again attribute the law of karma as the determining factor for which state of existence the soul enters. Reincarnationists who believe that the soul may only pass from one human state to another human state believe that the law of karma determines where and what condition the person re-enters the world. If the karma was bad, the re-entrance may be in an under-developed, poor country and perhaps in the poorest class of that country. If the karma was good, a person may be born in a flourishing country and in a wealthy family.

Shirley MacLaine informs her readers, "If you are good and faithful in your struggle in this life, the next one will be easier" (*Out on a Limb*, p. 45). New Age writer Alice Bailey said:

> The immortality of the human soul and the innate ability of the spiritual enable man to work out his own salvation under the Law of Rebirth, then in response to the Law of Cause and Effect, are the underlying factors governing all human conduct and all human aspiration (*The Reappearance of the Christ*, New York: Lucis Publishing Co., 1948, p.147).

Salvation in the New Age

Salvation in the New Age is to be released from the law of karma and reincarnation. The techniques to achieve this come from various measures in the New Age. Some call it God consciousness, God enlightenment, spiritual enlightenment, becoming one with the one, self-realization, self-actualization, and among other terms, personal transformation.

New Age writer David Spangler believes that Jesus found the same enlightenment that Buddha found: "Jesus was an individual who himself had to recapitulate certain stages. He built upon the pattern that Buddha had established. He himself had to become awakened. He had to, in his consciousness, touch this Christ pattern" (*Reflections on the Christ*, Moray, Scotland: Findhorn Publications, 1978, p. 6). Shirley MacLaine writes, "To become an enlightened individual first requires a focus of this inner spirituality, and that entails the belief that when we 'go within' ourselves there will be something there" (*Los Angeles Times*, August 19, 1987).

Marilyn Ferguson, author of *The Aquarian Con-*

spiracy, points out that the divergent methods of technology reach to the same consciousness: "Incantations, mantras, poetry and secret sacred words are all bridges that join the two brains—what counts is that something in us is wiser and better informed than our ordinary consciousness" (Boston: Houghton Mifflin Co., 1980, p. 81); "Meditation, breathing exercises and fasting are among the common technologies for shifting brain function" (ibid., p. 374).

Biblical Analysis of New Age Beliefs

The monism of the New Age (all is one) shows no objectivity for truth. The Bible says God is eternal and uncreated. Isaiah 40:28: "Do you not know? Have you not heard? The Everlasting God, the LORD, the Creator of the ends of the earth does not become weary or tired. His understanding is inscrutable." Genesis 1:1 and Colossians 1:16,17 both show that God is uncreated and eternal.

The monistic view of God says that God is impersonal. The Bible says that God is personal, otherwise love has no meaning; and neither would the word "Him" in reference to God. According to Scripture, God is a tri-personal being. The Father is God (Galatians 1:3). The Son is God (John 1:1; 5:18; 20:28). The Holy Spirit is God (Acts 5:3,4). There is but one God (Deuteronomy 6:4; Isaiah 43:10). Therefore, the three persons are the one true God (Isaiah 48:16—three persons as the true Jehovah; and in the New Testament, Jesus' statement in Matthew 28:19).

God is also a moral being in the Bible. Numbers 23:19 says lies are not found in God. The Book of Hebrews, showing the moral nature of Jesus Christ, says, "For we do not have a high priest who cannot sympathize with our weaknesses, but one who has been tempted in all things as we are, yet without sin"

(Hebrews 4:15). And Hebrews tells us clearly that it is impossible that God should lie (Hebrews 6:18).

The New Age world view teaches that the world is an illusion or that the world is maya. Most New Agers will say that the world is of the same essence as God, only at a slower vibration of energy. The higher vibration is supposed to be pure spirit whereas the lower vibration is supposed to be matter. However, the Bible makes a clear distinction between God and the matter that we encounter in the physical world (see Hebrews 1:10-12).

In reference to Jesus as the creator, Colossians 1:16,17 says that He created all things in heaven and earth, whether they are visible or invisible, He created them. They could hardly be a part of Himself if He created them. Spirit is not the invisible aspect of matter, and matter is not the visible aspect of spirit. What is invisible and created was made by Jesus Christ. What is visible and created was made by Jesus Christ. He made all things in heaven and earth, visible and invisible. Therefore, He could not be a part of created matter.

In regards to the source of authority in the New Age Movement, their monistic pantheism teaches that truth is within. This, however, provides no objectivity and therefore no verifiability of their "truths." God interacts with man according to what we read in the Bible. In all the miracles of the Bible, from the parting of the Red Sea to the raising of Lazarus from the dead, we find objective, testable events that took place before eyewitnesses. The events of the Bible are real and testable by historical evidences.

Peter confirms this by saying, "For we did not follow cleverly devised tales when we made known to you the power and coming of our Lord Jesus Christ, but we were eyewitnesses of His majesty" (2 Peter 1:16). The apostle Paul made an open declaration before King

Agrippa, boldly stating that these things were not done in a corner (Acts 26:26). His points out that God did not use subjectivism in the evidences of the resurrection, but rather He did it in an historical setting that could be tested and verified.

We saw that the New Age teaches man is basically good. The fact that man is not basically good is evident in history, since we have had no improvement. Things continue to get worse. It is also interesting to note that goodness is a term of morality. The New Age wants to eliminate absolute morals, yet it ascribes a moral term to the nature of man.

The Bible tells us that man is sinful in his nature. Romans 3:10-18 shows us that man is not righteous, not any one of us. In 3:23, Paul says, "For all have sinned and fall short of the glory of God." And 1 John 1:8 tells us, "If we say that we have no sin, we are deceiving ourselves, and the truth is not in us."

The New Age belief in reincarnation is unbiblical as well. Luke 16:19-31 contains the story of Lazarus and the rich man. The rich man wanted Abraham to send Lazarus back from the grave to warn his five brothers of their fate (verse 28), but his request was refused. According to the words of Abraham: "They have Moses and the Prophets; let them hear them." And then again in verse 31, "If they do not listen to Moses and the Prophets, neither will they be persuaded if someone rises from the dead."

This story offers an interesting parallel to reincarnation. New Agers seek after truth from those whom they claim have entered into and returned from the hereafter, just like the rich man wanted Lazarus to do. God refused to permit Lazarus to return to the rich man's brothers, so we should not expect Him to contradict this by permitting others to return through reincarnation.

Let us specifically deal with New Testament texts that deny reincarnation. Jesus contradicts the teaching of reincarnation in John 8:23: "You are from below, I am from above; you are of this world; I am not of this world." Jesus made it very clear that we are not all from the same place. He is the only one who is from above; all of the rest of us are from below. He is the only one not from this world; all of the rest of us are from this world.

First Corinthians 15:46 tells us that what came first is the natural body and after that the spiritual body, which we call the resurrected body. The reincarnationists have the message backwards. They believe in the spiritual body first and then the natural body. Hebrews 9:27 says, "It is appointed for men to die once, and after this the judgment." This perhaps is the single most condemning text that flies in the face of reincarnation. Man is appointed to die once, not many times. After his death, which is a single event, comes the judgment.

Reincarnation also denies several Christian doctrines of the Bible. The doctrine of hell, or eternal punishment for the wicked, is denied by reincarnationists, but we have already seen in Luke 16:19-31 that none shall return from the dead.

Another doctrine denied by reincarnation is the atonement of Jesus Christ. Hebrews 9:28 says, "So Christ also, having been offered once to bear the sins of many shall appear a second time for salvation without reference to sin to those who eagerly await him." The atonement of Jesus Christ was truly offered once for the sins of many. This refutes the law of karma which says that a person needs to return many times to work out his own salvation through each new reincarnation. Jesus Christ took care of our sins on the cross. First Peter 1:18,19 tells us that redemption is through the precious blood of Christ. We do not take care of our own sins by returning to earth.

Reincarnation denies the very purpose of Jesus Christ's coming to the earth. His mission is summarized in Revelation 13:8: "And all who dwell on the earth will worship him, everyone whose name has not been written from the foundation of the world in the book of life of the Lamb who has been slain." If reincarnation were true, then there would be no purpose in Jesus Christ coming and being called the Lamb slain from the foundation of the world. The fact that He did come shows us that we cannot save ourselves through the cycles of birth, death, and rebirth.

The bodily resurrection of Jesus Christ and our future bodily resurrection give the surest confidence to the Christian that reincarnation is false. In the resurrection, Jesus received the same body that He laid down. And in our future resurrection, we shall receive the same body only in a glorified state. The bodily resurrection of Jesus and our future resurrection as outlined in 1 Corinthians 15 refute the doctrine of reincarnation.

The plan of salvation, called self-realization or self-actualization, in the New Age Movement is unscriptural. Biblical salvation is faith in Jesus Christ. John 3:16-18 promises believers that we shall not perish, but have everlasting life through Jesus Christ, the Son. The Bible knows nothing of self-realization. The Bible only knows the realization of knowing the true God and knowing Jesus Christ in a personal way.

Acts 4:10-12 tells us that there is only one name under all heaven whereby we must be saved—and that is the name of Jesus. No New Age guru can help us. No former religious leader can help us. No future religious leader can help us. No New Age technique can help us. Only through faith in Jesus Christ, that one name given under heaven that all men might be saved, can we find genuine salvation.

Conclusion

The New Age is an old lie that leads to the same dead end that Adam and Eve faced. We are all going to die, so what will we say before God? New Agers believe their works under the law of karma will some-day justify them—they hope. The Christian has assurance of salvation in Jesus. We do not *hope* we will make it; we *know* we will (1 John 5:13). In conclusion, the New Age is a hopeless situation leading to a Christ-less eternity for millions of people. Only the message of salvation through the shed blood of Jesus Christ can help a New Ager come to the truth.

Witnessing Tips

We have found that the diversity in the New Age makes it highly improbable that you will know all the doctrines of the person you encounter. A New Ager talks with a matter-of-fact pretense about his experien-ces. Your point will be to ask him what makes his authority reliable. So let him talk. The more he talks, the more you can take mental or written notes. As you ask questions, pray for the Holy Spirit to lead you to ask the right follow-up questions.

One thing that will always happen is a New Ager will reveal his source for authority, ("I read . . . I had this experience . . . I heard my inner voice . . . I saw a dead relative . . . etc."). This is when you begin to show the reliability of the Bible as compared to his unreliable stories.

We know what makes the testimony of Scripture true—God has left us with a witness. We have to test the New Ager's experience by some objective authority, like the Bible. Begin with the solid evidence of the resurrection of Jesus Christ as a testable and reliable account of what took place (see *Evidence That Demands a Verdict*). If he objects to the biblical evidence, then give him homework and let him try to disprove it. Set an appointment and follow up your discussion the next week to see how he is doing.

Always define your terms as you talk with a New Ager. Ask him what he means by his terms and use the contrast between your definitions as you speak to him. This will solve communication difficulties from the start.

Try to get the New Ager to read a modern translation of the Bible with you. New Agers seem to enjoy building mystical interpretations around the old style of the King James Version. If you place a modern Bible in his hands, he may actually begin to understand and appreciate the Word of God.

16

Theosophy

The Theosophical Society is the fountainhead of the New Age Movement. Its teachings have been multiplied over and over in all of the smaller New Age cults.

History

Theosophy literally means "wisdom of God." The modern Theosophical movement was founded in 1875 by Helena P. Blavatsky. The wisdom of God, according to Theosophists, is to be found in all religions:

> What we desire to prove is, that underlying every once popular religion was the same ancient wisdom-doctrine, one and identical, professed and practiced by the initiates of every country who alone were aware of its existence and importance. To ascertain its origin and the precise way in which it was matured is now beyond human possibility (A. P. Sinnet, *The Purpose of Theosophy*, Boston, 1888, p. 25).

A Theosophist may pursue any religion he desires, since there is truth in all religions. This, however, did not stop Mrs. Blavatsky from detesting organized Christianity:

> The name has been used in a manner so intolerant and dogmatic, especially in our day, that Christianity is now the religion of arrogance, par excellence, a stepping-stone for ambition, a sinecure for wealth, sham, and power; a convenient screen for hypocrisy (H. P. Blavatsky, *Studies in Occultism*, Theosophical University Press, n.d., p. 138).

Source of Authority

There are no sacred books in Theosophy. Revelation comes from "adepts," who are "beings perfected spiritually, intellectually, and physically, the flower of human and all evolution" (*Theosophical Movement*, p. 112). Mrs. Blavatsky was the first individual in Theosophy who received messages from these adepts and passed them on to the world: "I confined myself to the Hindu scriptures, and in all cases I stated that I regarded these scriptures and the Hindu religion as the origin of all scriptures and all religions" (Annie Bessant, *The Daily Chronicle*, April 9, 1894).

The Teachings of Theosophy

A few sample quotations from Theosophical writings demonstrate their non-Christian character.

God

> We reject the idea of a personal ... God (H. P. Blavatsky, *Key to Theosophy*, Point Loma, CA: Aryan Theosophical Press, 1913).

> We believe in a universal divine principle, the root of all, from which all proceeds, and within which all shall

be absorbed at the end of the great cycle of being (ibid., p. 63).

Man

Theosophists teach that man consists of seven parts: 1. the body; 2. vitality; 3. astral body; 4. animal soul; 5. human soul; 6. spiritual soul; and 7. spring.

> Man is also equated with God ... for you are God, and you will only what God wills; but you must dig deep down into yourself to find the God within you and listen to His voice which is your voice (Krishnamurti, *At the Feet of the Master*, p. 10).

Man is evolving individually and corporately. Salvation is achieved when man's seventh stage is attained involving progressing from one body to another based upon his own self-effort. This is similar to the eastern doctrine of the law of Karma.

Jesus Christ

> For Christ—the true esoteric saviour—is no man but the DIVINE PRINCIPLE in every human being (H. P. Blavatsky, *Studies in Occultism*, Theosophical University Press, n.d., p. 134).

Reincarnation and Afterlife

> No one is to blame except ourselves for our birth conditions, our character, our opportunities, our abilities, for all these things are due to the working out of forces we have set going either in this life or in former lives (Irving S. Cooper, *Theosophy Simplified*, p. 55).

There is no heaven as such in Theosophy. The Theosophist can reach a state of "nirvana" in which the individual is absorbed by the impersonal world, losing all personal consciousness.

Biblical Analysis of Theosophy

Madame Blavatsky's statement on Hindu scriptures totally denies the basic premise of the Christian faith, namely, that God has given the world a unique revelation concerning who He is and who we are (Hebrews 1:1-3). The Bible and Christianity cannot be from Hinduism (as she claimed all religions are) because God's Word is set in direct opposition to the doctrines of Hinduism.

The rejection of a personal God is a rejection of the God of the Bible, the infinite-personal creator. Theosophy has no room for a God who has created man in His personal image: "Then God said, 'Let us make man in Our image, to Our likeness'" (Genesis 1:26).

There is nothing in Scripture to suggest that man has a seven-part constitution. Rather he consists of body, soul, and spirit: "Now may the God of peace Himself sanctify you entirely; and may your spirit and soul and body be preserved complete, without blame at the coming of our Lord Jesus Christ" (1 Thessalonians 5:23).

Mrs. Blavatsky, sounding like an adherent to Christian Science, attempts to separate Christ from the person of Jesus. However, Christ is merely his title, meaning "anointed one" or "messiah," designating the office Jesus held. There is no justification for making any distinction between Jesus and "The Christ." Furthermore, making Christ a principle rather than a true man is a denial of the whole purpose of His coming: "And the Word became flesh, and dwelt among us" (John 1:14).

The idea of reincarnation, that people must go through a series of lives to atone for their sins, is a denial of the work Christ accomplished on the cross. Salvation has been made complete by Christ's sacrifice.

There is nothing any of us can do to add or subtract from it. Consequently, there is no need for a series of births to accomplish what Christ has already completed.

The Bible teaches that there is an existence after death for everyone. Those who have put their trust in Jesus Christ will forever reside in God's presence while those who reject Christ will spend eternity apart from him. John's Gospel makes this plain: "He who believes in the Son has eternal life; but he who does not obey the Son shall not see life, but the wrath of God abides on him" (John 3:36).

Conclusion

When Theosophy beliefs are examined, we discover the whole Theosophical system is contrary to Christianity. There is, therefore, no possibility of reconciliation between the two, since the followers of Theosophy extol Buddhist and Brahmanic theories, and Christians follow Jesus Christ alone.

Witnessing Tips

When we witness to any cult member we must never forget to pray before we meet with them. The battle may look like it takes place in the intellectual realm or possibly the emotional realm, but behind it all is the most intense spiritual battle. You cannot expect to win a spiritual battle in the flesh (1 Samuel 17:47). The spiritual battle becomes even more intense when you deal with someone who is practicing the occult, such as Theosophists. Every experienced evangelist will testify that there is no power in their words without volumes of prayer beforehand. We must be committed to the same.

17

The
Forum/est

Although the Forum is not primarily religious in nature (it has no worship services), it nonetheless integrates Zen Buddhism and denies the basic beliefs of the historic Christian faith. It claims compatibility with Jesus Christ and Christianity, and it should be numbered among the New Age cults because of its self-transformation technique.

History

"But don't get me wrong, I don't think the world needs est; I don't think the world needs anything; the world already is and that's perfect."

"If nobody needs it, then why do you do it?"

"I do it because I do it because that's what I do" (Adam Smith, *Powers of the Mind, Part II: The est Experience*, New York, September 29, 1975, p. 284).

That last statement was made by former used car

salesman John Paul Rosenberg, now known as Werner Erhard, founder and director of the Forum (formerly called est, for Erhard Seminars Training). The Forum is one of the fastest-growing groups of the New Age/human potential movement in America. Thousands of people, including prominent public figures, have been giving glowing testimonies of the transforming effects of the Forum.

Dr. Herbert Hansher, psychology professor at Temple University, has called The Forum/est "one of the most powerful therapeutic experiences yet devised" (Adelaide Bry, *est: 60 Hours That Transform Your Life*, New York: Avon, 1976, p. 200). Singer/Songwriter John Denver has said of his est encounters: "It's the single most important experience of my life" (*Newsweek*, December 20, 1976).

By way of background, Erhard (or Rosenberg) traveled the religious merry-go-round of Scientology, Zen Buddhism, yoga, hypnosis, Silva Mind Control and a host of other religious movements before presenting the world with est in 1971 ("Werner Erhard—An Interview with the Source of est," part 1, *The New Age Journal*, No. 7, September 15, 1975, pp. 18-20).

The most recent development in their history is Erhard's retirement as the director of the Forum at the end of 1991. After a series of critical media reports and negative publicity, he sold his shares of the organization to his executive staff. Some reporters linked the public exposure of Erhard to investigators who were hired by the Church of Scientology (*Los Angeles Times*, December 29, 1991).

What Is the Forum?

The Forum consists of sixty hours of intensive training, usually on two successive weekends, where the initiate attempts to reach the goal of the Forum:

"getting it." It is, however, never clear exactly what one gets, for Erhard's system is a unique combination of Zen Buddhism, Scientology, and Vendanta Hinduism, coupled with the power of positive thinking.

Erhard has said, "We want nothing short of a total transformation—an alteration of substance, not a change of form" (Werner Erhard, *What's So*, January 1975). This alteration or transformation is accomplished during the training sessions by attempting to change the individual's concept of who he is. Once a person's belief system is shredded, the person becomes vulnerable to accepting Erhard's world view.

The Philosophy of the Forum

Erhard's world view of life is perfect, with no difference between right and wrong:

> Life is always perfect just the way it is. When you realize that, then no matter how strongly it may appear to be otherwise, you know that whatever is happening right now will turn out all right. Knowing this, you are in a position to begin mastering life (Werner Erhard, *What's So*, January 1975).

> Wrong is actually a version of right. If you are always wrong you are right (Adelaide Bry, *est: 60 Hours That Transform Your Life*, p. 192).

Accordingly, there is no objective truth, no absolutes except the absolute of "whatever is, is right." With this viewpoint one could argue that anyone has the right to do whatever he wishes, including killing six million Jews, because he is perfect. Such a world view opens the door to frightening possibilities.

At the heart of the Forum world view is the assumption that God is man and man is God, and that each individual must come to understand he is his own God. One follower illustrated this assumption in his statement, "I can do anything. One of these days, I'll be so complete I won't be human, I'll be a god" (*Newsweek*, December 20, 1976).

Erhard's seminars attempt to enlighten the uninitiated to this truth. As one est trainer told his trainees, "It ought to be perfectly clear to everyone that you are all [expletive deleted] and I'm God. Only an [expletive deleted] would argue with God" (Luke Rhinehart, *The Book of est*, New York: Holt Rhinehart and Winston, 1976, p. 47).

When people believe they are god, they feel justified in self-centered actions, since as a god they answer to no one.

God

If indeed we ourselves are God, the need to look to a supreme being for salvation is gone, and the God of the Bible is unnecessary. Erhard has stated, "For instance, I believe that the belief in God is the greatest barrier to God in this universe—the single greatest barrier. I would prefer someone who is ignorant to someone who believes in God because the belief in God is a total barrier, almost a total barrier to the experience of God" (Werner Erhard, *East-West Journal*, September 1974).

Jesus Christ

Jesus supposedly was saying the same sort of thing as Erhard. Consequently in the Forum there is no need to give Jesus Christ any special adoration:

> Church totally misinterpreted what Jesus said. He kept telling over and over that everybody was like He was: perfect. He was experiencing life, like Werner. He knew He was the total source, living moment to moment, and was spontaneous.

> Jesus is just another guru who happens to be popular

here in Western Civilization. I can't go into a church and praise Jesus. But I really got where he is coming from. He wants to let everybody know "I'm you." So my whole point of view about religion has totally altered (Adelaide Bry, *est: 60 Hours That Transform Your Life*, p. 182).

Biblical Analysis of the Forum

The Bible reveals not only that man is not God, but also that he can never become God. God is by nature infinite (unlimited) whereas man is finite (limited). God is the creator and man is the creature. We are dependent on Him for our every existence:

The God who made the world and all things in it, since He is Lord of heaven and earth, does not dwell in temples made with hands; neither is He served by human hands, as though He needed anything, since He Himself gives to all life and breath and all things (Acts 17:24,25).

It is difficult to understand how anyone who reads the Bible could believe Jesus said everyone was perfect, as Erhard said. The truth is that Jesus said:

For unless you believe that I am He, you shall die in your sins (John 8:24).

For from within, out of the heart of men, proceed the evil thoughts, fornications, thefts, murders, adulteries, deeds of coveting and wickedness, as well as deceit, sensuality, envy, slander, pride and foolishness. All these evil things proceed from within and defile the man (Mark 7:21-23).

Furthermore, as uniquely God in human flesh, Jesus deserves our worship:

At the name of Jesus, every knee should bow, of those who are in heaven, and on earth, and under the earth, and that every tongue should confess that Jesus

Christ is Lord, to the glory of God the Father (Philippians 2:10,11).

Conclusion

The entire Forum system centers around the self-centered individual rather than the biblical God. In the Forum the only god recognized is the god within the person. Any religious or psychologically-manipulating system that leads people away from the true and living God is functioning as anti-Christ and should be avoided.

The experience the Forum offers is a pseudo-answer to man's deepest need. Only a personal relationship with Jesus Christ can truly satisfy the longing of the human heart. Jesus said, "If therefore the Son shall make you free, you shall be free indeed" (John 8:36).

Witnessing Tips

The Forum graduates and all former est graduates try to carry on an upbeat life after their seminar ends. However, nobody lives their entire life trouble-free, so eventually the reality of everyday living challenges the seminar's world view.

Christians have sometimes been guilty of only telling the good things that the Bible speaks of and forgetting to let potential converts know that they will also face persecution for Christ's sake (Matthew 5:10). We need to be more honest and realistic than human potential seminars. The best part of the Christian life is regular communication to God through prayer, so use your answered prayers as examples of how God works in your life.

God will always do what is best for us, but not necessarily what we want the most. Use this as a contrast when witnessing to a person in the Forum. Show him that as a child of God he can have God's help through life, otherwise he has to rely on his own strength. Take a few moments to show why the ego-centered life goes nowhere fast.

18

The
Church Universal
and
Triumphant

T he Church Universal and Triumphant is the largest
of the older I AM movement. There are various
names used to identify these groups, such as The Great
White Brotherhood, the Ascended Masters, I AM, the I
AM Presence, and the Mighty I AM. These groups bear
the marks of the New Age cults and are sprinkled with
occultic practices.

Their books at one time were only available
through small occult/metaphysical bookstores or mail
order. Today they have gained a stronghold in major
bookstores found in large shopping malls. Thousands
of people follow the teachings of the Great White
Brotherhood without ever joining one of the organizations.

History

The roots of this following is the writings of
Helena Petrovna Blavatsky and the Theosophical

Society. She taught that a group of Ascended Masters governed the affairs of spiritual enlightenment and they only spoke through one human vessel at a time. She claimed this title for herself and said the Ascended Masters who contacted her most often were "El Morya" and "Koot Hoomi." Of the seven masters in the hierarchy, she placed Jesus in sixth place.

The Great White Brotherhood

Although the very name sounds racist, those in the movement make assurances that it has nothing to do with race but with the "white robes" of the Ascended Masters. The Ascended Masters of Blavatsky evidently became known as The Great White Brotherhood among the spin-off groups of Theosophy. There have been more than a hundred such groups with each one claiming special communication with the Ascended Masters or The Great White Brotherhood.

The mode of communication from the hierarchy varies. Blavatsky, the founder of Theosophy, said her revelations "precipitated" on paper (the blank page suddenly had printed words); Guy Ballard, founder of I AM, claimed revelation through "liquid" light; Alice Bailey, founder of Lucist Trust, used automatic writing (a spirit would move her hand); Jane Roberts, author of *Seth Speaks*, used automatic writing; Elizabeth Clare Prophet, founder of Church Universal and Triumphant, "channelled" (spirits spoke through her); while others claim visions of Ascended Masters.

The I AM Movement

One strain of splinter groups from the Theosophical Society occurred after Madame Blavatsky's death in 1891. Those that held closely to her teachings broke off into other societies with Blavatsky's co-founder, William Q. Judge, and later William Harley. Another parallel group, the Anthroposophical Society, was founded in 1914 by Rudolf Stiener and focused on the "school of spiritual science."

The other splinter groups emerged mostly from the revelations of Guy and Edna Ballard, founders of I AM. The Ballards said The Great White Brotherhood had designated them as messengers for the up and coming Golden Age. They drew many Theosophists away from Blavatsky's foundation.

Guy Ballard said he had encountered "St. Germain" (the last incarnation of Francis Bacon) while he was by a stream on Mount Shasta in California. St. Germain asked him to drink from a cup filled with Omnipotent Life. Ballard viewed his past lives through astral travel and concluded that the escape from reincarnation was to contact the Mighty I AM Presence.

The name is taken from Exodus 3:14: I am that I am. The words, "In God's name I AM commanding," form part of incantations said in unison during group meetings. This is intermixed with decrees about Ascended Masters, various light colors, and gods, in an effort of changing earthly circumstances.

The Church Universal and Triumphant

The Church Universal and Triumphant is led by Elizabeth Clare Prophet, who had a background in Christian Science and the I AM movement. Her late husband, Mark Prophet (1918-1973), had formed an I AM group in 1958 called Summit Lighthouse. He followed the tradition of the Ballards for the most part, which attracted his wife, Elizabeth Clare Wulf, in 1961. They married in 1962 and built the most successful of the I AM groups.

They believed they were the "two witnesses" spoken of in Revelation 11:3. In his previous incarnations Mr. Prophet had quite a reputation: He was a priest on Atlantis, Lot in Sodom, Aesop the Greek philosopher, Mark in the New Testament, Origen of Alexandria, King Louis XIV in France, and the celebrated poet Henry Wadsworth Longfellow before he was born as Mark Prophet in Chappawa Falls, Wisconsin.

When Mark Prophet died in 1973 he became an ascended master named Lanello, who now "channels" through Elizabeth. Mrs. Prophet is called "Guru Ma" by her followers, a Hindu expression for an enlightened messenger. A strong leader in the New Age movement, the group uses "the best crystals and gemstones at the best prices charged by Lords of the Seven Rays to your vibration," according to one advertisement.

Authoritative Sources in the Church Universal and Triumphant

All the "sacred" scriptures of the world are used in the Church Universal and Triumphant, but only to the degree that they benefit the movement. The books published by Summit University Press are too numerous to afford space, but *Climb the Highest Mountain* by Mark and Elizabeth Prophet (1972) is probably one of the most important works (all quotations from this work are indicated by page numbers only in this chapter). The Prophets believe this book "makes plain" the teachings of Jesus, "the Master of Galilee" (p. xvi).

The Bible is often quoted throughout the Prophets' works, but it is held in less esteem than their current revelations. Calling themselves "Messengers for the Spiritual Hierarchy," the Prophets have assured their readers that their writings contain "the unspeakable, to utter the unutterable, and to set forth in writing what no man has written. We have . . . penned the tongues of angels" (p. xviii).

Ever so confident of their revelations, the Prophets

add words to biblical quotations and attempt to present them as the original meaning. For example, eighteen words are added to the original seventeen words of John 1:3 to alter the meaning: "All things were made by Him [by the Word that comes forth through the union of the Father-Mother God]; and without Him [without this synthesis] was not anything made that was made" (p. 410).

They claim to give two sources of truth: "To publish the teachings of the Ascended Masters and to shed light on the lost or distorted teachings of Christ" (p. xxi). With this they believe theirs is the only genuine and true representation of Jesus' teachings. They published an unfounded collection of "The Lost Years and Lost Teachings of Jesus" (Summit University Press, 1985) and their other so-called revelations.

Biblical Analysis of Authority

The gospel message has already been delivered to the world (1 Corinthians 15:1-4). It cannot be improved upon by any new revelations, especially from an occultic source like the Prophets. God banished all those who contact spirits for information (Leviticus 20:6; Deuteronomy 18:11; Isaiah 8:19). We are to stay faithful to the faith that was "once for all delivered to the saints" (Jude 3). This means it has been delivered once, and will not be delivered again.

The Bible cannot be changed by adding words to it. Proverbs 30:6 says, "Do not add to His words lest He reprove you, and you be proved a liar." God takes a very dim view of those who pervert His Word (Galatians 1:6-8). Neither can the Bible be added to other "scriptures" of the world. Second Corinthians 6:14 says, "Do not be bound together with unbelievers; for what partnership have righteousness and lawlessness, or what fellowship has light with darkness?"

The Teachings of the Church Universal and Triumphant

Mark and Elizabeth Prophet tried to combine aspects of several religions into one.

God

God is given the impersonal form of pantheism (although they do not care to use the word):

> We who acknowledge Life as God and God as permeating His entire creation find no fault with this logic . . . But few among mankind would be willing to . . . accept the idea that there is conscious awareness within the heart of a rock, a tree, a flower, a mountain, a flaming bush, a drop of rain, or a wave upon the sea (p. 195).

From the teaching of dualism, the Prophets believe that God has a masculine and feminine nature: "We must include in our awareness the concept of the Father-Mother God—of a Being that is both masculine and feminine in nature" (p. 321).

In another statement Mr. and Mrs. Prophet address the trinity. Not the Trinity of Christianity, but a redefined trinity: "If God is Father-Mother, what, then, is the Trinity? When we refer to God as Father, God as Son, and God as Holy Spirit, we are actually referring to God as He is found in Spirit and in Matter" (p. 321).

Jesus

Jesus takes on a whole new personality in the Church Universal and Triumphant. He is one of several Ascended Masters who communicates to Mark Prophet (p. ix). Jesus, however, is not in the highest position. Their writings say that "El Morya" is "chief" over Jesus (p. 364). We find the gnostic teaching of separating Jesus from the Christ present in the Prophets' book: "Jesus had often explained to his close followers that the son of man ... was not greater than his Lord, his Christ Self. The Master's greatest desire was that they should not mistake the son of man (Jesus) for the Son of God (the Christ)" (p. 301). The "christ" principle is defined as "the Light of man's being" (p. 15). Every man has this same "christ" within him, "the Christ, the Real Image in you all" (p. 25).

The Holy Spirit

Mark and Elizabeth Prophet claim the Holy Spirit is an energy: "The Holy Spirit is the energy man uses either to expand Good or expand an energy veil" (p. 132). The impersonal Holy Spirit, an "it," is supposed to be within every living thing:

"The Holy Spirit," he begins, "is the ingredient of Life which is the Fire of Cosmos, the germinal power in nature; it is the power that beats the heart and infuses every form of Life with the essence of the Father-Mother God. The Holy Spirit is indigenous to every Life manifestation."

Man and Sin

Mr. and Mrs. Prophet define evil as, "All should realize that darkness can also be a misqualification of Light, as such it forms the energy-veil we call evil ... it is *live* spelled backwards" (p. 14). Sin has no real existence in their writings, it is only real to the synthetic image (the human body): "Man's origin is in God. Where, then, original sin? Only in the synthetic image that is no more. There is no sin in the generation of the sons and daughters of God" (p. 25).

Man is a spark of God, a part of the nature of God:

Each man is a manifestation of God (a manifest action of God), the image of the Higher Cosm reflected in the lower cosm (p. 27).

Billions of Spirit-sparks spiraled thorough Cosmos,

trailing clouds of glory and chanting . . . And so the Spirit of man was born, and so God was borne in man (p. 19).

As a part of God, the Prophets feel that man is not a sinner: "Contrary to the lie that man is a sinner and gravitates to the baser elements of his nature, man is inherently Good" (p. 59).

Salvation

Salvation is accomplished in the Church Universal and Triumphant by release from reincarnation. The blood of Jesus is repudiated,

> And the erroneous doctrine concerning the blood sacrifice of Jesus—which he himself never taught—has been perpetrated to the present hour, a remnant of pagan rite long refuted by the word of the Lord. God the Father did not require sacrifice of His son Christ Jesus, or of any other incarnation of the Christ, as an atonement for the sins of the world (pp. 279-280).

Jesus is seen as equal with Buddha by the Prophets and they came to "take upon themselves a certain portion of mankind's planetary karma" (p. 443).

The way for man to get rid of his bad karma is through works: "God's grace . . . is the natural resource given to man freely in order that man might fulfill the pattern of his individuality through faith and good works. If man were saved by God's grace alone, then everyone would be saved" (p. 161). When man dies he eventually becomes a god: "Only man can become God because only man has free will" (p. 197).

Biblical Analysis of Teachings

The confusion of the Church Universal and Triumphant is the mixture of Christian terms with New Age thinking. Nobody, perhaps, has so blended the two as Mark and Elizabeth Prophet have. They gained many converts for the movement from weak Christians in liberal denominations.

A solid understanding of the Trinity, as we presented in Chapter 6 and in other parts of this work, will refute the dualism of the Prophet's impersonal Father-Mother god. Matthew 28:19 is a clear example from the words of Jesus that there are three Persons under the one name, the name of God. In what appears to be the only reference to all eastern religions in the Bible (all are east of Jerusalem), God rebukes Judah for being "filled with influences from the east" (Isaiah 2:6). God will not bless any mixture of eastern customs with His Holy Word.

The way of salvation is through the shed blood of Jesus. It would do the followers of the Church Universal and Triumphant well if they read what Jesus said about His own crucifixion. The Prophets were wrong when they said Jesus never referred to it. Our Lord, hardly refuting it, made reference to His death and blood for the remission of sins: Matthew 20:28; 26:28.

Conclusion

Chanting positive affirmations and using the words "I AM" does not provide eternal life for anyone. It only deceives the soul into believing salvation can be self-made outside of faith in Jesus. We recognize the I AM movement as a cult that separates man from a true relationship with God, through His Son Jesus Christ.

Witnessing Tips

People in the Church Universal and Triumphant usually have some familiarity with the Bible. Sadly, this is because so many of their members had a Protestant or Catholic background before joining the movement.

When you witness to members in the Church Universal, try to stress the importance of the sinless nature of Jesus, which then means He never lied. If He always told the truth, then what He said about Himself, the sinfulness of man, and salvation can be believed.

The only way for the person in the Church Universal to get around the claims of Jesus is to deny the reliability of the Bible. One argument that seems to run through the rank and file members of the Church Universal is, "The Bible has been changed through the years." This is your opportunity to show him how reliable the Bible is. For additional information on why the Bible can be believed, see *Evidence That Demands a Verdict*, Volume 1.

19

Religious Science

The Church of Religious Science is rooted in gnosticism, metaphysics, Hinduism, and the occult. It belongs with the New Age cults because it combines the teachings of eastern mysticism and the Bible. The Bible, however, does not have any special place in their literature. The transformation in Religious Science is through the mind and positive thinking rather than an actual technique so common to New Agers. Religious Science does not bar its members from using objects like New Age crystals, however.

History

From the outset Religious Science claims to be a melting pot of ideas. It draws from Christian Science, Quimby, the transcendentalism of Ralph Waldo Emerson, Unity School of Christianity, Theosophy, and New Thought. It claims to be a "correlation of laws of science, opinions of philosophy, and revelations of religions applied to human needs and the aspirations of man" (*What Religious Science Teaches*, p. 1).

Ernest Holmes, the founder of Religious Science, was born in Maine in 1887. In his early years he was fascinated with the writings of Ralph Waldo Emerson. His growing doubts about Christianity caused him to reject it by the age of twenty.

He studied Christian Science, hypnotism, psychic phenomenon, Theosophy, and spiritism. After attending some seances he decided they were too limited, so he turned "inward" for truth.

In 1916 he began to teach metaphysics and culminated his work ten years later with the publication of *Science of Mind* (1926), which is the main text of Religious Science. The Church was incorporated the following year and soon began to spread with a vigorous popularity.

Theology of Religious Science

Mr. Holmes attempted to harmonize all truths. He felt there were good ideas in all religions and he tried to locate the one faith: "Religion is one faith, faith is one. Truth is one. There is one reality at the heart of all religions, whether their name be Hindu, Mohammedan, Christian or Jewish" (ibid., p. 10).

The Trinity

Holmes denied every major doctrine of Christianity, beginning with the Trinity. He redefined the Trinity and made God impersonal:

> Turn it as we may, we are confronted with the necessity of a Trinity of Being. Throughout the ages, this Trinity has been taught. Every great religion and every great spiritual philosophy has taught this Trinity. Father, Son and Holy Ghost is the Christian Trinity. It is the Thing, the Way It Works, and What It Does. The Thing is

Absolute Intelligence; the *way* It works, is Absolute Law; and What It does, is the result—manifestation. The action of the Thing Itself is what the Bible calls "The Word" . . . Absolute Intelligence (Holmes, *Science of the Mind*, 1926, p. 80).

He said again:

NATURE OF GOD—We have already discovered that the Nature of God is "Triune"—Spirit, Soul and Body . . . Father, Son and Holy Ghost . . . or The Thing, How It Works, and What It Does (ibid., pp. 613-614).

God, in Religious Science, is actually impersonal Himself, because He is the person of Human, having person of His own: "We begin to see that there is an Infinite Personalness . . . where our life is personified, God is personified. If man did not exist, God would be impersonal!" (*Words That Heal Today*, p. 6)

Jesus Christ

Holmes denied the true deity of Jesus Christ by claiming that Jesus was only a man: "Jesus was a man, a human being . . . Jesus never thought of himself as different from others" (*What Religious Science Teaches*, p. 19). Jesus only lived better than others: "As Jesus, the man, gave way to the Divine Idea the human took on the Christ Spirit and became the voice of God to humanity" (ibid., p. 20).

The gnostic cults teach that Jesus is separate from the Christ. This found its way into Holmes's teachings: "Christ is God in the soul of man . . . JESUS—the name of a man. Distinguished from the Christ. The man Jesus became the embodiment of the Christ, as the human gave way to the Divine Idea of Sonship" (ibid., p. 603). In another work, we find, "Christ is the unseen principle in Man . . . Christ is the reality of every man, his *true inner self*" (*What Religious Science Teaches*, p. 65).

The Holy Spirit

There are only a few cults that claim the Holy Spirit is the female aspect of God. Moonies are notorious for this and some gnostic cults, like Religious Science, teach their own variation of this:

> The *Holy Ghost* signifies the feminine aspect of the Divine Trinity. It represents the divine activity of the higher mental plane . . . The Spirit is, "the supreme Law of Cause and Effect" . . . the divine creative fertility of the universal soul when impregnated by the Divine Ideas (*What Religious Science Teaches*, p. 65).

Man Is God

Mr. Holmes picks up the metaphysical concept that the divine nature exists in man, sometimes called the Christ: "The inner Spirit, *which is God*, bears witness to the divine fact that we are the sons of God, the children of the Most High" (*Science of the Mind*, p. 485). "As the human gives way to the Divine, in all people, they become the Christ" (ibid., p. 360).

Salvation

Religious Science teaches salvation is accomplished by becoming like God and becoming part of the whole:

> Every question is in man, because man is within Spirit, and Spirit is an Invisible Whole! The solution to every problem is within man; the healing of all disease is within man; the forgiveness of all sin is within man; the raising of the dead is within man; Heaven is within man . . . each of us, then, represents the Whole (ibid., p. 365).

Salvation Is Universal

> We believe the ultimate goal of life to be a complete emancipation from all discord of every nature, and that this goal is sure to be attained by all (ibid., p. 43).

If one would know God, he must penetrate deeply into his own nature, for here alone can he find Him ... The only way to know God is to be like Him (ibid., p. 443).

Biblical Analysis of Religious Science

Every cult thinks it can redefine the Trinity into its own terminology, thereby destroying the truth of the doctrine for its members. Mr. Holmes did just that. The nature of God is not to be altered or redefined; it is blasphemous to do this. It is considered such a sin to blaspheme the Holy Spirit that Jesus promised judgment upon those who do such (Matthew 12:31,32).

Man is not a god (Numbers 23:19; Hosea 11:9); neither is man a Christ. Jesus said all those who claim to be Christ are deceivers (Matthew 24:5). He that denies that Jesus is the only Christ is a liar and an anti-Christ (1 John 2:22).

Salvation, according to the Bible, is first to recognize that we are totally incapable of meeting the holiness of God because we have been separated from Him by sin (Romans 3:23; 6:23). The only way of salvation is through the atonement of Jesus' shed blood for our sins (Hebrews 10:10; 1 John 1:7), which is provided by God's grace, and not by anything we have done (Ephesians 2:8,9).

The Failed Philosophy

The largest Religious Science Church used to be that of Terry Cole Whittaker, in El Cajon, California. She had built her congregation from remnants of other congregations.

In February, 1985, Terry Cole Whittaker was quoted as saying, "I'm gonna keep on going, 'cause I know this stuff works." She also said that Religious Science will create heaven on earth by the year 2020.

"Of course," she adds, "all the present systems and religions will have to collapse first" (*Los Angeles Times*, February 10, 1985, Calendar, p. 5). This would mean that Christianity would have to collapse in order for Religious Science to succeed.

On March 17, one month after she made those statements, Ms. Whittaker stood before her congregation and resigned from her position as pastor! She had recently returned from India and while there had discovered that people in poverty can be happy. This discovery pulled the plug on her philosophy that "prosperity" is a divine right. She thought her philosophy was perfect, until it failed before her eyes.

Conclusion

Religious Science denies every essential doctrine of our faith. The philosophy of Religious Science does not work. It is a failed system in the eyes of God and man.

Witnessing Tips

Witnessing to members of the Church of Religious Science is like witnessing to a positive-thinking humanist. They both have an upbeat attitude about life while being dead-wrong on theology.

The Bible is used mainly for "claiming" prosperity and health for the members of Religious Science. Sit down with the person and show him the real message of the Bible. Go directly to the gospel message and explain that the purpose of the Bible is the redemption of mankind.

Groups
in
Transition

It is not strange to us that the Holy Spirit might move upon a group of people to reexamine their doctrines by the Word of God. This has occurred in several epochs of church history, especially when doctrinal issues were raised at the historic church councils. Some of those who were wayward came back into fellowship through discovering their error. Others rejected the council results and became all the more polemic.

A group that was largely held as a cult in its early years is the Seventh-day Adventists. Several dedicated Christian authors have included Seventh-day Adventists in their writings on the cults (Hoekema, Irvine, Van Baalan, DeHaan). They correctly and rightfully take the false doctrines of Ellen G. White to task with a painstaking biblical analysis.

We do not know if it is due to the writings of Christians, or whether the Seventh-day Adventists discovered it independently, but it is undeniable that there has been a change taking place in Seventh-day Adventist thinking since the 1960s. A large sector of the group has forsaken the writings of Ellen G. White while remaining within the church. Many of them have become devout evangelical believers in Jesus Christ.

This, no doubt, has caused unrest within the group and has all but sharply divided it into two churches. While it remains a single entity, there is an evangelical wing that authors like Walter R. Martin and Donald Grey Barnhouse recognize, and there is the old school that remains ever-so-faithful to Ellen G. White.

There appears to be a similar movement within the Worldwide Church of God, whose beliefs are commonly called Armstrongism. We do not challenge the description of Armstrongism given in our former book *Understanding the Cults* (reprinted in *Handbook of Today's Religions* and *The Best of Josh McDowell: A Ready Defense*). We labeled it a cult in unison with other respected authors in the field (Martin, Hoekema, Tucker, Hopkins).

However, Dr. Ruth A. Tucker, author of *Another Gospel* and visiting professor at Trinity Evangelical Divinity School in Deerfield, Illinois, began to see a change in Armstrongism after the founder, Herbert W. Armstrong, had passed away. She invited two representatives of the Worldwide Church of God to the 1991 Tanner Lecture Series (an annual symposium on cults) to explain their recent changes to a group of noted Christian scholars and apologists.

Although they have not come as far as Seventh-day Adventists by accepting the doctrine of the Trinity and other essentials to the faith, we wish to recognize their open-minded effort in meeting with Christian scholars to reexamine their teachings. Yet if their talks with Christian leadership swing into an unrepentant denial of the essentials of Christianity, we would have to reconsider whether they are truly a group in transition or a group that has made up its mind to remain under the umbrella of false doctrine.

20

The
Worldwide
Church
of
God

In February of 1991, two authorities of the Worldwide Church of God were invited to Trinity Evangelical Divinity School (Deerfield, Illinois) to speak about their doctrinal changes at the Tanner Lecture Series. Dr. Ruth A. Tucker, along with several noted theologians and apologists, listened and responded with questions to the speakers. The Worldwide Church of God was changing their position on doctrines and was asking for the input of Christian leaders. While some at the lecture series were skeptical and sought for ulterior motives, others were willing to put in the necessary time for constructive dialogue.

Dr. Tucker was the first to publish the changes in recent Armstrongism. She points out that under Mr. Armstrong's leadership, the Worldwide Church of God gained a respectability "that few cults have achieved." But, she adds, after his death "there does appear to be a shift away from some of his doctrinaire views" (*Another Gospel*, p. 192).

Dr. Tucker suggests that several doctrinal issues were under revision at the time she wrote her book: "At the time of this writing the Worldwide Church of God is revising its doctrinal statement, so it is impossible to assess how significant any changes in church doctrine will be" (ibid., p. 216). She demonstrates that the printed literature of the church is incompatible with the stated changes of the church. She wisely cautions readers that changes may "be more cosmetic than real." And the Worldwide Church of God "continues to reject the orthodox view of the Trinity" (ibid.).

Previous to the publishing of *The Deceivers*, the Associate Director of Public Affairs for the Worldwide Church of God, Mr. Michael A. Snyder, sent us a letter. His stated purpose was to invite our investigation of the recent changes in doctrine for the Worldwide Church of God.

We believe that this rare opportunity to engage in direct dialogue with the leadership of a church of their magnitude was no small step in evangelism. In response to his letter we set up a personal meeting with writer Kurt Van Gorden, accompanied by Dr. Alan Gomes, Associate Professor of Historical Theology at Talbot School of Theology (La Mirada, California).

Mr. Snyder's letter suggested that we change eight points in our former work, *Understanding the Cults*, which did not reflect the "current doctrinal teachings" of his church. We sent twenty questions in advance of our meeting with their church authorities. The Worldwide Church of God representatives were Michael A. Snyder, David Hulme (Director of Communications and Public Affairs), and J. Michael Feazell (Executive Assistant to Joseph Tkach, Pastor General). One advantage we had over the Tanner Lecture Series

(1991) and Dr. Tucker's book (1989) is that the Worldwide Church of God's revised doctrinal statement was released three weeks before our meeting (January 13, 1992).

Even in consideration of the meeting, we still believe the group fits our definition of a cult as outlined in Chapter 1, but we also see a move toward orthodoxy in parts of their theology. We were hopeful that they would stop rejecting the Trinity and the Person of the Holy Spirit, but they did not. In fairness, we wish to represent the changes they have made.

There will be ongoing dialogue with the leadership of the Worldwide Church of God. Since their doctrines are in a stage of transition, we have placed them in this special section of our book. In this chapter we will give a brief history and an outline of beliefs in the Worldwide Church of God. Following that we will show the direction of their doctrinal changes.

History

The founder of the Worldwide Church of God is Herbert W. Armstrong, born on July 31, 1892, in Des Moines, Iowa. As a young man, Armstrong worked in the advertising business and showed little interest in spiritual things. In a dispute with his wife over the issue of keeping the seventh-day Sabbath, Armstrong began an intensive personal study of the Bible. This resulted in his agreeing with his wife on observing the Saturday Sabbath. Further Bible study convinced Armstrong that much of what he had been taught in traditional churches was wrong.

According to Armstrong, the Worldwide Church of God began in September 1933. The World Tomorrow Radio program began in January 1934, which Mr. Armstrong saw as a fulfillment of the book of Revelation, when the "Sardis" era of the church ended and the

"Philadelphia" era began (a reference to the seven churches listed in Revelation 2 and 3 that some see as a
prefiguring of eras of church history). Armstrong put it
this way:

> Back in 1934 . . . Jesus Christ (Revelation 3:8) was
> opening the gigantic mass media DOOR of radio and the
> printing press for the proclamation of His same original
> GOSPEL to all the world! (*The Autobiography of Herbert W.
> Armstrong*, Pasadena: Ambassador College Press, 1967, p.
> 503)

Armstrong at this time began his radio broadcast
and the publishing of the magazine *The Plain Truth*.
Since its inception, the Worldwide Church of God has
experienced significant growth, reaching into millions
of homes through the distribution of its magazine and
the World Tomorrow radio broadcast.

The Claims of Armstrong

Herbert W. Armstrong makes no small claim for
his work in the Worldwide Church of God:

> A.D. 69, the apostles and the church fled to Pella from
> Jerusalem according to Jesus' warning (Matthew
> 24:15,16). That was the END of the organized proclaim-
> ing of Christ's gospel by His church to the world! . . . For
> eighteen and one-half centuries, all worldwide organized
> proclaiming of Christ's gospel was stamped out" (ibid.,
> pp. 502-503).

Armstrong reiterated his belief that his work was
to restore the lost gospel and prepare for the second
coming of Christ:

> For eighteen and one-half centuries that gospel was
> not preached. The world was deceived into accepting a
> false gospel. Today Christ has raised up his work and
> once again allotted two nineteen-year time cycles for

proclaiming His same gospel, preparatory to His second coming.

He also states:

"No man ever spoke like this man," reported the officers of the Pharisees regarding Jesus. The multitudes were astonished at his doctrine.

It is the same today, the same living Christ through *The World Tomorrow* broadcast, *The Plain Truth Magazine*, and this work proclaims in mighty power around the world the same gospel preached by Peter, Paul and all the original apostles ... *The World Tomorrow* and *The Plain Truth* are Christ's instruments which he is powerfully using. Yes, His message is shocking today. Once again it is the voice in the wilderness of religious confusion (*The Inside Story of The World Tomorrow Broadcast*, pp. 2,7).

The lines are clearly drawn. If you do not believe the message of Herbert W. Armstrong then you do not believe the true message of Christ to this age.

Mr. Armstrong led his church for more than fifty years, having died at the age of ninety-three in January 1986. The successor of his position as "pastor general" is Joseph W. Tkach, who appointed David Hulme and three others to take over the television broadcast.

Changes in Theology

It is not easy for a group to hold its membership together while making changes in theology. We were given access to a "membership only" publication, which tells the members of some of the changes. Mr. Tkach told the church:

If a doctrine is changed, does that mean the doctrine has been watered down? ... Brethren, we all understand that Herbert W. Armstrong never claimed to be perfect ... He let God guide him by remaining open to correction from the Bible . . . When we find that we've been wrong, regardless of how small the point may be, regardless of how big the point may be, regardless of how dearly held the point may be, we have the obligation before God to change (*The Worldwide News*, June 24, 1991, pp. 1,5).

In another issue, Mr. Tkach, said the *Plain Truth* (while under Armstrong's direction) was "overly enthusiastic . . . speculative and narrow . . . the mistake that has been made so often before—crying wolf" (*Plain Truth*, March 1991, p. 1,25). Some have already begun to leave the Worldwide Church of God and form their own followings based upon the teachings of Mr. Armstrong. Mr. Tkach took a position on this: "Though they still use the Bible, in their emotional distress, they have placed Mr. Armstrong ahead of the Bible in their own minds" (*The Worldwide News*, May 21, 1990).

Old Positions vs. New Positions

In order to see where the Worldwide Church of God stands today, we feel it's necessary to examine and compare the old positions with the new positions.

Old Position: The position of Mr. Armstrong having the only truth for eighteen centuries, from the above quotations, is now being challenged by current leadership of his church.

New Position: Mr. Snyder's letter to us, dated April 29, 1991, stated: "The Church no longer makes the claim that the gospel was not preached for eighteen and a half centuries." According to Mr. Snyder, they are not in the business of judging those outside of their organization. He said, "We want to look beyond groups and see that the Body of Christ transcends denominational barriers."

Our Comment: We frankly are troubled by what appears to be a double standard in the Worldwide Church of God material. Mr. Snyder said they do not have the only truth, but articles still appear by Mr. Tkach that take shots at Christian denominations (*The Worldwide News*, May 21, 1990, and *The Plain Truth*, February 1992). It may take time before the slamming of denominations stops, but we would at least expect this if the new position of the Worldwide Church of God is consistent. Only time will tell us the sincerity of the statement.

Old Position: "You are setting out on a training to become creator—to become God!" (Herbert W. Armstrong, *Why Were You Born*, p. 22).

New Position: Mr. Snyder's letter said, "The Church no longer promulgates the statement that man will become God. The Church believes and teaches that the Christian inheritance is eternal life as sons of God."

Our Comment: In questioning the church authorities we found this is a real change for the better in their theology. Mr. Feazell said, "The whole concept is something we do not accept. A Christian is one who is sanctified and saved." Our follow up question was concerning how they see our sonship as distinct from Jesus as the Son of God. Their answer was, "Jesus is the unique, eternal Son of God by nature and by right. We become sons of God by grace. We will, by grace, not by right, become like Christ. We will receive the communicable attributes of God, such as glorification and love. We will never receive any of God's incommunicable and unique attributes."

We find these statements more in line with Scripture than Mr. Armstrong's. If their theology later changes to the idea that man in any way absorbs or acquires the unique attributes of God, then it has to be rejected as heresy.

Old Position: "God is a family—not a trinity. God's family will not be limited to an intractably closed circle of three . . . God's family is open" (B. McDowell,

"Is the Holy Spirit a Person?," *Tomorrow's World*, September 1970, p. 31).

New Position: Mr. Snyder's letter said, "The Church does not teach that the Godhead is an 'open' entity."

Our Comment: The doctrine of the "open" entity in God seemed to be totally rejected through a series of questions we addressed to the church authorities. They maintained that the monotheism and oneness of God throughout the Bible is what drove them to this conclusion.

When we got to the rejection of the Trinity, we found that there were some unsettled questions among the authorities. We were assured that they are still studying it and it is not a closed subject with them. But nevertheless, they still rejected the doctrine of the Trinity and the Person of the Holy Spirit. This statement, of course, we find unscriptural.

On the subject of the Holy Spirit we saw that one of the authorities was willing to call Him by the personal pronouns found in John 14, 15, and 16—He, Him, His. This gentleman said he cannot deny what John has written and promised more study in the future. Their doctrine of God is what we call *binitarianism.* They freely call the Father and Son two Persons within God's nature. The Holy Spirit is called the mind, power, or essence of God in their theology, but not a person. If they come to the conclusion that the Holy Spirit is a person, then they will be Trinitarian. At this point, they still reject the Trinity as one God in three Persons.

Old position: "God commands water baptism; and for one who is able to either defy the command and refuse, or neglect . . . certainly would be an act of disobedience which would impose the PENALTY of sin, and cause loss of salvation" (ibid., p. 19).

New Position: Mr. Snyder's letter said, "Concerning your statement that the Church has some alleged belief in salvation by works (which it emphatically does not) . . . "

Our Comment: During our discussion on this subject we became convinced that a real change had taken place on the subject of grace and works for salvation. The authorities in the church maintained that salvation is by grace through faith in Jesus Christ. We asked specifically if baptism is a prerequisite to salvation. They said it was not. They used to teach that a person was not born again until the resurrection, but this has been changed too.

We were dismayed to find statements in print that seemed to challenge their denial that baptism is a prerequisite. In recent articles (*Plain Truth*, January 1992, p. 9), baptism is still essential for salvation. Their newly published booklet, *Why You Should Be Baptized*, also teaches "baptism is a vital part of the process of salvation" (p. 5). We will watch this inconsistency in the future to see what corrections are made.

Old Position: Herbert W. Armstrong advanced the doctrine of Anglo-Israelism in several publications (*Where Are the Lost Ten Tribes?*, Pasadena: Ambassador College, n.d.), wherein he taught that the lost ten tribes went through Europe to Britain and eventually the United States.

New Position: All the publications on Anglo-Israelism have been pulled from circulation and a two-year study committee has been assigned the task of reassessing the issue.

Our Comment: Although this doctrine is not essential to salvation, it is commendable that it is being examined. Not knowing where the committee will end up, it is too early to make any further comment.

Old Position: Mr. Armstrong denied the bodily resurrection of Jesus: "Now notice carefully, God the

Father did not cause Jesus Christ to get back into the body which had died . . . Nowhere does the Scripture say He was alive and active, or that God had Him get back in to the human body, that had died and was now resurrected" (*Plain Truth*, November 1963, pp. 11-12).

New Position: In our discussion with the Worldwide Church of God authorities, they consistently said that Jesus was raised bodily from the grave, glorified and immortal. Their proof that His raised body was real is Luke 24:39, where He calls His body "flesh and bones."

Our Comment: This was a good change in their doctrines. We also asked about the "spiritual body" mentioned by Paul in 1 Corinthians 15:44. They continued to maintain that it would be like Jesus' body, a physical resurrection of "flesh and bones."

False Doctrines Still Taught

Even with the changes that have been made we still see room for major changes in the future—especially in the doctrine of the Trinity, one God in three Persons.

Mr. Armstrong taught other doctrines that we consider to be false by scriptural standards.

Eternal Judgment

Armstrong rejects any idea of eternal punishment for the wicked:

"The wages of sin is death" (Romans 6:23) and the death, which is the absence of life, is for ALL ETERNITY. It is eternal punishment by remaining DEAD for all eternity—not remaining alive and being tortured in a fictitious, burning hell-fire! (Herbert W. Armstrong, *Immortality*, p. 7).

The fires of hell spoken of in the Bible will eventually burn themselves out, he says:

> They (the fires in the valley of Hinnom) were never quenched or put out by anyone! The flames merely died out when they had nothing more to consume. Even so, it will be with the Gehenna fire. It will be unquenched—but it will finally burn itself out" (Herbert W. Armstrong, ed., *Ambassador College Correspondence Course*, Lesson 6, p. 14).

The idea that hell will eventually burn itself out is not scriptural: "And these will go away into eternal punishment, but the righteous into eternal life" (Matthew 25:46). If there is no eternal punishment, then certainly there is no eternal life for this verse uses the same word to describe both. Jesus said the fire is unquenchable:

> And if your eye causes you to stumble, cast it out; it is better for you to enter the kingdom of God with one eye, than having two eyes to be cast into hell, where their worm *does not die, and the fire is not quenched* (Mark 9:47,48, italics ours).

For a thorough refutation of the annihilation doctrine, see "Evangelicals and the Annihilation of Hell" by Dr. Alan Gomes (*Christian Research Journal*, Spring and Summer 1991).

The Sabbath

Armstrong believes observing Sunday as the day of worship is the Mark of the Beast: "Sunday observance—this is the Mark of the Beast ... you shall be tormented by God's plagues without mercy, yes, you!" (Herbert W. Armstrong, *The Mark of the Beast*, Pasadena: Ambassador College Press, 1957, pp. 10-11).

Since there are other cultic groups which teach a

similar doctrine about the Sabbath, we feel it necessary to demonstrate that it was the policy of the New Testament believers and the early church to observe Sunday rather than Saturday as their day of worship.

The teaching that the day of worship was changed from Saturday to Sunday during the reign of the Roman Emperor Constantine (c. A.D. 325) does not fit the facts. The fact that the early church believed the Hebrew Sabbath was not binding on the Christian is demonstrated by the following quotations:

> At the beginning of the second century, Ignatius, bishop of Antioch, wrote to the Magnesians:
>
> > Be not deceived with strange doctrines, nor with old fables. For if we still live according to the Jewish law, we acknowledge that we have not received grace . . .
>
> He then goes on to categorize his readers as "those who were brought up in the ancient order of things" but who "have come to the possession of a new hope, no longer observing the Sabbath" (*The Ante-Nicene Fathers*, Volume 1, pp. 62-63).

During the middle of the second century, Justin Martyr explained why Christians did not keep the law of Moses and the Sabbath observance in *The Ante-Nicene Fathers*, Volume 1, pp. 199,200,204, 207; and *Dialogue With Trypho*.

The same is true with Cerenalus, Bishop of Lyons, at the end of the second century (*Against Heresies*, Book IV, Chapter 16). Also Clement of Alexandria (*The Stromata*) and Tertullian (*On Idolatry*, Chapter 14 and *An Answer to the Jew*, Chapter 2), testify of the early Christians' attitude concerning Sabbath observance. It was basically a Jewish institution.

Biblical Analysis

Since there are so many of Mr. Armstrong's booklets in circulation, we will answer some of the points of his church's former positions.

The accusations leveled by Armstrong against the doctrine of the Trinity are unfounded. Rather than being the invention of false prophets and heretics, as Armstrong said, the doctrine of the Trinity is the clear teaching of Scripture on the nature of God. Simply stated, the Bible teaches there exists one God who is three distinct persons: the Father, the Son, and the Holy Spirit, and these three persons are the one God (Matthew 28:19). See our section about the Trinity in Chapter 3, "The Beliefs of Orthodox Christianity."

There is no teaching whatever in Scripture that suggests God is a family. This doctrine would make God changeable, which is contrary to Malachi 3:6. God does not change.

The views of Armstrongism concerning the Holy Spirit fly right into the face of true biblical teaching. The Bible clearly portrays the Holy Spirit as God while maintaining personal distinction from both the Father and the Son.

This can be observed in Acts 5:3,4 where the Holy Spirit is spoken of as God, "But Peter said, 'Ananias, why has Satan filled your heart to lie to the Holy Spirit? . . . You have not lied to men but to God.' "

The idea that man will some day be God can be found nowhere in the Bible. God is God by nature. He was, is and always will be God. Man cannot attain Godhood for he is finite, limited by his nature. There is no other God, neither will there be any other God: " 'You are My witnesses,' declares the LORD, 'and My servant whom I have chosen, in order that you may know and believe Me and understand that I am He. Before Me there was no God formed, and there will be none after Me' " (Isaiah 43:10).

According to the Worldwide Church of God, sal-

vation is only a process beginning in this life and cul-
minating in the resurrection. Salvation consists of
repentance, faith and water baptism. No one is saved in
this life. The doctrine of "simply" coming to Christ for
salvation is rejected by Armstrong in the strongest of
terms.

Contrary to Armstrong's statements, the Scriptures
teach that salvation is a free gift from God. The Scriptures further declare that salvation cannot be earned by
doing any work, whether it be water baptism or the
keeping of the Sabbath. Salvation comes as a result of a
person simply placing his faith in Jesus Christ:

> For by grace you have been saved through faith; and
> that not of yourselves, it is the gift of God; not as a result
> of works, that no one should boast (Ephesians 2:8,9).

> He saved us, not on the basis of deeds which we
> have done in righteousness, but according to His mercy,
> by the washing of regeneration and renewing by the
> Holy Spirit (Titus 3:5).

Salvation, therefore, is totally a work of God. Man
can add nothing to what Christ has already done when
He died in our place on the cross.

Conclusion

While the changes in doctrine have been significant to the members of the Worldwide Church of
God, we must still classify them as a cult. They cannot
be embraced as fellow believers until they shed more of
the doctrines of their founder. We began by showing
that the new leadership of the Worldwide Church of
God told their members, in 1988, and Christians, in
1989, that their doctrines were changing. For these to be
other than "cosmetic" changes, we would have to see
direct denials of their false doctrines and acceptance of
orthodox doctrines on the major issues of the Trinity,

the person of the Holy Spirit, the necessity of baptism for salvation, and the church.

Witnessing Tips

Usually the people in the Worldwide Church of God are willing to study the Bible by invitation. Those who believe in Armstrongism seem to know more reasons for why they worship on the Sabbath or abstain from eating pork than why they do not believe the Holy Spirit is a Person. God is our only reason for meeting with anyone, so center your discussion on the nature of *who* God is.

When we ask *what* God is, we answer with His attributes—holy, eternal, omniscient, omnipresent, omnipotent. When we ask *who* God is, we answer with three Persons—the Father is who He is, the Son is who He is, and the Holy Spirit is who He is. Since the Worldwide Church of God denies the Person of the Holy Spirit, emphasize that subject the most.

21

Seventh-day Adventists

D o Seventh-day Adventists belong in a book about cults and deception? We feel this question cannot escape our attention since so many Christian authors have placed Seventh-day Adventists among the cults of our age (Irvine, Talbot, Gerstner, Hoekema, Van Baalen, DeHaan, Breece). However, there has been a recognizable change in Seventh-day Adventist theology that reveals an evangelical movement emerging within its ranks. Recent authors have recognized this change that began in the late 1950s (Barnhouse, Martin, Tucker, Spitzer).

Kenneth R. Samples, who writes for the *Christian Research Journal*, wrestled with the question of whether the Seventh-day Adventists are a cult or evangelical. He gives us a third alternative and calls them a "heterodox [i.e., departing from accepted doctrine] Christian denomination." He also says that their internal evangelical movement is a positive contribution to their

otherwise controversial beginning; while simultaneous-
ly, the traditional faction is "cultic" in its reverence of
Ellen G. White's writings and may "one day be fully
deserving of the title 'cult.'" He points out that certain
Seventh-day Adventist writers of the 1980s stirred a
controversy causing their excommunication from the
movement for denying the teachings of Ellen G. White
(*Christian Research Journal*, Summer 1988).

There may indeed come a day when the traditional
Seventh-day Adventists separate themselves from the
evangelical Adventists. Even then, though, there will be
problems with the evangelical Seventh-day Adventists
that will prevent them from being recommended as a
place for Christian fellowship and growth by Protestant
pastors.

It is true that they hold to a sound doctrine of the
Trinity, the deity of Jesus Christ, and the Person and
deity of the Holy Spirit. Where they depart from the
Scriptures is on a variation of grace. That is, they are
saved by grace through faith, but kept in grace by their
works. We find this untenable as well as other variant
doctrines, such as: Jesus possessing a "sinful nature,"
Satan as the "scapegoat" for our sins, Jesus having the
preincarnate name of Michael (but not a created being),
an "investigative judgment" of each person's life on
earth, conditional immortality of the soul, unconscious
state of the soul (soul-sleep) until the Second Advent,
keeping a strict dietary and Sabbath law as a condition
for salvation, worship on Sunday as the "mark of the
beast," and annihilation of the unjust instead of eternal
punishment in hell.

Any born-again student of the Bible will see from
the above list that there are too many false doctrines
mingled with the doctrines of the Trinity and grace to
recommend the Seventh-day Adventists as an evangelical church. Their isolation from other Protestants is

troubling as well. It was taught by Ellen G. White that they are the "remnant" of God's true church. While we recognize that there are some born again believers in their midst, this separation attitude prevents us from recommending the Seventh-day Adventist Church as a place of true Christian fellowship.

For a thorough appraisal of the Seventh-day Adventists, we recommend *Kingdom of the Cults* by Walter R. Martin (Minneapolis: Bethany House Publishers, 1985). He presents a meticulous overview that is balanced by a fair objective analysis. He states:

> It is my conviction that one cannot be a true Jehovah's Witness, Mormon, Christian Scientist, Unitarian, Spiritist, etc., and be a Christian in the biblical sense of the term; but it is perfectly possible to be a Seventh-day Adventist and be a true follower of Jesus Christ despite certain heterodox concepts (p. 409).

Appendix A

Cult Ministry Referrals

The following ministries deal with all of the major cults: Mormonism, Jehovah's Witnesses, Mind Science groups, New Age groups.

Answers In Action, P. O. Box 2067, Costa Mesa, CA 92626

C.A.R.I.S., P. O. Box 1659, Milwaukee, WI 53201

Christian Research Institute, P. O. Box 500, San Juan Capistrano, CA 92693

Institute for Contemporary Christianity, P. O. Box A, Oakland, NJ 07436

Jude 3 Missions, P. O. Box 1901, Orange, CA 92668

Personal Freedom Outreach, P. O. Box 26062, St. Louis, MO 63136

Spiritual Counterfeits Project, P. O. Box 2418, Berkeley, CA 94702

The following ministries specialize in Mormonism:

Marvin Cowan, P. O. Box 21052, Salt Lake City, UT 84121

Ex-Mormons for Jesus, 14106 Whittier Blvd., Whittier, CA   90605. Ex-Mormons for Jesus maintains two visitor centers: 14106 Whittier Blvd., Whittier, CA; and 226 W. Chapman Ave., Orange, CA (Open daily, 10 A.M.—5 P.M.).

Frontline, P. O. Box 1100, La Canada Flintridge, CA 91011

Utah Gospel Mission, P. O. Box 1901, Orange, CA 92668 or P. O. Box 17503, Salt Lake City, UT 84117

Utah Lighthouse Ministry, P. O. Box 1884, Salt Lake City, UT 84110

Watchman Fellowship, P. O. Box 13251, Arlington, TX 76013

The following ministries specialize in Jehovah's Witnesses:

Edmond Gruss, Los Angeles Baptist College, P. O. Box 878, Newhall, CA 91321

Witness Incorporated, P. O. Box 597, Clayton, CA 94517

Appendix B

Select Cults Bibliography

General Cults

Bjornstad, James. *Counterfeits At Your Door*. Ventura, CA: Gospel Light Publications, 1979.

Enroth, Ronald. *Evangelizing the Cults*. Ann Arbor, MI: Servant Publications, 1990.

Gruss, Edmund. *Cults and the Occult in the Age of Aquarius*. Nutley, NJ: Presbyterian and Reformed Publishing Company, 1974.

Hoekema, Anthony A. *The Four Major Cults*. Grand Rapids, MI: Eerdmans Publishing Company, 1963.

Martin, Walter R. *The Kingdom of the Cults*, fifth ed. Minneapolis: Bethany House Publishers, 1985.

-----. *Martin Speaks Out on the Cults*. Ventura, CA: Vision House/Gospel Light Publications, 1983.

-----. *The New Cults*. Ventura, CA: Vision House/Gospel Light, 1980.

Passantino, Robert and Gretchen. *Answers to the Cultist at Your Door*. Eugene, OR: Harvest House Publishers, 1981.

Tucker, Ruth A. *Another Gospel: Alternative Religions and the New Age Movement*. Grand Rapids, MI: Zondervan, 1989.

New Age Cults

Chandler, Russell. *Understanding the New Age*. Waco, TX: Word, 1988.

Groothuis, Douglas. *Unmasking the New Age*. Downers Grove, IL: InterVarsity Press, 1986.

-----. *Confronting the New Age*. Downers Grove, IL: InterVarsity Press, 1988.

-----. *Revealing the New Age Jesus*. Downers Grove, IL: InterVarsity Press, 1990.

Hoyt, Karen, ed. *The New Age Rage*. Old Tappan, NJ: Fleming Revell Company, 1987.

Martin, Walter R. *The New Age Cult*. Minneapolis, MN: Bethany House Publishers, 1989.

Miller, Elliot. *A Crash Course on the New Age*. Grand Rapids, MI: Baker Book House, 1989.

Mormonism

Cowan, Marvin. *Mormon Claims Answered*. Cowan Publications, P. O. Box 21052, Salt Lake City, UT 84121, 1975.

Hunt, Dave and Decker, Ed. *The God Makers*. Eugene, OR: Harvest House Publications, 1982.

Martin, Walter R. *The Maze of Mormonism.* Ventura, CA: Gospel Light Publications, 1978.

Tanner, Jerald and Sandra. *The Changing World of Mormonism.* Chicago: Moody Press, 1980.

-----. *Mormonism—Shadow or Reality?* Utah Lighthouse Ministry, P. O. Box 1884, Salt Lake City, UT 84110, 1985.

Van Gorden, Kurt. *The Christian and Mormon Theological Debates.* Jude 3 Missions, P. O. Box 1901, Orange, CA 92668, 1991.

Jehovah's Witnesses

Bowman, Jr., Robert M. *Understanding Jehovah's Witnesses.* Grand Rapids, MI: Baker Book House, 1990.

Gruss, Edmund. *Apostles of Denial.* Nutley, NJ: Presbyterian and Reformed, 1978.

Martin, Walter R. and Klann, Norman. *Jehovah of the Watchtower.* Minneapolis, MN: Bethany House Publishers, 1981.

Magnani, Duane. *The Watchtower Files.* Minneapolis, MN: Bethany House Publishers, 1985.

Armstrongism

Benwar, Paul. *Ambassadors of Armstrongism.* Nutley, NJ: Presbyterian and Reformed Publishing Company, 1975.

Hopkins, Joseph. *The Armstrong Empire: A Look at the Worldwide Church of God.* Grand Rapids, MI: Eerdmand Publishing Company, 1974.

Unification Church

Bjornstad, James. *The Moon Is Not the Son: A Close Look at the Teachings of Rev. Sun Myung Moon and the*

Unification Church. Minneapolis, MN: Bethany House Publishers, 1976.

Yamamoto, J. Isamu. *The Puppet Master: An Inquiry into Sun Myung Moon and the Unification Church*. Downers Grove, IL: InterVarsity Press, 1977.

Transcendental Meditation

Lewis, Gordon R. *What Everyone Should Know About Transcendental Meditation*. Ventura, CA: Gospel Light Publications, 1975.

Miller, Calvin. *Transcendental Hesitation: A Biblical Appraisal of TM and Eastern Mysticism*. Grand Rapids, MI: Zondervan Publishing House, 1977.

Would You Like
to
Know God
Personally?

Here are four principles that clearly explain the gospel message and the truth of what God has done through His Son Jesus Christ for each and every human being. We've had great success sharing these principles with those who are involved in the cults, and we've lead many to the love of the one true God. It is our prayer that you'll find them helpful as you witness.

1. *God loves you, and created you to know Him personally.*

While the Bible is filled with assurances of God's love, perhaps the most telling verse is John 3:16:

For God so loved the world, that He gave His only begotten Son, that whoever believes in Him should not perish, but have eternal life.

God not only loves each of us enough to give His

only Son for us; He desires that we come to know Him personally:

> Now this is eternal life; that they may know you, the only true God, and Jesus Christ, whom you have sent (John 17:3, NIV).

What, then, prevents us from knowing God personally?

2. *Men and women are sinful and separated from God, so we cannot know Him personally or experience His love.*

We were all created to have fellowship with God; but, because of mankind's stubborn self-will, we chose to go our own independent way and fellowship with God was broken. This self-will, characterized by an attitude of active rebellion or passive indifference, is evidence of what the Bible calls sin.

> For all have sinned and fall short of the glory of God (Romans 3:23, NIV).

The Bible also tells us that "the wages of sin is death" (Romans 6:23, NIV), or spiritual separation from God. When we are in this state, a great gulf separates us from God, because He cannot tolerate sin. People often try to bridge the gulf by doing good works or devoting themselves to religious or New Age practices, but the Bible clearly teaches that there is only one way to bridge this gulf . . .

3. *Jesus Christ is God's ONLY provision for our sin. Through Him alone we can know God personally and experience His love.*

God's Word records three important facts to verify

this principle: (1) Jesus Christ died in our place; (2) He rose from the dead; and (3) He is our only way to God:

> But God demonstrates His own love toward us, in that while we were yet sinners, Christ died for us (Romans 5:8).

> Christ died for our sins . . . He was buried . . . He was raised on the third day, according to the Scriptures . . . He appeared to Peter, then to the twelve. After that He appeared to more than five hundred . . . (1 Corinthians 15:3-6).

> Jesus said to him, "I am the way, and the truth, and the life; no one comes to the Father, but through Me" (John 14:6).

Thus, God has taken the loving initiative to bridge the gulf which separates us from Him by sending His Son, Jesus Christ, to die on the cross in our place to pay the penalty for our sin. But it is not enough just to know these truths . . .

4. We must individually receive Jesus Christ as Savior and Lord; then we can know God personally and experience His love.

John 1:12 records:

> But as many as received Him, to them He gave the right to become children of God, even to those who believe in His name.

What does it mean to "receive Christ"? The Scriptures tell us that we receive Christ through faith—not through "good works" or religious endeavors:

> For by grace you have been saved through faith; and

that not of yourselves, it is the gift of God; not as a result of works, that no one should boast (Ephesians 2:8,9).

We're also told that receiving Christ means to personally invite Him into our lives:

(Christ is speaking): Behold, I stand at the door and knock; if anyone hears My voice and opens the door, I will come in to him (Revelation 3:20).

Thus, receiving Christ involves turning to God from self and trusting Christ to come into our lives to forgive our sins and to make us the kind of people He wants us to be.

If you are not sure whether you have ever committed your life to Jesus Christ, we encourage you to do so—today! Here is a suggested prayer which has helped millions of men and women around the world express faith in Him and invite Him into their lives:

Lord Jesus, I want to know You personally. Thank You for dying on the cross for my sins. I open the door of my life and receive You as my Savior and Lord. Thank You for forgiving my sins and giving me eternal life. Take control of the throne of my life. Make me the kind of person You want me to be.

If this prayer expresses the desire of your heart, why not pray it now? If you mean it sincerely, Jesus Christ will come into your life, just as He promised in Revelation 3:20. He keeps His promises! And there is another key promise to write indelibly in your mind:

And the witness is this, that God has given us eternal life, and this life is in His Son. He who has the Son has the life; he who does not have the Son of God does not have the life. These things I have written to you who believe in the name of the Son of God, in order that you may **know** that you have eternal life (1 John 5:11-13).

That's right—the man or woman who personally receives Christ as Savior and Lord is assured of everlasting life with Him in heaven. So, in summary, when you received Christ by faith, as an act of your will, many wonderful things happened including the following:

1. Christ came into your life (Revelation 3:20; Colossians 1:27).

2. Your sins were forgiven (Colossians 1:14).

3. You became a child of God (John 1:12).

4. You received eternal life (John 5:24).

5. You began the great adventure for which God created you (John 10:10; 1 Thessalonians 5:18).

If you have received Jesus Christ as your Savior and Lord, we'd like to welcome you to the family of God! We heartily encourage you to attend and participate in a church where the Lord Jesus Christ is glorified, where the Holy Bible is honored and taught, and where believers love, encourage, and pray for one another. Study God's Word regularly and apply it to your daily life. Share His love with your family, friends, and neighbors.

The answers that the cults seek can only be found in the Lord Jesus Christ. We rejoice with you that you've made this discovery of truth in your own life.

These four principles are adapted from *Would You Like to Know God Personally?* (San Bernardino, CA: Here's Life Publishers, 1987). Used by permission.